# Content

E-book Download & Bonus Content .................................................
My Story .................................................
Who Is This For? .................................................................................... 8
The Goal ................................................................................................. 8
Inflation .................................................................................................. 9
    Inflation – Linked Bonds (ILB) ........................................................ 11
Index Investing ..................................................................................... 12
    How Is an Index Calculated? ........................................................... 12
    Advantages Of Index Investing ....................................................... 13
    Disadvantages Of Index Investing ................................................... 17
    Where To Find the Most Important Indexes? ................................. 24
    How To Choose the Right Country (Index) To Invest in? ................. 26
        Interest Rates ............................................................................. 26
        Rating ......................................................................................... 30
        Additional Info ........................................................................... 32
        Indexes - A Final Note ................................................................ 32
Introduction To Stock Investing ........................................................... 33
    Advantages To Stock Investing ........................................................ 33
    Disadvantages To Stock Investing ................................................... 34
    Economic Models? Don't Make Rocket Science of It! ..................... 35
    How Are We Going to Do This ........................................................ 36
    Our Edge .......................................................................................... 36
Stock Screeners .................................................................................... 37
How To Filter Out Stocks Using FINVIZ Stock Screener ....................... 38
FINVIZ: Descriptive Tab ........................................................................ 38
    Market Capitalization ...................................................................... 40
    Dividend Yield .................................................................................. 41
    Sectors ............................................................................................. 43
        Basic Materials ........................................................................... 44

- Communication Services ........................................... 49
- Consumer Cyclical ........................................... 53
- Consumer Defensive ........................................... 57
- Energy ........................................... 60
- Financial ........................................... 63
- Healthcare ........................................... 68
- Industrials ........................................... 73
- Real Estate ........................................... 77
- Technology ........................................... 82
- Utilities ........................................... 86

## FINVIZ: Fundamental Tab ........................................... 90
- P/E (Price to Earnings Ratio) ........................................... 91
- P/B (Price to Book Ratio) ........................................... 93
- Earnings Per Share (EPS) Growth ........................................... 95
- Return On Assets (ROA) ........................................... 95
- Return On Equity (ROE) ........................................... 97
- Debt/Equity ........................................... 98
- Net Profit Margin ........................................... 99

## Picking Stocks with Stock Screener: Step-By-Step Examples ........................................... 101
- Companies from the Basic Materials Sector ........................................... 102
- Companies from Communication Services Sector ........................................... 107
- Companies from Consumer Cyclical Sector ........................................... 112
- Companies from Consumer Defensive Sector ........................................... 116
- Companies from Energy Sector ........................................... 120
- Companies from Financial Sector ........................................... 122
- Companies from Healthcare Sector ........................................... 124
- Companies from Industrials Sector ........................................... 128
- Companies from Real Estate Sector ........................................... 132
- Companies from Technology Sector ........................................... 135
- Companies from Utilities Sector ........................................... 139

## Picking the Right Time to Make Your Investment ........................................... 144

## Price Action – How to Read a Simple Chart ................................................ 144
### Why Does the Price Move? ................................................ 144
### The "BIG" Guys ................................................ 147
### How to Spot Institutional Activity with Price Action ................................................ 147
#### Rotation ................................................ 148
#### Trend ................................................ 151
#### Strong Rejection (of Higher or Lower Prices) ................................................ 153
#### The Complete Picture ................................................ 155

## How to Use Volume Profile in Stock Investing ................................................ 156
### Volume Profile Introduction ................................................ 156
### What Does Volume Profile Look Like? ................................................ 156
### What Does Volume Profile Tell Us? ................................................ 157
### Different Volume Profile Shapes ................................................ 158
#### D-Shaped Profile ................................................ 158
#### P-Shaped Profile ................................................ 159
#### b-Shaped Profile ................................................ 159
#### Thin Profile ................................................ 160
### What Makes Volume Profile Different from Other Trading Indicators? ................................................ 160
### Why Care About Volumes and What the Big Institutions Are Doing? ................................................ 161
### Where to Get Volume Profile ................................................ 162
### Where to Get Data ................................................ 162
### Where to Get Data for Non-US markets ................................................ 163

## Volume Profile Trading Setups ................................................ 164
### Volume Profile Setup #1: Volume Accumulation Setup ................................................ 166
#### The Logic Behind Volume Accumulation Setup ................................................ 169
#### Why Not Trade This as a Breakout Strategy? ................................................ 172
#### EXAMPLES: The Volume Accumulation Setup ................................................ 172
### Volume Profile Setup #2: Trend Setup ................................................ 179
#### EXAMPLES: The Trend Setup ................................................ 181

## When to Sell Your Stocks? ................................................ 187
## Recap of the Steps We Have Already Taken ................................................ 190

- Fundamental Criteria ............................................................................................................ 190
- Volume Profile Criteria ......................................................................................................... 194

## Building a Portfolio .................................................................................................................. 195
- Money Management ............................................................................................................ 195
- 20% Reserve ......................................................................................................................... 196
- The Problem With the "Standard Portfolio Theory" ............................................................ 197
- No Leverage ......................................................................................................................... 197
- No Stop Loss ........................................................................................................................ 197
- Limit Orders ......................................................................................................................... 197
- Alerts .................................................................................................................................... 198
- Free Capital Allocation ......................................................................................................... 198
  - Bond ETFs ....................................................................................................................... 199
  - Other Markets to Diversify ............................................................................................. 200
- Difference Between Stocks and Stock CFDs ........................................................................ 201
- How Much Money You Need ............................................................................................... 202
- Fractional Shares .................................................................................................................. 202

## The Most Common Mistakes ................................................................................................... 204

## Bonus Content ......................................................................................................................... 212

## What to Do Next ..................................................................................................................... 213

## Thank you! .............................................................................................................................. 215

# E-book Download & Bonus Content

A quick note before we begin: If you bought a printed version of this book, then you may also want to have an electronic version of it.

The e-book could come in handy because it has colored pictures which you can zoom in on to see more details. You can also download it to your phone or computer and have it around when you need it.

You can download this book (for free) along with some extra video material on a special page that I set up for you.

**Link:** https://www.trader-dale.com/investing-book

**Password:** happy trading

# My Story

Hello, my name is Dale, and I've been a full-time investor and trader since 2008. I have always been very passionate about economics, finance, investing and trading. I obtained a university degree in finance and also became a certified portfolio manager and an investment manager. Unlike most of the other "gurus," I am proud to say that I have a proper education and industry certifications.

Fresh out of university, I started to work as a market analyst for a major brokerage company that was dealing mostly in stocks. I remember that many people applied for this job, but they picked only me. The reason wasn't that I was the cleverest applicant (I wasn't). They later told me that they chose me because they saw how passionate I was and how eager I was to learn. That was true, and it is still true.

One of the best things I learned working at this company was how different real investing was from what they taught us at the university. It was only then I saw the huge gap between academic theories and the real world.

My colleague analysts taught me many practical and useful things during my time there. Those guys were clever, and I am grateful I could learn from them. Those guys were the smartest in the whole company.

Another thing I learned there was not so shiny. It was how such a big company works – how it does its business. There were just a couple of us – analysts, and then there was a huge open-office hall full of people whose only job was to call a client and make him buy something. Their superiors went as far as having a big board on which they would write the names of the "best performing" people from the salesforce. "Best performing" meant that they had talked their clients into investing the most money. There was also a bell that rang every time a certain threshold was met. Crazy, right?

Want to hear a juicy story? BTW it's a secret. I signed a contract where I promised not to tell those things to anyone. But I am telling you anyway.

A client called one of those sales guys (who called themselves managers), and he considered buying stocks of Bank of America. He wasn't exactly sure about it, so he wanted to talk it through with this "manager." So, this manager went to my office and told me that he needed ten arguments in bullet points about why Bank of America was a worthwhile investment. If he asked my opinion at that time, then I would say that it was not an investment I would recommend – but he did not ask for my opinion. That was not how the game was played. He wanted arguments to make the client invest. After I gave him the list, he called the client and played the clever guy, and yes, they made the deal. Such practices were part of the reason I quit the company and started to do things on my own.

Those sales guys had received some training in investing and had a background in the field. They needed to have a certain degree of certification to be allowed to do their job. They weren't just random sales guys found on the street.

The disturbing thing was that when I asked them if they were investing their money, they usually answered "no." But, how can those people play the clever guys, and give investment advice when they don't invest their own money? I was one of the youngest guys there and I had already been investing and trading when I got there. Why not them? They weren't as interested in investments as they tried to appear when they talked to their clients. It was an 8-5 job for them.

I was a bit disappointed to see how things were behind the curtain. Also, I don't think other brokerages do their business too differently.

After I quit this company, I focused all my efforts on my own investing and trading. I was on it for 12-15 hours every day. But don't worry. You won't need to invest as much time as I did. I learned many things the hard way and I spent a lot of time trying things that never led to success.

Back then I focused on long-term stock investing, investment certificate investments, automated trading systems and currency trading. Today, I mostly focus on long-term stock investing, and on long-term and short-term currency trading.

You may have heard of me as the "Volume Profile guy" – which would be pretty accurate. Volume Profile is a tool that I would recommend to anybody. No matter if you are a long-term investor doing stocks, or if you are a day trader who is trading currencies.

Discovering Volume Profile was a breaking point in my life, and I am sure it will also be a breaking point in yours. Once you learn how it works, you will never look at the markets the same as before. I can promise you that.

In 2017 I started a website www.trader-dale.com which focuses on investing and trading education. My courses and books cover stock investing, and both long-term, and short-term currency trading.

In all my courses I focus mostly on tracking the BIG trading institutions who move and manipulate the markets. I do this with my custom-made tools – Volume Profile, VWAP, and Order Flow. I believe that tracking the institutions and trading alongside them is the key to consistent success. This strategy has worked for many years, and I can honestly say that I haven't found a strategy that is better than it.

# Who Is This For?

I have always been into the economy, finances, investments and trading and I cannot imagine doing anything else in my life. However, I am sure that most people aren't like that and their goal isn't to be full-time traders. That's fine! This book is mostly for people who want to dedicate their professional lives to something else than investments and trading.

The impulse to start working on this book and course came from my family and friends. Most of those guys are not investors or traders. They are regular people with regular jobs. The thing they have in common is that they wanted to do something with the money they saved instead of just waiting for inflation to slowly devalue and consume their savings. They kept calling me, visiting me and asking for investment advice.

Their questions were like: should I buy Bitcoin? "Will it be $70k by this Christmas? Should I buy Gold? Tesla? Should I invest my money in real estate? Should I hold or sell that stock of this one company I have been investing in the last X years?" Or – "Check out those companies (giving me some info leaflets with no proper info whatsoever) – I put my money on them, what should I do now?"

All they wanted was simple yes/no answers. But I am not an oracle. Nobody is.

Hearing their questions, I realized that what they needed was proper training. A proper strategy to follow. This was the reason I started working on this course. What you are going to learn in this course is exactly what I do and what I recommend my family and friends to do with their free money.

It's not rocket science, and I assume that many of you are beginners. So, we are going to take it slow, step-by-step, using many real examples. I will mentor you as I would mentor a friend who came to me for advice.

# The Goal

The goal of this course is to teach you how to invest your money smartly, how to build and manage your portfolio, and how to do all this with as low effort as possible. Once you have learned my method, you will see that it's not time-consuming, that it is easy to grasp and most importantly, that it is highly effective and universal.

It is important to care for your money and obtain at least some education about investment.

# Inflation

The reason you need basic knowledge about investing is that the real buying power of the money you hold in your bank account is slowly deteriorating. This is called inflation. Inflation is the reason an average house in the US was $40.000 in 1975 and is now $400.000 (2022).

Inflation is a tax on people who save money. It slowly eats up your savings until one day you realize that the pile of money you have been saving has lost 50% of its real value over the last ten years.

More money in the economy makes the nominal prices rise. Currently, the money supply in the economy is enormous as central banks all over the world have been lending money to banks almost for free (super low or zero interest rates). This leads to rising inflation which will diminish your savings over time.

The long-term average inflation worldwide is 5.4%. This is an average since 1981.

Currently, inflation is rising fast, and I don't think it will go down anytime soon. Your money is losing value quickly and you need to do something about it now!

If you would like to check the long-term data on inflation, you can do so here:

https://www.macrotrends.net/countries/WLD/world/inflation-rate-cpi


I would like you to check out this chart I made. It shows how $10.000 gets diminished by inflation over time. The top row shows inflation – from 1% to 6%. Below that you can see how much the inflation takes from the initial capital of $10.000.

| Years | Inflation in % | | | | | | | | | | |
|---|---|---|---|---|---|---|---|---|---|---|---|
| | 1 | 1.5 | 2 | 2.5 | 3 | 3.5 | 4 | 4.5 | 5 | 5.5 | 6 |
| 1 | 9900 | 9850 | 9800 | 9750 | 9700 | 9650 | 9600 | 9550 | 9500 | 9450 | 9400 |
| 2 | 9801 | 9702 | 9604 | 9506 | 9409 | 9312 | 9216 | 9120 | 9025 | 8930 | 8836 |
| 3 | 9703 | 9557 | 9412 | 9269 | 9127 | 8986 | 8847 | 8710 | 8574 | 8439 | 8306 |
| 4 | 9606 | 9413 | 9224 | 9037 | 8853 | 8672 | 8493 | 8318 | 8145 | 7975 | 7807 |
| 5 | 9510 | 9272 | 9039 | 8811 | 8587 | 8368 | 8154 | 7944 | 7738 | 7536 | 7339 |
| 6 | 9415 | 9133 | 8858 | 8591 | 8330 | 8075 | 7828 | 7586 | 7351 | 7122 | 6899 |
| 7 | 9321 | 8996 | 8681 | 8376 | 8080 | 7793 | 7514 | 7245 | 6983 | 6730 | 6485 |
| 8 | 9227 | 8861 | 8508 | 8167 | 7837 | 7520 | 7214 | 6919 | 6634 | 6360 | 6096 |
| 9 | 9135 | 8728 | 8337 | 7962 | 7602 | 7257 | 6925 | 6607 | 6302 | 6010 | 5730 |
| 10 | 9044 | 8597 | 8171 | 7763 | 7374 | 7003 | 6648 | 6310 | 5987 | 5680 | 5386 |
| 11 | 8953 | 8468 | 8007 | 7569 | 7153 | 6758 | 6382 | 6026 | 5688 | 5367 | 5063 |
| 12 | 8864 | 8341 | 7847 | 7380 | 6938 | 6521 | 6127 | 5755 | 5404 | 5072 | 4759 |
| 13 | 8775 | 8216 | 7690 | 7195 | 6730 | 6293 | 5882 | 5496 | 5133 | 4793 | 4474 |
| 14 | 8687 | 8093 | 7536 | 7016 | 6528 | 6073 | 5647 | 5249 | 4877 | 4529 | 4205 |
| 15 | 8601 | 7972 | 7386 | 6840 | 6333 | 5860 | 5421 | 5012 | 4633 | 4280 | 3953 |
| 16 | 8515 | 7852 | 7238 | 6669 | 6143 | 5655 | 5204 | 4787 | 4401 | 4045 | 3716 |
| 17 | 8429 | 7734 | 7093 | 6502 | 5958 | 5457 | 4996 | 4571 | 4181 | 3822 | 3493 |
| 18 | 8345 | 7618 | 6951 | 6340 | 5780 | 5266 | 4796 | 4366 | 3972 | 3612 | 3283 |
| 19 | 8262 | 7504 | 6812 | 6181 | 5606 | 5082 | 4604 | 4169 | 3774 | 3414 | 3086 |
| 20 | 8179 | 7391 | 6676 | 6027 | 5438 | 4904 | 4420 | 3982 | 3585 | 3226 | 2901 |
| 21 | 8097 | 7280 | 6543 | 5876 | 5275 | 4732 | 4243 | 3803 | 3406 | 3048 | 2727 |
| 22 | 8016 | 7171 | 6412 | 5729 | 5117 | 4567 | 4073 | 3631 | 3235 | 2881 | 2563 |
| 23 | 7936 | 7064 | 6283 | 5586 | 4963 | 4407 | 3911 | 3468 | 3074 | 2722 | 2410 |
| 24 | 7857 | 6958 | 6158 | 5446 | 4814 | 4253 | 3754 | 3312 | 2920 | 2573 | 2265 |
| 25 | 7778 | 6853 | 6035 | 5310 | 4670 | 4104 | 3604 | 3163 | 2774 | 2431 | 2129 |
| 26 | 7700 | 6751 | 5914 | 5177 | 4530 | 3960 | 3460 | 3021 | 2635 | 2297 | 2001 |
| 27 | 7623 | 6649 | 5796 | 5048 | 4394 | 3822 | 3321 | 2885 | 2503 | 2171 | 1881 |
| 28 | 7547 | 6550 | 5680 | 4922 | 4262 | 3688 | 3189 | 2755 | 2378 | 2052 | 1768 |
| 29 | 7472 | 6451 | 5566 | 4799 | 4134 | 3559 | 3061 | 2631 | 2259 | 1939 | 1662 |
| 30 | 7397 | 6355 | 5455 | 4679 | 4010 | 3434 | 2939 | 2512 | 2146 | 1832 | 1563 |

If we take, for example, inflation of 2.5 %, then after 10 years the $10.000 is only worth $7.763. Nominally you still have $10.000, but real buying power is $7.763.

After 20 years (with inflation of 2.5%) you only have $6.027.

Mind that we are still talking about quite low inflation. If the inflation was for example 4%, then $10.000 would be down to $6.648 after 10 years, and to $4.420 after 20 years.

Inflation is quite the killer, isn't it? The worst thing is that you don't even notice it.

Inflation is a reason it is so important to invest your money, not just sit on it.

Our goal will not be just to beat inflation. That's not too difficult, but we will strive to make solid investments that make our money grow and work for us. Not just to cover the inflation.

# Inflation – Linked Bonds (ILB)

If your only goal is to beat inflation (and there is nothing bad about doing just that!), then you may want to look for "Inflation-Linked Bonds" or "Inflation-Protected Bond ETFs."

Inflation-Linked Bonds are usually issued by governments. Those bonds are linked to inflation and their purpose is to protect you from inflation.

Here is a couple of the biggest ETFs to cover inflation:

- **SPDR® Bloomberg 1-10 Year TIPS ETF**
  https://www.ssga.com/us/en/intermediary/etfs/funds/spdr-bloomberg-1-10-year-tips-etf-tipx

- **Schwab U.S. TIPS ETF**
  https://www.schwabassetmanagement.com/products/schp

- **Vanguard Short-Term Inflation-Protected Securities ETF (VTIP)**
  https://investor.vanguard.com/etf/profile/VTIP

If covering inflation is your only goal and if you don't want to bother with any other stuff, then you may just get one of the Inflation-Protected ETFs and just end there. And again, there is nothing wrong with that! It's super easy and you can focus on other things you like.

If you want to go a bit further, then the next chapter is for you. It's about index investing and it's somewhere in the middle between getting inflation-protected bonds and building a stock portfolio.

# Index Investing

The simplest way to effectively start investing your money is by investing it into a stock index.

A stock index is a basket of stocks. In this basket, there are the biggest companies in the country or economy you choose (for example USA, Europe and Australia). When you buy the index, you don't buy stocks of those companies separately. You buy the whole basket of stocks. This enables you to invest in many companies easily.

**Example:** The most important index to gauge the US economy is the American index S&P 500. This index comprises the 500 biggest US-based companies (for example, Apple, Microsoft, Amazon and Meta). If you want to know how the US economy is doing and how its companies prosper, then look at this index. One look is enough to have a good picture.

The picture below shows the development of the S&P 500 index. You can easily spot areas where the US economy was in trouble, and where it was booming:

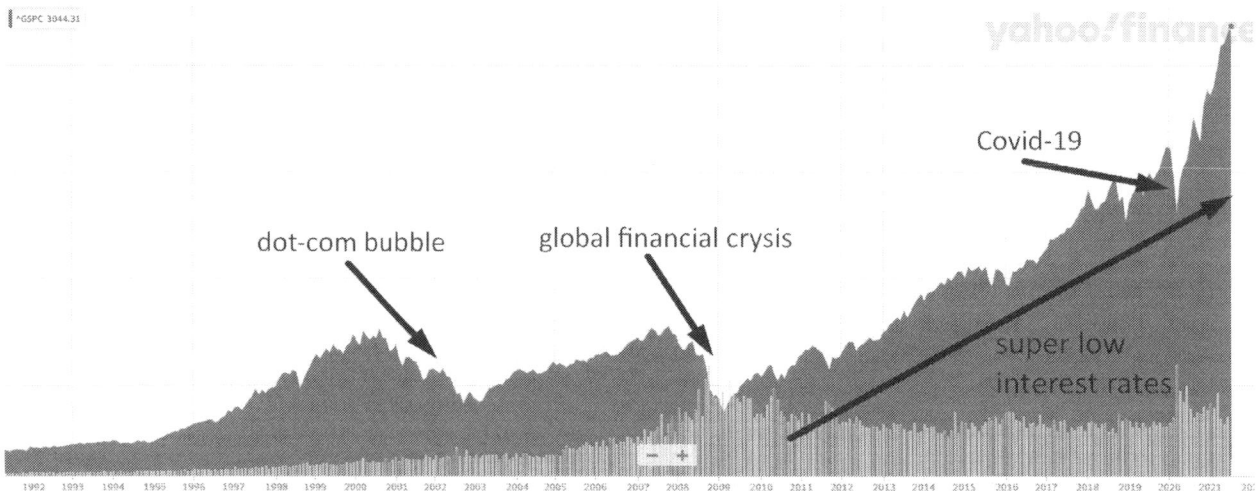

When you invest in the index, you buy tiny parts of each company that is listed in the index. If you buy the S&P 500 index, then you have a little part of Apple, Microsoft, Amazon, Meta and many more stocks that are part of the S&P 500. All that with one click. Easy.

## How Is an Index Calculated?

Most indexes are value-weighted. This means that the bigger the market value a company has, the bigger percentage the company represents in the index.

Simply put: a rise or fall of a big company affects the index more than the rise or fall of a small company.

For example – Apple has around 6% weight in the S&P 500 (it is currently the biggest company there). If Apple falls, then it will drag the S&P 500 down as well. On the other hand, if for example, Electronic Arts (EA) falls, then it won't hurt the index so much, because EA only has 0.1% weight in the index.

# Advantages Of Index Investing

### Advantage #1: No cherry picking

You don't need to be an expert on stocks when you invest in indexes. You don't need to analyze all the single stocks, filter them and search for the best ones. You don't even need to know how to do a stock analysis! Nothing like that. You simply buy the whole basket where all the biggest companies of the given economy are.

Index investing is ideal for those who want to invest their money themselves, but who don't want to spend too much time and energy on learning how to do it. Those are typically "busy professionals" – people who have their own business and some extra money to invest, but who have very little time to learn how to manage their investments more actively. There is absolutely nothing bad about this approach. I have many close friends who are exactly like this and my advice to them has always been: "invest your money into an index and do it yourself!"

### Advantage #2: It's better than investing with a fund

The main goal of most funds is to outperform an index. A sad fact is that in most cases they fail. It is also an interesting fact, isn't it?

Imagine all those "professionals" who use complex models for stock analysis, who spend all their time going through various company reports, balance sheets and other similar things, only to fail to beat a simple index in the end!

**Interesting fact:** There was a $1 million bet in 2008 between Warren Buffet and a couple of hedge funds on who will get a better gain in ten years – whether the hedge funds or the S&P 500 index. Buffet (who betted on the S&P 500) won since neither of the funds managed to beat the index. Here is the result:

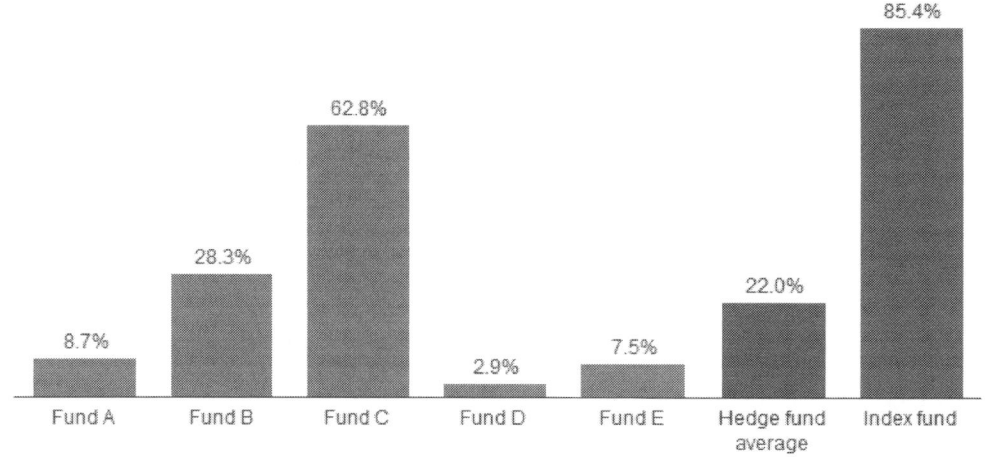

### Advantage #3: No management fees

If you manage your investments yourself then there is no management fee for you to pay.

If you give your money to a fund to manage it for you, then you will need to pay them!

The standard price for an actively managed fund is a 2% manager fee (you pay this every year no matter how the fund performs) plus a 20% performance fee (paid from the gain they make).

Some funds follow the index closely and have results that are similar to the index. But having their fees, they can never beat the index! They will always underperform.

This is another reason I say you better invest your money yourself. Even if you put your money into a simple index, chances are you will end up better than giving your money to an actively or passively managed equity fund.

### Advantage #4: you can do this with a very small amount of money

A wonderful thing about index investing is that you can buy the whole basket with a small amount of money. You can do this even if you have just a couple of hundred USD.

You can buy a very small share in, for example, 500 companies (S&P 500 index) for just a couple of American dollars.

If on the other hand, you wanted to buy every single stock from the index yourself, then you would need a lot of money and you would also spend a lot of money just on the fees for all the transactions.

With index investing though, you can easily diversify your money between many strong companies with a negligible transaction fee. This is a huge advantage index investing has.

## Advantage #5: Indexes consist of strong companies

Another advantage of index investing is that major stock indexes consist of superior quality stocks (they are referred to as "blue chips").

This is an advantage because beginner investors don't need to worry too much about spending their money on a bad company.

Simply put, if you buy the S&P 500 index, then you will have a small share in 500 big and stable companies. If, on the other hand, you try to find solid companies to invest in, then you may end up picking bad companies, companies with hidden risks, unstable companies and very easily make a very bad investment.

With index investing, the risk is lower as the companies in the index are usually the strongest and most stable companies in the given economy.

But let's not pretend that big and stable companies from indexes can't have their problems and that they can't fail miserably. Because they can fail too! However, the chances are that a big company from a renowned index will perform better than, for example, some unknown startup company with just an idea, a couple of employees and no capital.


## Advantage #6: Indexes and stocks are good protection against inflation

There is one significant difference between stocks (and stock indexes) and other trading instruments like commodities, raw materials, currencies and cryptos.

That enormous difference is how all those instruments react to inflation.

When there is inflation, then it means that there is more money in the economy and this inflates the prices of everything – all the things ordinary people buy like food, clothes, cars and houses. If you hold your money in a bank account, then it simply deteriorates and loses its value.

You can imagine inflation as a sort of "invisible tax." This is a way governments tax people who have cash.

If you buy a company or a basket of companies (an index), then you will be protected against inflation. The reason is that stock prices are tightly connected and correlated with the amount of money that central banks print and pump into the economy.

The chart below shows the Monetary base (amount of money pumped into the US economy) compared to US stock prices. It nicely demonstrates how close those two are.

Simply put: the more money gets pumped into the economy (inflation), the more stock prices rise.

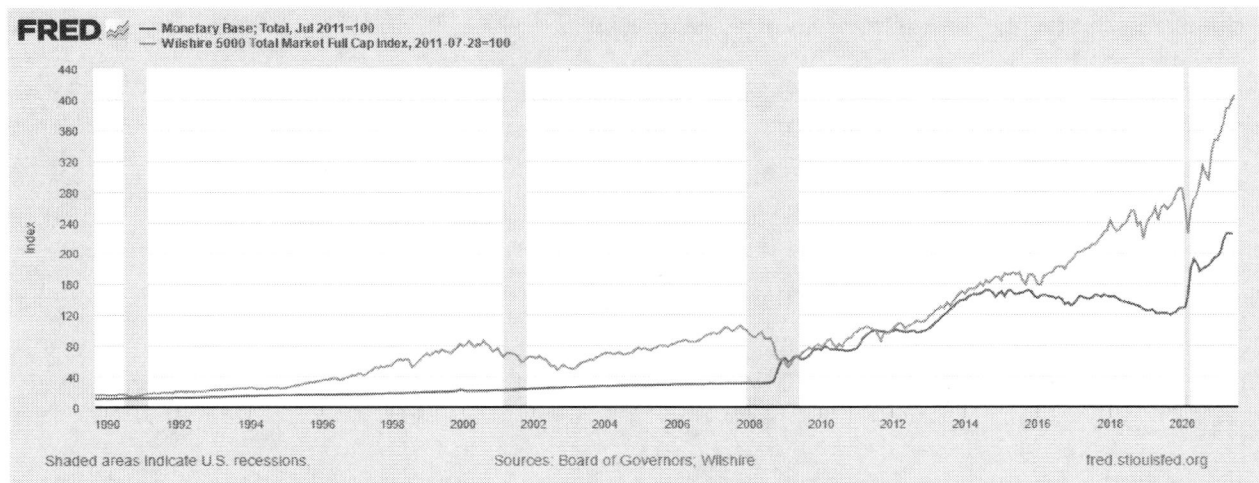

If you don't have cash, but you own shares in some companies, then inflation won't hurt you. It will help to drive the prices of stocks up, protecting you from inflation.

Inflation will cause the companies to make more money (because with inflation all things cost more, so companies make more and more).

People also tend to invest more when there is a good supply of cheap money, and this also helps stock prices to rise. Do you know what happened when the US sent people money to help them deal with the covid crisis? People just took it and pumped it into stocks! Increasing the money supply helps stocks.

Central banks and governments use inflation and other stimuli to help the economy and drive stock prices upwards. This is also one of the reasons I always prefer buying stocks and stock indexes rather than speculating on their fall. The reason is that "invisible power" that drives the stock prices naturally upwards.

I am not trying to say that stock prices cannot fall. Sure, they can! I am just trying to explain that specifically for stocks and stock indexes it is more natural to go up and to react positively to inflation.

**NOTE**: Currently, we are in a unique situation where we have big inflation and increasing interest rates. The increasing interest rates go against stocks (because it's more expensive for companies to borrow money). For this reason, stock prices do not rise as much. The rising interest rates slow their growth down. Still, central banks are very limited in how much they can raise the rates. They know that rising interest rates would hurt the economy too much and possibly cause it to collapse. So, they are not likely to increase the interest rates too much. Simply put, the tool to battle inflation can be used only in an extremely limited way. For this reason, the big inflation we are facing now is not going to go away anytime soon.

# Disadvantages Of Index Investing

There is one huge disadvantage to index investing. The thing is, that when you buy the basket of stocks (index), then there will inevitably be stocks that you don't want to own.

It is not just about the number of stocks that you don't want in your basket rather than their weight.

The thing is, that all stocks don't have an equal share in the basket. For example, if you invest in the S&P 500 index, then your basket will inevitably have around 7% Apple stocks and 5.6% Microsoft stocks.

The two biggest companies make up over 12% of your basket of 500 companies. I, for example, don't really like investing in companies from the "Technology" sector – where those two companies belong (I will discuss the reason later). However, if I buy the S&P 500, then I am forced to invest HUGELY into the Technology sector since that's just how the basket is!

Another sector I don't like investing in is the "financial sector." Unfortunately, the financial sector along with the "technology sector" very often takes most of the "space" in the basket. The reason is that the biggest giant companies are usually banks or huge technology firms.

The chart below demonstrates this very clearly. It is a visualization of all the companies in the S&P 500 index. The bigger the tile, the bigger share the company takes in the index. Link to the chart here: https://finviz.com/map.ashx?t=sec

You can see that the companies that take most of the space are Apple, Microsoft, Amazon, Google, Meta and Tesla.

If we talk about sectors, then the biggest ones are "Technology" and "Financial."

Unfortunately, the S&P 500 is by a huge part driven by sectors I am very hesitant to invest in!

The technology and financial sectors take around 40% of the whole S&P 500 index.

What this means is that if technologies and financials get hit hard in an economic crisis, then they will drag the whole index down (because those sectors represent over 40% of the index). Also, when there is a crisis, those sectors will most likely go down first (we will talk about the reason later).

In short, if you invest in an index, then you need to be prepared that a huge chunk of the index will be risky stocks from Technology and Financial sectors.

Let me make one little demonstration and show you what the S&P 500 would look like without those risky sectors:

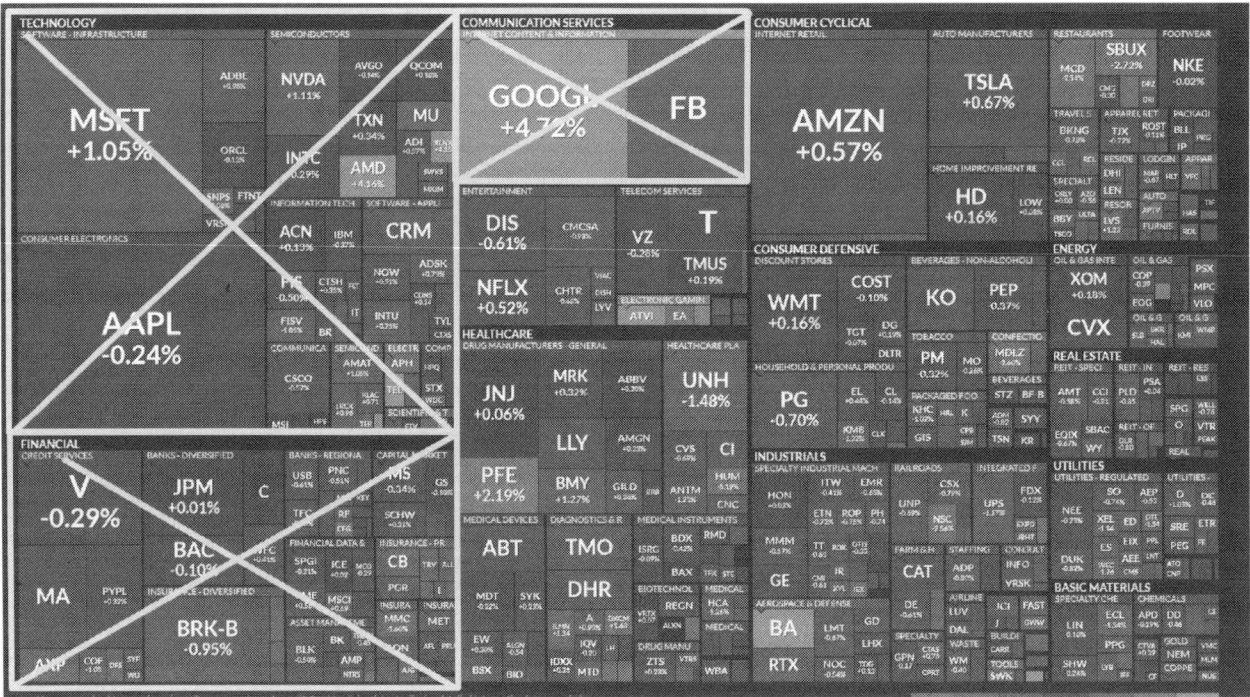

Now you are probably thinking, "Sure, so I can invest in a different index. I don't need the S&P 500."

You are right about that and that's why we are going to talk about other stock indexes.

Let me show you some more leading indexes and their structure.

## ASX 200

The most important index gauging the Australian economy comprises 200 of the biggest Australian stocks.

Again, the financial sector takes a massive chunk of the whole index – around 30%.

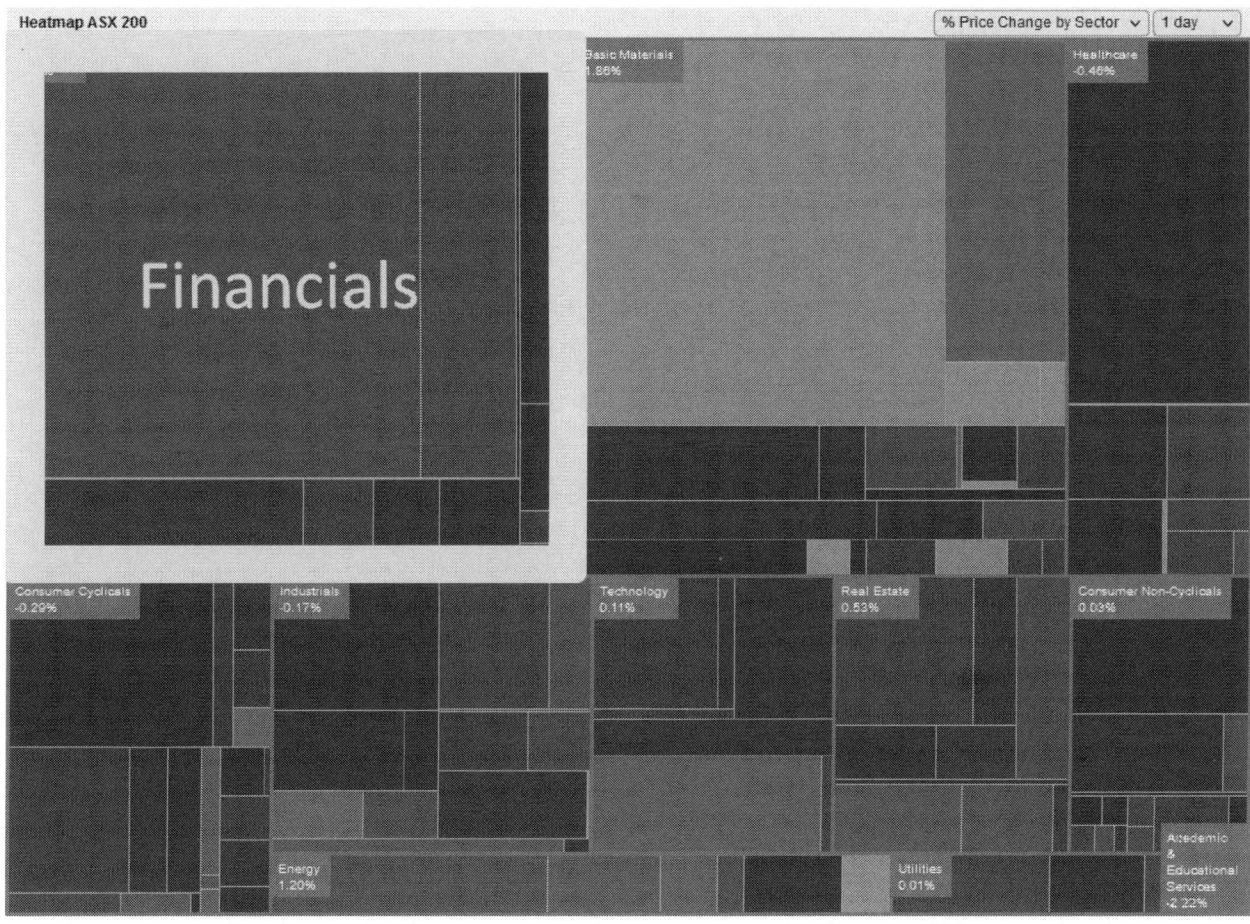

## Hang Seng index

This one gauges the Chinese economy. Notice that over 70% of this index is just Financials and Technology! If there is an economic crisis, then the financial sector will go down first and drag down the whole index. The reason is that companies from the financial sector represent a substantial chunk of this index!

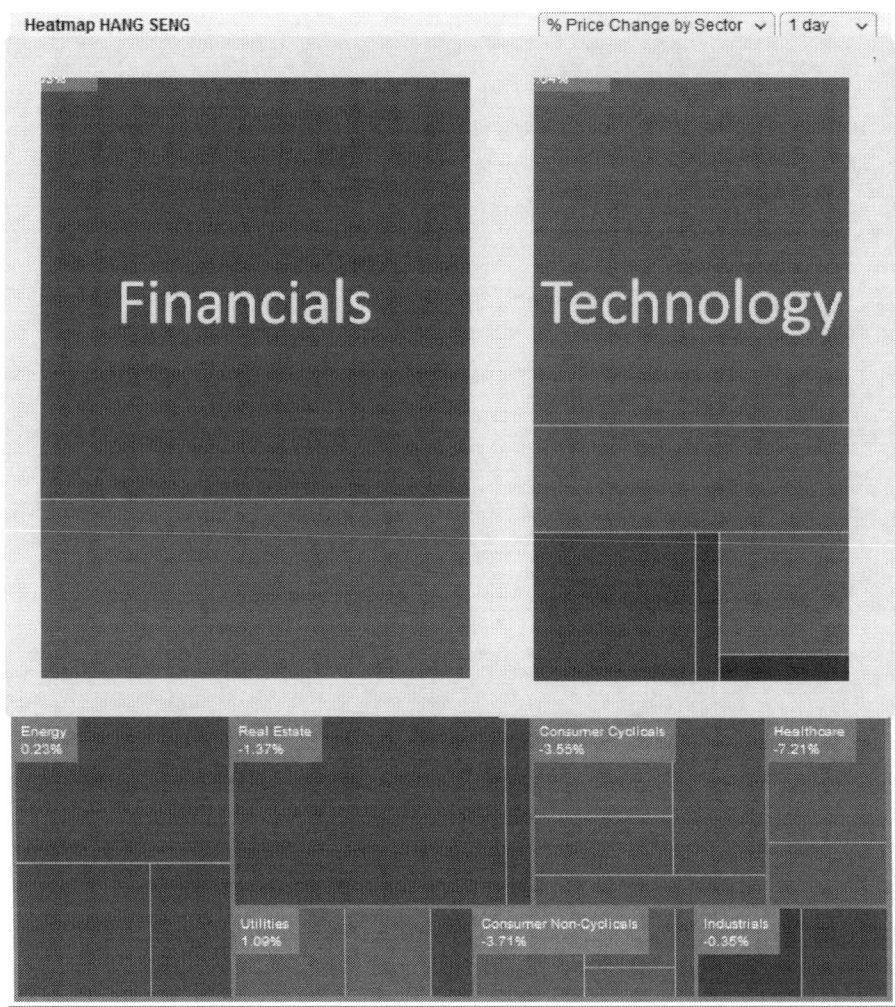

## DAX

This is the most important index to gauge the German economy (30 biggest companies). Dax doesn't have such big exposure to the risky financial sector, and the percentage of Technology companies is "bearable."

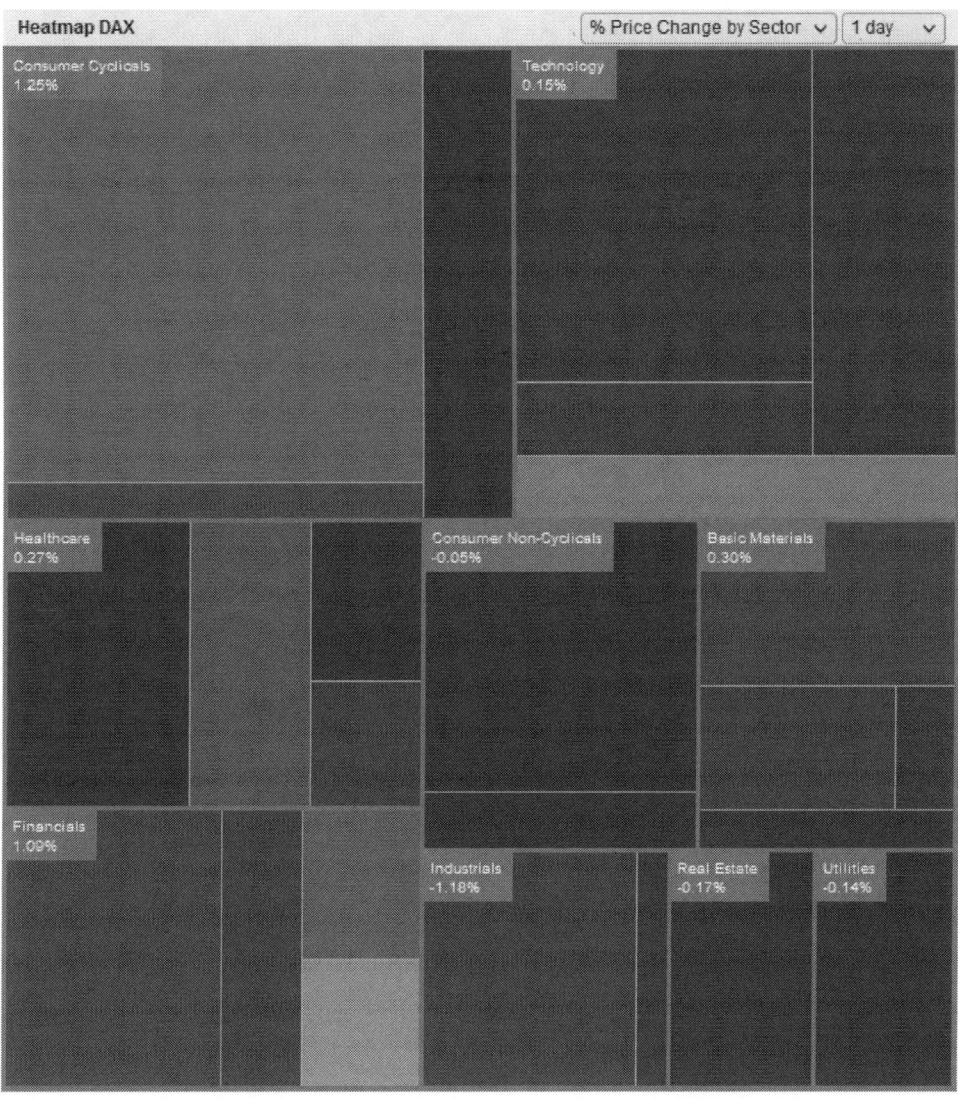

## FTSE

This index gauges the British economy and represents the biggest companies listed on the London exchange. Again, note how much space the financial sector takes.

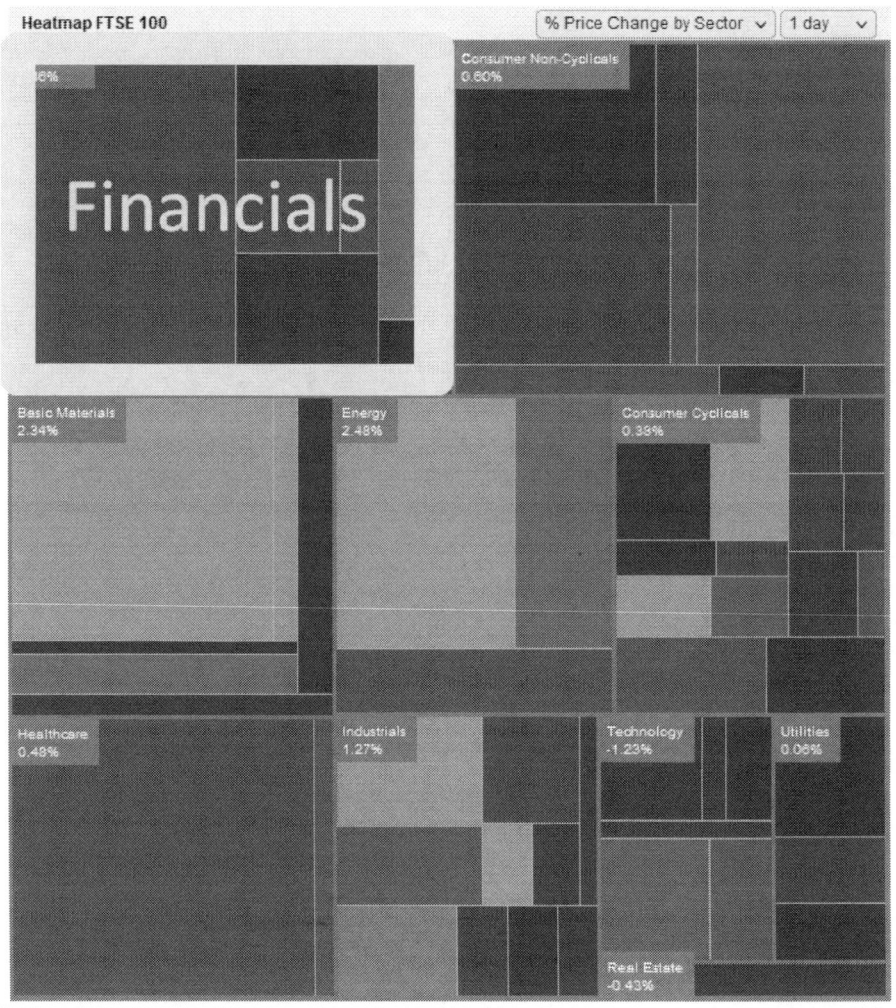

## BOVESPA

BOVESPA is a Brazilian index that gauges the performance of stocks quoted on the Brazilian Stock Exchange. If you buy this index, then you will be exposed to the performance of their financial sector by around 20%. Another thing to notice is that the technology sector represents only a marginal part of this index.

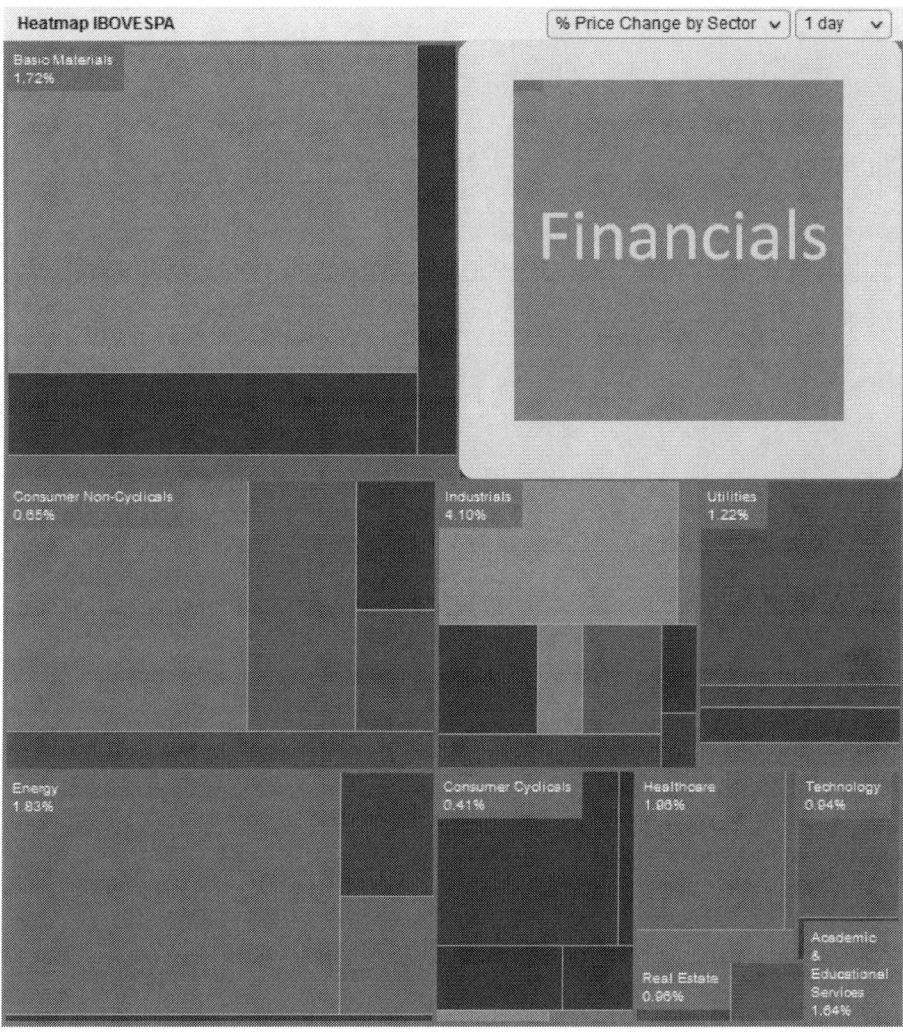

If you like these "heatmaps" and if you would like to learn about the sector structure of some index you are interested in, then go to this website: https://www.marketscreener.com

What you need to do is to search for the index you are interested in (in their search console), and then click "Heatmap".

As you can see, those heatmaps can be useful as they can tell you how big the sectors in that index are.

If there are one or two dominant sectors, and if you think those sectors are too risky for you to invest in (for me, that's the financial and technology sectors), then you may reconsider investing in that particular index and search for some different index to invest in.

To sum this up – the big disadvantage to index investing is that you are sort of "forced" to buy the stuff you don't want to. The risky stuff is the financial and technology sectors – and those often take up a big chunk of the index.

If there is a problem in the economy, then who goes down first? It's the banks (financial sector). And if the financial sector has a big weight in the index, it will inevitably drag the whole index down.

## Where To Find the Most Important Indexes?

There are two nice websites where you can find the names of indexes.

The first web page is: https://countryeconomy.com/stock-exchange

This page gives you a list of the world's biggest and most well-known indexes. If you scroll down, there is an interactive map that shows the most important index of any economy.

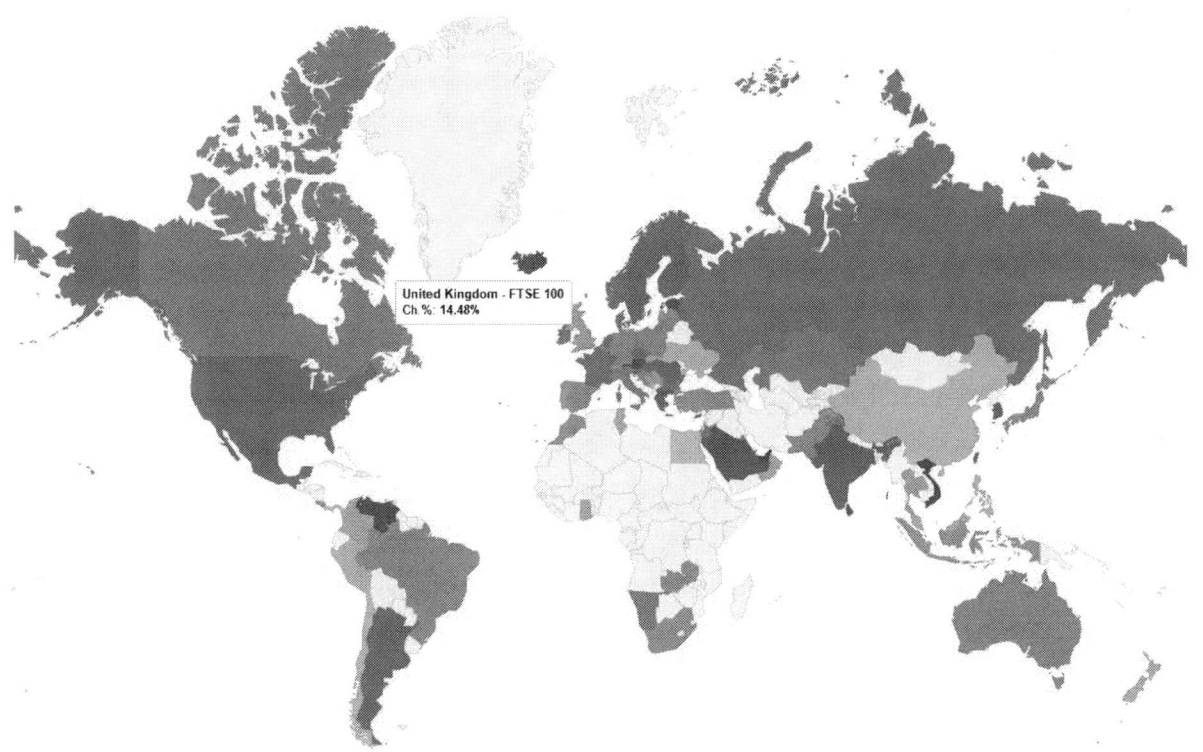

The second webpage (https://markets.ft.com/data/world) is better in the way that it gives you more indexes. Most of the bigger countries have more than one index to gauge their economy. This page reflects that. There is also an interactive map, and this one shows you all the leading indexes that gauge the selected country's economy. Not just the biggest and most well-known index. The interactive map looks like this:

# How To Choose the Right Country (Index) To Invest in?

The performance of the stock index depends on the economy of the country and its companies. That's why it's important to pick the country carefully.

There are two good starting points for you to check – Interest rates and Ratings.

## Interest Rates

Rule number one here is that you shouldn't invest in an economy that a stimulus drives. Such stimulus is most often very low or zero interest rates (rates at which the central bank lends money to other banks).

The stimulus is often used to boost the economy and should be used only for short-term boosts. What we are seeing now is many advanced countries (with the USA in the lead) pumping money into their economy at low rates for years! And yes, this helps the economy, companies and the stock market. But you need to realize that this is a stimulus. It is not sustainable. Right now, many economies and countries are "addicted" to such stimuli. But what happens when the stimulus is withdrawn (and it will be withdrawn)? A collapse. Like when a drug-addicted person can't get more drugs.

What I am trying to say here is that you want to invest in an economy that is healthy and that does not need such a stimulus. You want to look for a country that has "normal" interest rates.

I want this book to be universal and useful even after a couple of years. That's why I cannot say something like "look for economies with rates around 2% - because that's what I consider healthy." The reason is that everything is ever-changing. and what I consider normal and healthy now could easily be ordinary in a couple of years.

However, the basic rule that stays no matter what is: don't invest in countries that use extreme measures - like zero or negative rates. Those countries can have booming economies with rising and steady indexes, but those indexes will inevitably crash after the stimulus (drug) is withdrawn.

Here is a link to a webpage where you can quickly check the interest rates. Again, it comes with a nice interactive map: https://countryeconomy.com/key-rates

Let me show you a couple of charts where you can see how low-interest rates affect stock indexes.

### USA – S&P 500 index:

The chart below shows the S&P 500 index (blue) and interest rates (red). There are a couple of interesting things to notice.

1. Rates are declining. There have never been as low rates as they are now (start of 2022). Before the year 2000, it was quite normal to have a rate over 4%.
2. Every time the FED started their "free money" policy the stock index went up.

3. The zero-rate policy was usually applied after a crash to prevent a crisis or economic catastrophe.
4. The biggest, longest and steepest bull run was until the end of 2021 – when the rates were close to zero.

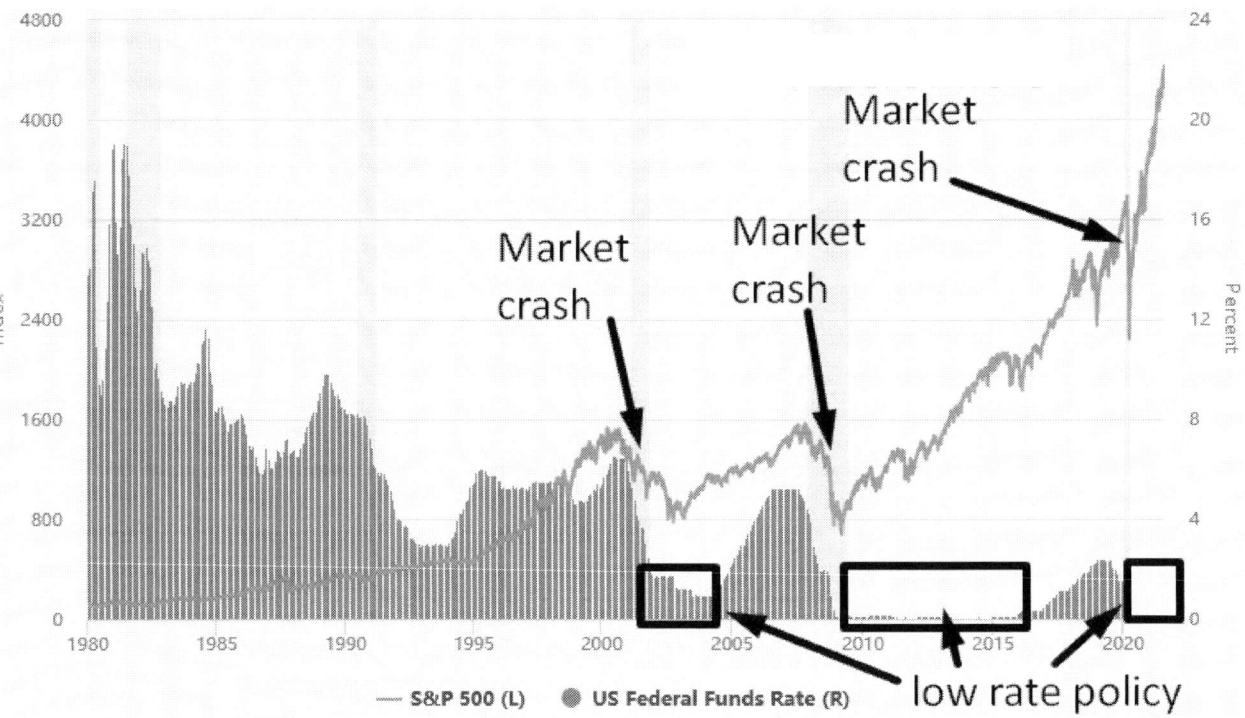

The US central bank (FED) is afraid to raise the rates more. Central bankers know how badly the economy, stocks and indexes would react to it. They are very limited in what they can do. Simply put - they need to raise rates, but they can't (at least not adequately) because the economy would collapse.

This is a typical example of a risky investment into an index in which life depends on constant stimulus.

## ECB (European Central Bank) rates:

Another example of economies whose growth is depending on zero or minimal rates is currently the Euro zone. Here the central bank ECB held zero rates from 2016 up until 2022 (when it rose slightly to 0.5%).

ECB rates chart:

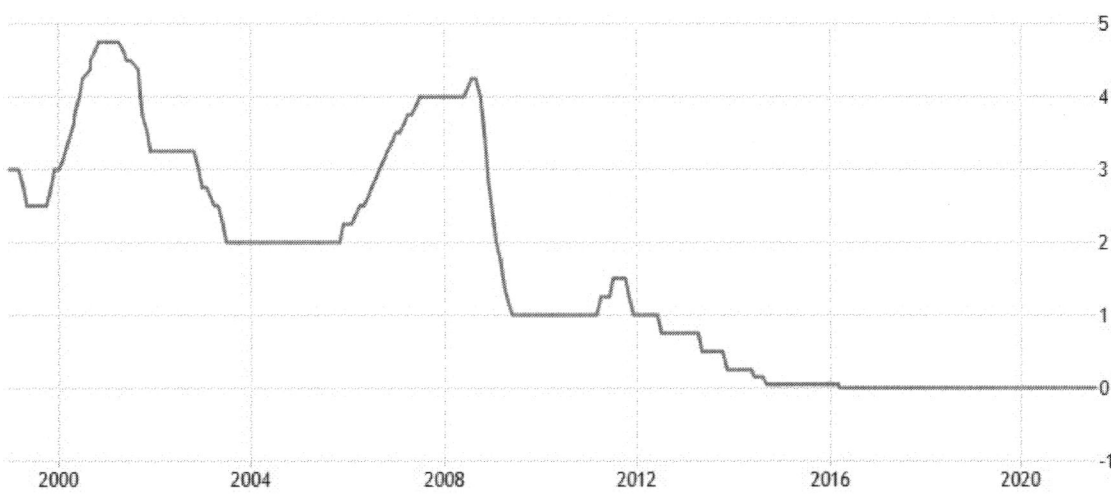

## BOJ (Bank of Japan) rates:

Another typical country where the central bank is stimulating the economy to the extreme is Japan. The Bank of Japan has been holding zero, or even slightly negative rates since the year 2000.

Would you want to invest in an economy where its performance is so hugely dependent on the Central bank stimulus? I hope your answer is "no."

# Rating

Another thing you should check before investing in a country through an index is the "rating" of the country.

There are three main rating agencies that rate countries and their credibility. Those agencies are Moody's, S&P and Fitch. Those are the so-called "big three." Those agencies are completely independent and neutral. They have their models of how they evaluate countries (and companies). The models they use for the credibility evaluation are not public so we can only guess what plays a role in their assessment and their final rating.

Here is the rating they use:

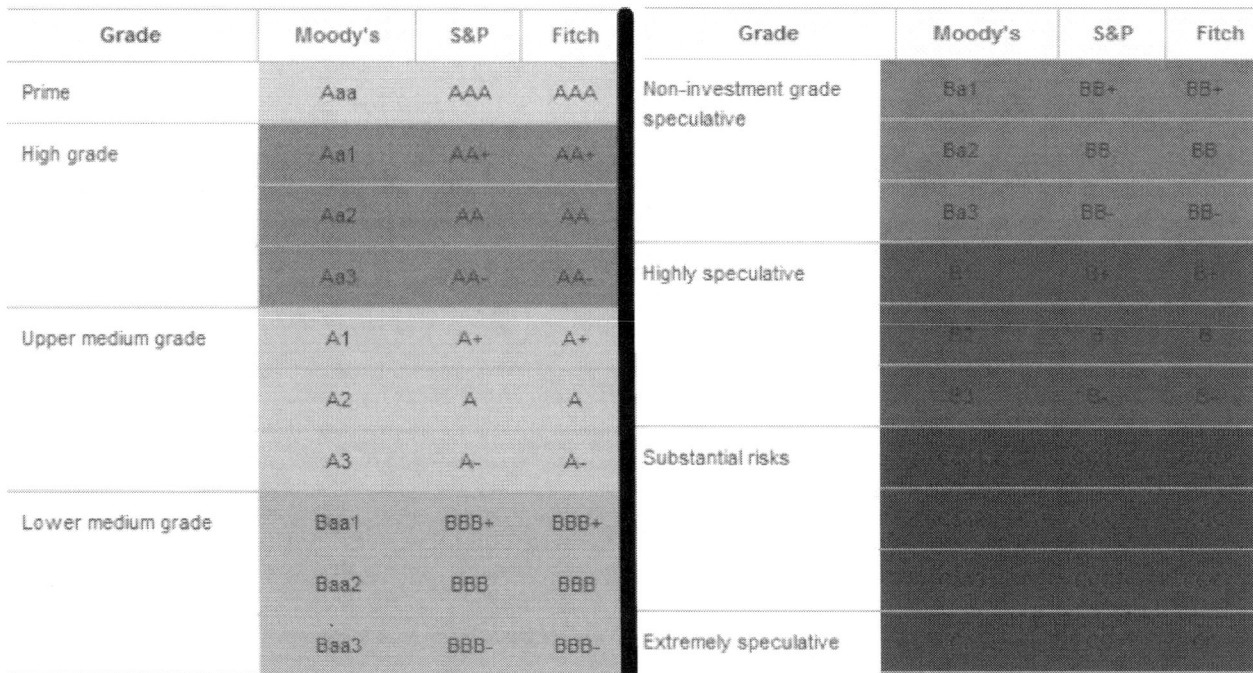

Even though professionals who focus solely on calculating risks and giving ratings run those agencies, it doesn't mean that they cannot make a mistake.

One of their biggest failures so far was that they were not able to spot companies who owned "toxic assets" and who caused the economic crisis in 2008. Those rating agencies are not all-knowing and without error!

What I am trying to say with this is that you definitely should look at the rating of the country you are going to invest in, but don't base your analysis and evaluation solely on the rating the agencies give the country. This should only be another piece of the puzzle into the bigger picture you want to create.

What you want to look for is a country with a good rating. My recommendation is to look only for countries that have the "non-investment" grade (speculative) or better.

This step will help you cut the riskiest countries out of your search.

Don't get me wrong – you definitely can make good money if you invest in a risky country with a bad economy. But if you invest there, then prepare for a very risky and wild ride! My goal here is not to get you on a crazy ride though. My goal is to help you build a stable portfolio with good risk/gain potential. If you want a crazy ride, then you are at the wrong place.

Here is a list of ratings of some picked countries. You can look at the full list on this webpage:

https://countryeconomy.com/ratings

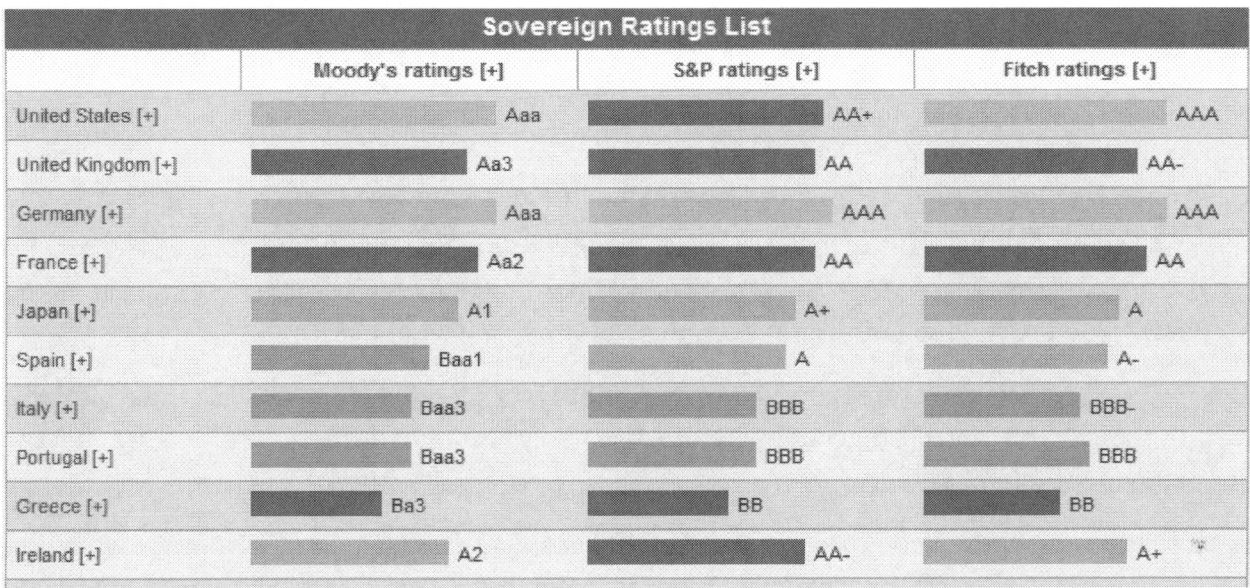

| Sovereign Ratings List | | | |
|---|---|---|---|
| | Moody's ratings [+] | S&P ratings [+] | Fitch ratings [+] |
| United States [+] | Aaa | AA+ | AAA |
| United Kingdom [+] | Aa3 | AA | AA- |
| Germany [+] | Aaa | AAA | AAA |
| France [+] | Aa2 | AA | AA |
| Japan [+] | A1 | A+ | A |
| Spain [+] | Baa1 | A | A- |
| Italy [+] | Baa3 | BBB | BBB- |
| Portugal [+] | Baa3 | BBB | BBB |
| Greece [+] | Ba3 | BB | BB |
| Ireland [+] | A2 | AA- | A+ |

An interesting thing to point out is that some of the best ratings were given to countries with enormous debts and countries whose economies run on zero-rate stimulus. This should give you an idea of how much trust you should put in those ratings...

To be frank, I sometimes get the feeling that those guys were doing a weather forecast for yesterday. They tell us that yesterday was raining and that it was wet and that today is probably going to be wet too...

So, check their ratings out, cut out the countries that are too risky to invest in and move on. Don't give this more attention than it deserves.

## Additional Info

There is much more info you can look at before you make your investment. I wouldn't delve too much into it but I understand there are a lot of true analytical people who need to do their super deep research before making their investment decision.

This is for them - deep but well-structured info about all countries: https://countryeconomy.com/

If you want to learn as much as you can about a single specific country, then go to this page: https://countryeconomy.com/countries

Just click the desired country and you will get all the info well-structured and all in one place.

## Indexes - A Final Note

I prefer economies that have solid companies with a business model I can understand easily. For example, Australia. This country has plenty of natural resources so they mine and provide energy, agriculture, and services mostly to the Asian market. Their biggest sector in the ASX index is "Basic Materials" – which is good (as it is not Technology or the Financial sector).

They manage to hold their rates above zero, their debt is not too big (compared to the rest of the world), they are an advanced economy with AAA (Prime) rating, and they have a quite healthy unemployment rate of around 5%.

Even though I would not consider the ASX index a bad investment, I don't think now would be the best time to invest in this index. The reason is that it is at its near its maximum. If I am to buy it, then I want it for a better (lower) price.

After selecting the right stock index to invest in, we need to open a price chart and do some analysis there. The goal is to find a price level where we would be willing to invest. More on how to do this later in this book!

# Introduction To Stock Investing

When a company needs additional funds to grow or simply more money for its business activities it has essentially two options. Option number one is to issue bonds which represent a debt the company will need to pay back in the future (including interest). The second option is that the company issues stocks.

The advantage of issuing stocks is that the company doesn't need to pay anything back. It's not a debt. The disadvantage of issuing stocks is that the company is selling a part of itself.

Imagine, for example, that you run a small coffee shop. You are good in the business and you would like to expand – to build a second one. Sure, you could be saving money and eventually after a couple of years build another one. What you could also do is to tell your rich friend to give you 1 mil USD in exchange for 30% of your whole business. Such a step would help you expand way quicker and you would never need to pay him back. This would cost you 30% of the company. 30% of all the money (net income) would go to him.

That 30% would belong to him forever unless he sold his 30% share back to you – for a different price than the 1 mil USD he paid before. It would be a price you both agree on. If your business prospers it could be for example 3 mil USD. If it doesn't, then the price could be 0.5 mil USD. Those are just random numbers and a very simplified case, but they should demonstrate the essence of how stocks work.

A lot of investors don't realize that by buying stocks they own a very small part of the company. For them, it's something intangible - just a ticker and a number that tells how much it costs.

A good piece of advice I once heard was that when you are considering buying a stock, then you should look at it as if you were buying the whole company. You should do your analysis as if you were considering buying the whole thing. If you think of it, then it's pretty good advice, since it doesn't matter if you are buying the whole company or just 0.0000001% of it. If the company strives, then you will strive too, no matter how big a part of it you own. I would like you to adapt this approach and always look at buying stocks as if you were buying the whole company.

## Advantages To Stock Investing

### Pick only stocks you like

The big advantage of stock investing to index investing is that with stock investing we can pick only the stocks we want to own. Only the ones we like the most. With index investing, on the other hand, you always need to buy all stocks from the index. No cherry picking. You buy all of it. The good and the bad.

### Outperform index

If you pick the right stocks, then you can outperform the index. The goal of stock investing should always be to make more money than you would make if you just bought the whole stock index.

### Endless opportunities

Another advantage to stock investing is that there is a huge amount of them to pick from. Hundreds and thousands of good quality companies! With this many stocks to pick from, you will never run out of opportunities.

## Disadvantages To Stock Investing

### Fees

A disadvantage to being an active stock trader is the fees that you pay each time you Buy or Sell a stock. The more active you are, the more fees you pay. This is simple with indexes as you can buy or sell the whole thing paying only one fee. With stocks, the number of transactions is bigger.

### Time-consuming

Another disadvantage to stock investing is that you need to spend time learning how to do this properly. You will also need to spend some time managing your portfolio and looking for new stocks and new opportunities. It's not too terrible, but compared to index investing, this approach is more time-consuming.

### Diversification

Another disadvantage is diversification. A diversified portfolio means you don't put all your eggs in one basket – you have more companies across more sectors.

With index, it is simple as when you buy an index you buy a whole basket of stocks from many different sectors. With stocks though, you need to invest in more different companies to have a diversified portfolio. Investing in more companies means more fees and more time spent on picking the right stocks and managing your portfolio.

# Economic Models? Don't Make Rocket Science of It!

As you progress further in this book, you will maybe start to think that my approach to investing and analyzing stocks is a bit simplistic. There are so many models to evaluate stocks, so why don't we use any?

It's not that I wouldn't know them. Believe me, I have learned my share of them at the Economic university. A huge chunk of my studies was about those models.

The problem I see with those models is that they were developed mostly by academic economists. It's a theory. They work theoretically, not in real life.

Do you know what "ceteris paribus" means? It's a very popular phrase used with these models. It means that everything outside of the model stays the same. But in the real world, everything is connected. Everything has an impact on everything and even the most complex models can't possibly contemplate that.

All the unexpected events simply can't be calculated into a model.

A couple of examples: An active volcano on an Island stops Airlines from flying, a COVID-19 pandemic, Donald Trump or Elon Musk tweets, or a scandal with one automobile company negatively affects the stock prices of other, completely unrelated automobile companies, … This stuff happens very often but you can't put it into a model.

Another thing I just can't get my head around is how risk is measured in those models. It's usually measured by Beta. Simply put, the more volatile the stock is, the riskier it is. Does it make sense? Not to me…

Imagine this: You want to invest in a strong company. Let's say Coca-Cola. The standard price is more or less steady at around $45 per stock. Now, there is a crash in the S&P 500 index, which affects and drags down everything in it (Coca-Cola included). Suddenly Coca Cola stock is at $20. What happens in a model is that Beta (risk) rises dramatically and suddenly Coca Cola would appear a bad investment. But in real life, Coca-Cola is still the same company. They still sell the same products; they still have their worldwide business and they still have stable earnings. Why is it riskier now? I would say Coca-Cola just got discounted so I better buy some! It's less risky, not more!

After university, I worked as an analyst in a brokerage company. Our senior analysts I worked with and learned from were pretty clever guys. And guess what? None of them was using economic models.

So, if not economical models, how are we going to determine if a company is any good?

We will use stock screeners to filter out the bad companies and find the good ones. And we won't make a rocket science of it!

## How Are We Going to Do This

I am going to tell you the main idea behind the method I am about to teach you. Just to give you a quick overview so you know what to expect.

First, we are going to use a market screener to filter out the bad stocks and find the potentially good ones. We will cut out risky sectors like Financials or Technology sectors. We will also filter out stocks that are not healthy. Those are stocks of companies with too big debt, too small income, companies that are losing money, companies without tangible assets, etc.

In the end, we will end up with a couple of companies that we like and that we are ready to invest in – if the price is right.

How do we tell if the price is right? By using Volume Profile, but more on that later.

## Our Edge

Many people all over the internet conduct unnecessarily thorough stock analysis. They make rocket science of it. What they don't realize is that they will never have all the info and that their analysis will never be perfect. Our goal will not be to surpass those guys in the complexity of the analysis.

The edge we will have over those guys is that we will be picking good and healthy stocks and using an advanced trading tool – Volume Profile to pick the best timing for the investment.

# Stock Screeners

A stock screener is a freely available online tool for looking for viable stocks to invest in. Screeners have a huge database with hundreds, even thousands of stocks and detailed info about each of them.

The reason I like to use screeners is that you can filter out bad and risky stocks with only a few clicks and narrow down your search very easily. And the best part is that you don't need to be an expert to do this!

There are more stock screeners around, each a bit different. Here are some good ones to pick from:

**Finviz**: https://finviz.com/screener.ashx

This screener is one of the most popular ones and it's the one I will show you how to work with. I like it because it's very intuitive and well-arranged. A little disadvantage is that it only includes stocks that are quoted on US stock exchanges (AMEX, NASDAQ, NYSE). This does not mean you won't be able to analyze stocks from different countries. You will be able to do that as long as those stocks are quoted (available to trade) on one of the three American exchanges.

If you are looking for something a bit more exotic (stocks that are not quoted on AMEX, NASDAQ or NYSE), then you will need to use another screener.

**Yahoo Finance**: https://finance.yahoo.com/screener/new

Yahoo screener is the biggest screener around. It includes data on stocks from all around the world. This is also one of my favorite screeners and I use it to filter out stocks as well as to learn more details about them. Their database is huge. If you are looking for some specific stock, and you can't find info about it anywhere, then you will find it here.

There are a couple of different Yahoo finance websites – based on the country. For example, if you want specific info about some Australian stocks, then you go to the Australian version of the Yahoo finance website (https://au.finance.yahoo.com/australia). If you want Canadian stocks, then it is (https://ca.finance.yahoo.com).

**MarketInOut:** https://www.marketinout.com/stock-screener/stock_screener.php

This is a stock screener with a huge database of stocks quoted on exchanges from all over the world. If you don't want to be limited to searching only American exchanges (using Finviz), then use the Market InOut. Here, you will be able to search through stock from stock exchanges from all over the world. What I recommend is to save the tickers (names) of the stocks you found there and go to Yahoo.com where you should be able to find more detailed info about them.

# How To Filter Out Stocks Using FINVIZ Stock Screener

The Finviz stock screener has three tabs to use when looking for stocks or filtering them out. The tabs are the **Descriptive** tab, **Fundamental** tab, and **Technical** tab. We won't be using the Technical tab as I don't think it is any good. Instead of this tab, we will use our tool – the Volume Profile.

In the Descriptive and Fundamental tabs, there are many parameters and filters to help you narrow down your search for stocks. Some of them are useful, and some of them are not.

Our goal is to make things simple, so I won't bother you by describing each parameter from the long list. This would only make it overwhelming and not helpful at all. Instead, I will focus only on the parameters I find useful and that I use.

# FINVIZ: Descriptive Tab

This tab focuses mostly on the big picture rather than the company details. This is what it looks like:

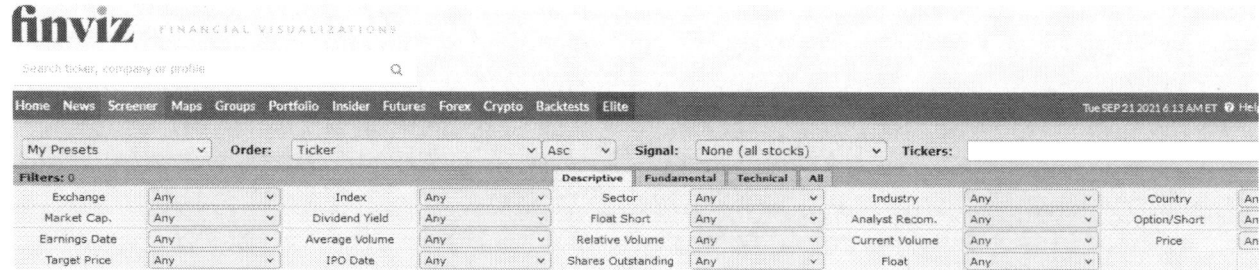

**All the parameters you can set up are:**

Exchange, Index, Sector, Industry, Country, Market Capitalization, Dividend Yield, Float Short, Analyst Recommendations, Optionable/Shortable, Earnings Date, Average Volume, Relative Volume, Current Volume Price, Analyst mean Target Price, IPO Date, Shares Outstanding, Float.

Feeling overwhelmed already? Don't worry I am here to tell you what parameters are important. It's just a few of them.

**Recommended parameters to use:**

- Market Capitalization
- Dividend Yield
- Sector
- Industry

Yea – just four. The obvious question is – what about the rest? Aren't those parameters important as well? Not really. Take for example the "**Analyst recommendations**" and their "**Target Price**". We know nothing about their analysis, about models they used, we don't know who those guys are, we know nothing. Those guys can just point a finger at the screen and write down the price where their finger landed. Also, in the end, their target price differs dramatically! What Finviz does next is they make an average out of it. That doesn't make any sense. It's like you wanted a blue car, your wife a red one, so you buy a purple car because that's what comes if you mix red and blue.

Let's have a look at another example - the "**Average Volume**". For investing, it is not that important to seek stocks that trade at higher volumes. This is important for day trading, but not for investing. Also, Finviz only has data on stocks that are quoted on the biggest US stock exchanges. No small stock will make it there. For those reasons, there is no point in setting up this parameter/filter.

Another example is the parameter "**Float**" – this one tells you how many shares are available to trade for the public. This may be an interesting piece of information, but that's about it. I don't see a point in picking a stock based on this.

Another example: "**IPO date** "– this tells you when the stock initially went public (when it became available to trade for the public). In my opinion, this is also not that important. Sure, you can use this one if you want to look only for the old and time-proven companies and I am not saying it's a wrong approach. But in the end, if we want to focus only on the most important parameters, then this is not one of them.

I would say that most of the parameters are quite interesting, but only a few are helpful.

Let's now have a closer look at the ones I do find helpful. These are Market Capitalization, Dividend Yield, Sector, and Industry.

# Market Capitalization

I recommend looking only for companies with a Market Capitalization **bigger than $300 mln**. In Finviz, they are categorized as "**Small**". What I prefer even more, though, are companies that are one step bigger: **$2bln** and more. Those are categorized as "**Mid**" companies.

Many people like to search through the little (called junk or penny stock) companies, looking for a hidden gem that will one day soar and shoot through the roof making them rich. I am not saying it is impossible, because such things are happening. But the chances that you or I will find that gem is small. Investors that trade such "penny stock" strategies usually buy hundreds or thousands of those tiny companies to have a solid chance of picking a few gems. Those few gems should pay for the rest of the penny stocks that never really performed or went bankrupt and, of course, for the exchange fees. If the investor is successful, then he ends up with some extra money after he covers all those costs.

I am not saying this is a bad strategy, but it's not something I would prefer. For me, it feels like you were shooting 1000 bullets blindfolded hoping for one or two successful hits. What I prefer is to shoot 20 bullets and hit the target 15 times.

The bigger companies have the advantage, that they have already proved to have a good product and that their business is scalable – it can grow. Bigger companies are also often older companies, which means they are already "time-tested" or "battle-tested". Simply put they are less likely to fail than the smaller companies.

That's why I recommend looking for stocks of the bigger and more stable companies. In Finviz, this would be companies with a Market Capitalization of at least over $300m and preferably over $2b.

# Dividend Yield

A dividend is a part of the profit the company made distributed to shareholders.

**Calculation:** It is calculated as the latest yearly Dividend divided by the current price of the stock. If the last yearly dividend was $10 (per share) and the stock price is currently (today) $100, then Dividend Yield is 10/100 = 10%.

$$\text{Dividend Yield} = \frac{\text{Annual Dividends per Share}}{\text{Price per Share}}$$

An important message this formula tells us is that Dividend Yield relies not only on the dividend the company pays out but also on the price of shares you bought the stock for. The cheaper you buy, the bigger the dividend!

Later, I am going to teach you how to best time your stock investments. You will learn that the best time to invest is when there is a drop in prices. When prices drop, then dividend yield rises (look at the formula above)! Isn't this a very good reason to invest when the market drops?

I like companies that pay dividends. At least 2% to cover the inflation (or a part of it). When I search for stocks, I usually set the dividend filter to show only companies that pay a bigger dividend than 2%.

BTW the majority of S&P 500 stocks vary between 1% and 2% dividend yield.

You can go for more here if you like. Even a 3-4% dividend is fine and sustainable. No problem there. If it's more than that, then it may be too good to be true. Higher dividend yields may not be sustainable in the long run. Remember, the equation to calculate Dividend yield uses only the latest company statement. It doesn't tell you the whole history and how big the dividends were before.

Another thing I would like you to consider is that when a company earns money, it has two options. Either keep the money in the company – which should use it for its growth or give the money to shareholders. There is not a good or a bad option. (BTW this is called "Payout ratio" = ratio between how much the company pays to shareholders and how much it keeps).

It's quite common and healthy that companies that are still growing and expanding don't pay a huge dividend. They need the money to expand (which should eventually show in the growth of the stock price).

On the other hand, huge companies that have already built their business and have a big chunk of the market share tend to pay a lot more to the shareholders.

It's simply not black or white. A big dividend doesn't always need to be a sign of a well-managed company.

One more thing to mention here is that there are also companies that heavily rely on the economic cycle – as far as their dividends are concerned. This is most typical for REIT companies (Real Estate Investment Trust). Those pay huge dividends (they pay around 90% of their income to shareholders!). Their dividends could range from 5-10% even. However, they can only pay huge dividends when the main interest rates are low. But this is not sustainable, is it? When interest rates rise it's not unicorns and rainbows anymore and these companies are forced to significantly cut their dividend.

I am not saying REITs are bad. I am only trying to say that I recommend looking for a more stable and sustainable dividend yield.

On a final note, if something looks too good to be true, then there is probably something you missed or some accounting trick you did not get. If you stick roughly to the 2-4% range, then you should be fine.

# Sectors

There are 11 sectors that the Finviz screener recognizes. Those sectors are:

Basic Materials, Communication Services, Consumer Cyclical, Consumer Defensive, Energy, Financial, Healthcare, Industrials, Real Estate, Technology, and Utilities.

**Recommended sectors**

Basic Materials, Consumer Defensive, Healthcare, Industrials (to some extent), and Utilities.

**Not Recommended**

Financial, Technology, Consumer Cyclical (to some extent).

When you are screening for stocks, you will always need to select one sector. You cannot select multiple. So, for example, you will be looking for stocks in the Basic Materials first. When finished, you will select another sector, for example, Communicational Services and do your screening again.

I recommend investing in more than one sector. Putting all your eggs in one basket would be too risky. However, I don't recommend spreading your portfolio too wide into too many sectors. If you do this, then you might as well buy the index which would be cheaper. I recommend you choose 4 -5 sectors and pick stocks from those.

Each sector consists of industries. I am now going to give you some more detailed info about each sector and its industries:

## Basic Materials

The basic materials sector includes companies that specialize in the discovery, extraction, and processing of raw materials.

Raw materials are natural resources such as Gold, Silver, Iron Ore, Coal, Oil, Natural gas, Stone, and Wood, ...

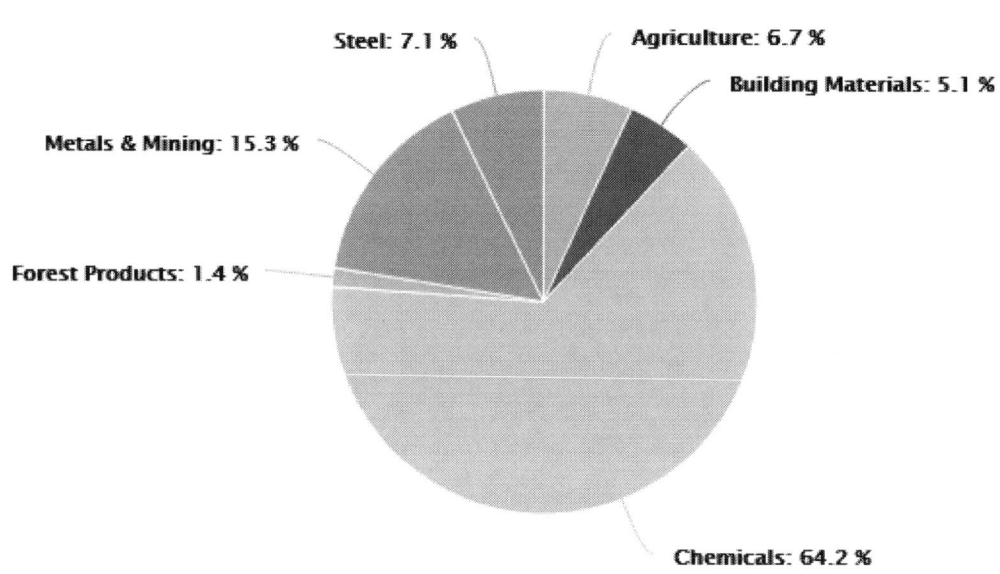

**Industries**

- Agricultural Inputs
- Aluminum
- Building Materials
- Chemicals
- Coal
- Copper
- Gold
- Lumber & Wood Production
- Other Industrial and Precious Metals & Mining
- Paper & Paper Products
- Silver
- Steel

**Leading companies**

- Linde plc (LIN) – Specialty chemicals, United Kingdom
- BHP Group (BBL, BHP) – Industrial Metals & Mining, Australia
- Rio Tinto Group (RIO) – Industrial Metals & Mining, United Kingdom
- Vale S.A. (VALE) – Industrial Metals & Mining, Brazil
- The Sherwin-Williams Company (SHW) – Specialty Chemicals, USA
- Ecolab (Inc. (ECL) – Specialty Chemicals, USA

## Sector Specifics
**Sensitive to the business cycle**

Companies from this sector provide materials mostly for companies dealing in construction. This makes the Basic Materials sector **sensitive to the business cycle**. When the economy is expanding, companies are growing. There is a lot of construction being done (housing, industrial & commercial buildings, infrastructure, …) which results in high demand for Basic materials. In this scenario, the companies in the Basic materials sector thrive.

If the economy is not doing well, then there is not so much new construction going on and demand for Basic materials is low. This negatively impacts companies in this sector.

**Easy to grasp**

What I like about this sector is that it is quite **easy to understand** – I mean the business model. Nothing complicated here – companies simply discover and get the materials (wood, coal, stone, …) and then they process them and sell them. Simple business model, right? I think it is important to be able to understand the basics of how each sector works. With Basic Materials, I think it is pretty straightforward.

**Difficult & expensive entry for companies**

What I also like is that it is quite complicated for new companies to get into the Basic Materials sector and create new competition. This sector is very hard for a new company to get into. The main reason is that it is expensive. For example, it is super complicated and expensive to create a company that would drill and sell oil. The same goes for mining gold, stone, etc.

This means that the companies that have already made it into this sector are likely to keep their market share. The risk of a new competitor entering this market and endangering the market positions of the current leading companies is quite low.


**Good book value**

Companies in the Basic Materials sector need to own a lot of tangible and expensive assets to operate (machinery, buildings, land, …). This is sort of a universal fact in this sector. Having a lot of tangible assets means that the company has a good book value.

If it makes it easier for you to understand this, then you can imagine the book value as a sort of "real value".

A good investor should be aware of the book value. Why? Because if in a critical scenario a company goes bankrupt, then investors won't lose all their investment. What will happen is that all the assets of the company will get sold (machines, buildings, land, other properties…), the company debt will be paid, and then the rest of the money will go back to the investors. The bigger the book value, the more money will go back to investors.

**Simplified example:** Company's market value is $10 bln. It owns machines, factories, buildings and land with a total value of $5 bln. It also has a debt of $1 bln. If this company went bankrupt, then shareholders would get $4 bln. back from their investment ($5 bln. – $1bln. = $ 4bln).

What does this mean for you as a shareholder? It means you get your cut as well as the other shareholders. How big your cut would depend on how many stocks you own (how big a portion of the company you own). If you own 1% of the company, then you get $40 mil.


**P/B Ratio (Price to Book ratio)**

Currently, the average Price/Book ratio (P/B) in this sector is around 1.9 (August 2022). This means that stock prices in this sector are 1.9 times bigger than the company's Book value. Book value is an accounting term and it means the stuff the company can in the worst-case scenario sell (this is a bit simplified, but it's the gist of it).

1.9 is quite a good number. For example, the Technology sector had a P/B ratio of around 5 just a month ago.

Here is a long-term chart of the P/B ratio in the whole Basic Materials sector:

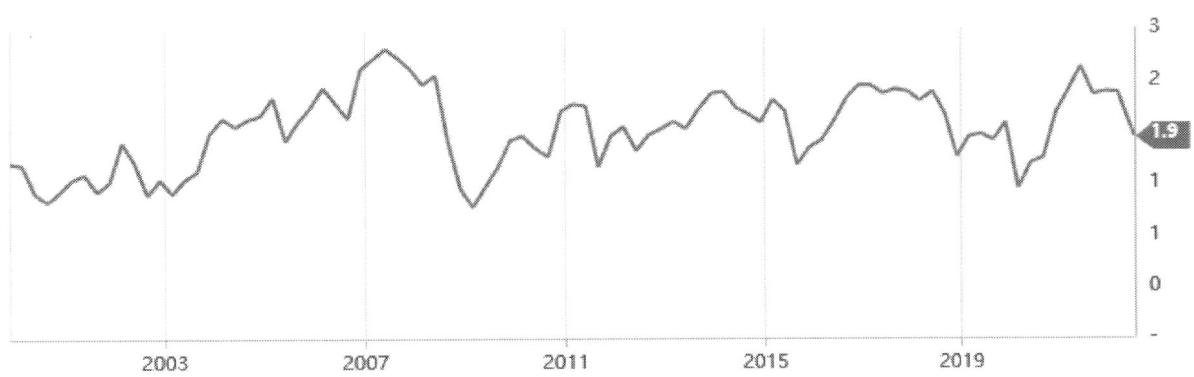

## Dividend

The average dividend in this sector is currently 1.8%. To stay up to date and find the newest numbers, go here:

https://www.gurufocus.com/industry_overview.php?sector=Basic-Materials&region=USA

For your comparison, most companies in the S&P 500 index have their dividend between 1-2%.


## P/E Ratio (Price to Earnings ratio)

We will talk more about the ratios later, but to give you a brief info about this: the P/E ratio tells us how much you pay now to receive $1 of the company earnings.

You can also look at it this way: How many years will it take the company to earn you the money you paid for your stocks?

**Example**: Stock price is $100. One stock of the company makes $10/year in Earnings. In this case, it will take 10 years to cover the investment. In 10 years, the company will earn you the money you invested in it ($100/$10) = 10 years.

The average P/E ratio in this sector is currently 12.4. If you buy an average stock from this sector, it will take 12.4 years (based on the current earnings) to make you the money back. In other words, you now pay $12.4 to receive $1 of the company earnings.

The P/E ratio in the Basic Materials sector does not change that much over time. It is quite stable as you can see in the chart below:

**PE Ratio**
- Basic Materials

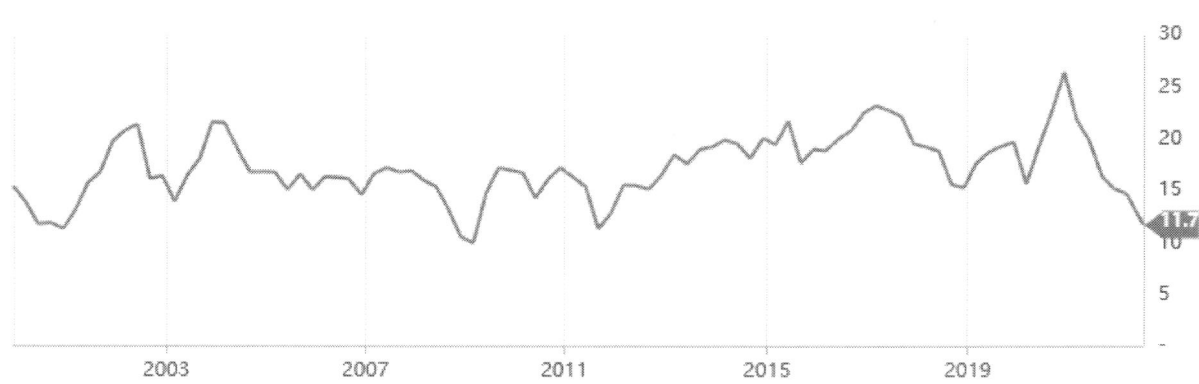

Just for your comparison, the long-term average P/E in the whole S&P 500 index is around 16.

# Communication Services

This sector has three main sub-sectors. It's Telecommunication services, Internet Media, and Diversified Media.

Companies in the **Telecommunication sector** transmit text, audio, and video to make communication possible. They do it through phone, internet, wire and wireless (Verizon, AT&T, ...)

**Diversified Media** includes companies that provide internet entertainment – mostly movies, television, and internet broadcasting ... (Disney, Netflix, Comcast, ...)

**Interactive Media** is from the biggest part just two companies – Google and Meta.

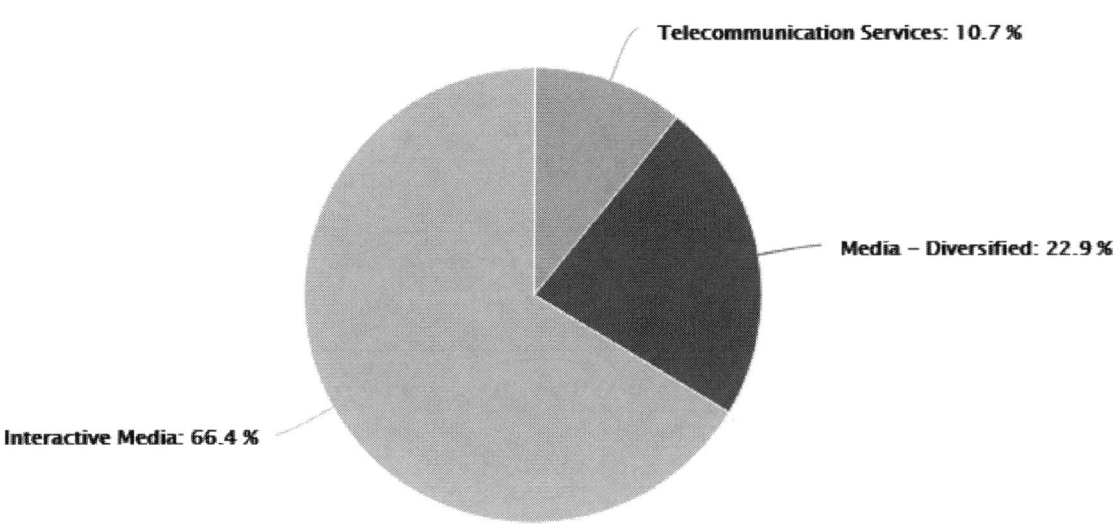

### Industries

- Advertising Agencies
- Broadcasting
- Electronic Gaming & Multimedia
- Entertainment
- Internet Content & Information
- Publishing
- Telecom Services

**Leading companies**

- Alphabet Inc = Google (GOOGL) – Internet Content & Information, USA
- Meta (FB) – Internet Content & Information, USA
- The Walt Disney Company (DIS) – Entertainment, USA
- Comcast Corporation (SMCSA) – Entertainment, USA
- Netflix (NFLX) – Entertainment, USA
- Verizon Communications (VZ) – Telecom services, USA
- AT&T (T) – Telecom services, USA

## Sector Specifics

**Not sensitive to the business cycle**

What I like about this sector is that it is not too sensitive to the business cycle. No matter if there is a crisis or if the economy is booming, people will always be using phones, and the internet and they will always be watching television. Interactive media (Google, Meta) is also a strong trend on the rise, so I don't expect much change there either – regardless of the phase of the business cycle.

**Fast-growing sector**

This sector is growing fast. Just look at what the leading companies in this sector are. It's Google and Meta. Those are the biggest companies in the world. Also, video streaming platforms are becoming more and more popular.

**Difficult & expensive entry for companies**

It's not easy for a new company to make it into this sector. Customers now demand high standards regarding speed, availability and quality of internet connection, data flow, video streaming resolution and quality, … All this is not cheap. Big investments are needed to deliver such standards. Only companies that can keep up with the rising standards can survive in this sector. It's very hard for new companies to make it here.

This is good for the current companies who already have their share in this sector. Still, they need to keep up with the competition if they don't want to be left behind.

This sector is not as stable and simple (in its essence) as the Basic Materials sector. As an investor, you need to have at least some basic knowledge about this sector and the companies in it.

## P/B (Price to Book ratio)

The average Price to Book ratio in this sector is currently 1.6. If you look at Price to Tangible-Book (this is just tangible stuff), then it is 3.6 on average. This shows that companies in this sector are a bit inflated concerning the tangible stuff they own. In other words – if a company from this sector goes bankrupt, you won't get too much out of it.

This does not mean the companies here are bad. It just shows how this sector works overall.

Below is the development of the P/B ratio in the long run (since 2000). Notice the drop after the Dot-com bubble after 2000 and then after the financial crisis in 2007-2008. Especially after the crisis in 2007-2008, there were great opportunities to buy stocks very close to their actual book value! Buying stocks close to their book value greatly reduces the risk of your investment (even though economical models using Beta to calculate risk will tell you otherwise).

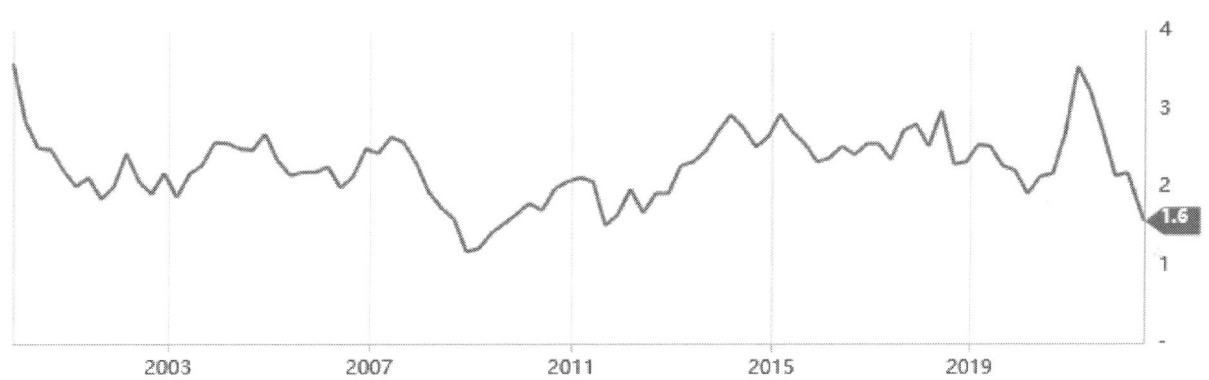

## P/E Ratio (Price to Earnings ratio)

The P/E ratio in this sector is currently averaging around 15. This is more or less around the long-term average of the whole US economy. I think investors are quite optimistic about this sector – or at least they were until stock prices and also the P/E started to drop dramatically from over 25 to 15.

Let me tell you why they were willing to buy for inflated prices: If they bought stocks with the P/E = 25 and if earnings doubled in the future (the company started to make twice as much as when they bought the stock) then it would be like if they bought the stock with P/E 12.5, which would not be bad at all!

This is what investors were hoping for. They were too optimistic because it is a growing and popular sector. This is the reason prices were until recently inflated (and therefore P/E was inflated as well).

The chart below shows the P/E ratio in this sector since 2000.

**PE Ratio**

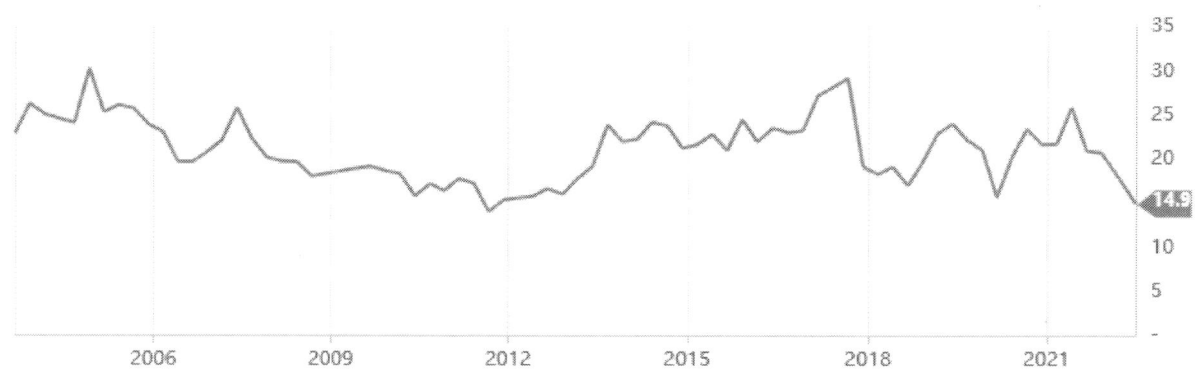

### Dividend

Dividend in this sector is currently averaging around 2.3%. There are differences between the three sub-sectors though. The biggest average dividend is in the Telecommunication services (3.3%), then Diversified Media (2.8%), and what brings the average down is the Interactive Media with Google and Meta in the lead, paying out only 0.8% dividend.

The reason Telecommunication services can give such a nice dividend is that they are partly regulated and this gives them sort of a stable share on the market, allowing them to keep their margins from which they pay dividends to the shareholders.

## Consumer Cyclical

Typical Consumer Cyclical companies are car manufacturers, airlines, furniture retailers, clothing stores, hotels, and restaurants, ...

When the economy and people are doing well, then they buy cars, travel, buy clothes and go out to restaurants. If they are not doing good, then they can easily cut those expenses because they are not essential.

This is why I am a bit skeptical about this sector. I prefer companies that are stable no matter what. I am not too much into companies that thrive only when the economy is doing well and that have serious problems when it's not.

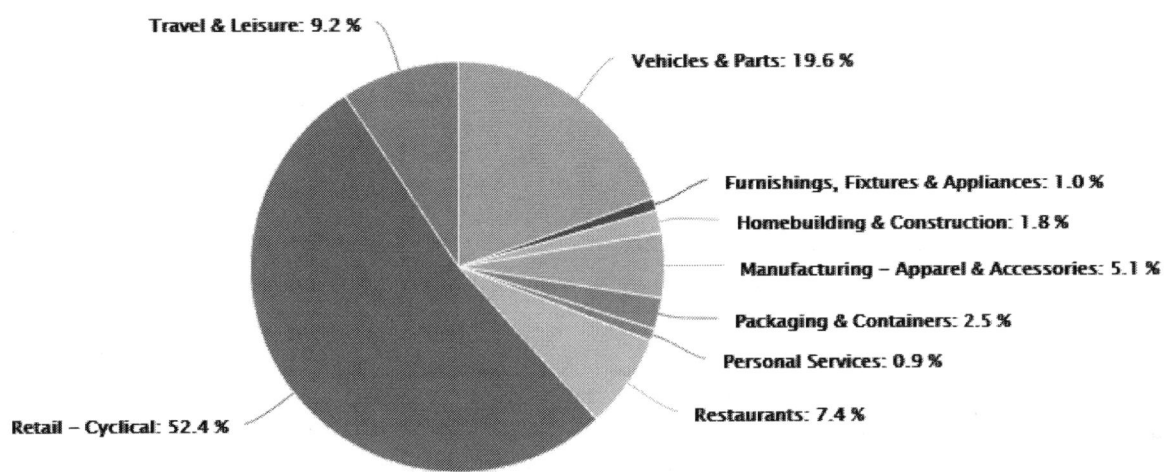

### **Industries**

- Apparel Manufacturing & Retail
- Auto Manufacturers & Parts
- Auto & Truck Dealerships
- Department Stores
- Footwear & accessories
- Furnishings, Fixtures & Appliances
- Gambling
- Home Improvement Retail
- Internet Retail
- Leisure
- Lodging
- Luxury Goods

- Packaging & Containers
- Personal Services
- Recreational Vehicles
- Residential Construction
- Resorts & Casinos
- Restaurants
- Textile Manufacturing
- Travel Services

**Leading Companies**

- Amazon.com (AMZN) – Internet Retail, USA
- Tesla (TSLA) – Auto Manufacturers, USA
- Alibaba Group (BABA) – Internet Retail, China
- The Home Depot (HD) – Home improvement Retail, USA
- Toyota (TM) – Auto Manufacturers, Japan
- Nike (NKE) – footwear Accessories, USA
- McDonald's (MCD) – Restaurants, USA
- Starbucks (SBUX) – Restaurants, USA

**P/B (Price to Book ratio)**

The current P/B ratio in this sector is around 2, and if we look at the tangible stuff, then it is 3.5. This is around the long-term average in this sector. It was not like this a couple of months back though (P/B was around 3). The reason it was way higher was that the FED was stimulating the economy and printing cheap money. People had money to spend and they spent it. That's why this sector was thriving and stock prices were rising.

Recently, the US started to raise interest rates, which forced the market to sober up a bit and bring prices and the P/B ratio back to the long-term average - which has been around 2 for the last 20 or so years.

Here is the historical P/B ratio in the Consumer Cyclical sector since 2000:

**PB Ratio**
* Consumer Cyclical

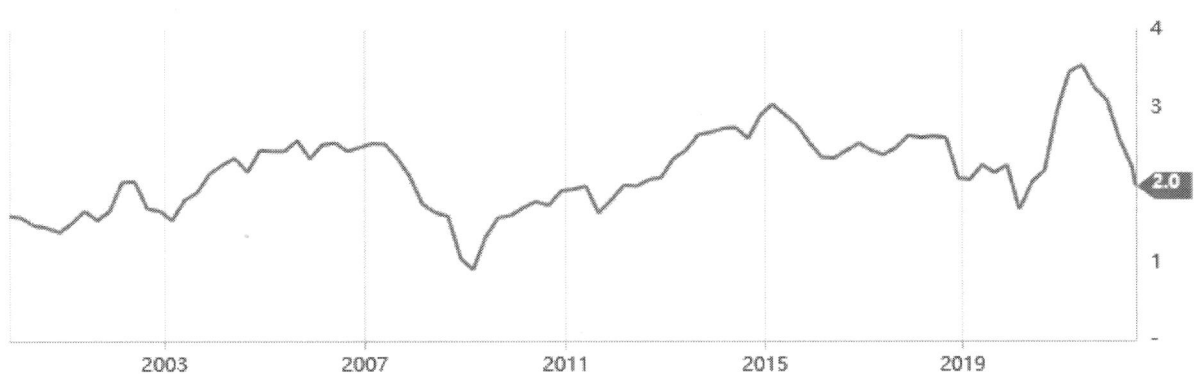

## P/E Ratio (Price to Earnings ratio)

The P/E ratio in the Consumer Cyclical sector is currently around 12.

If you look at the historical chart of P/E development, you can see how this ratio reacted to all crises. The best visible is the reaction after the dot-com crisis around 2000, then the financial crisis in 2007-2008, the covid crisis, and now the rise of interest rates (big impact on this sector!). So far, there has always been a quick recovery after each dip as the banks briskly started to provide cheap money to the economy to avoid a catastrophe. But now things may be different because the era of super cheap money seems to be ending (central bankers fear rising inflation and for this reason, they are rising interest rates).

**PE Ratio**
* Consumer Cyclical

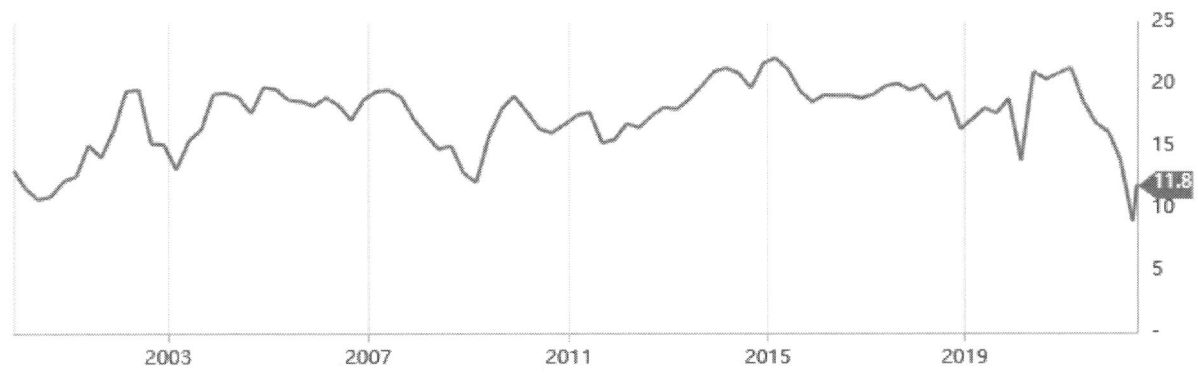

**Dividend yield**

The dividend yield in this sector is currently averaging 2.1% which is a bit above the S&P 500 index average. One thing to keep in mind is that now the era of cheap money could be ending, or at least the money printing machines are slowing down. So far, people were spending on non-essentials. This meant companies from the Consumer Cyclical sector had money to pay dividends. Now, the situation could be changing. With diminishing earnings, companies may not have enough to keep paying out dividends.

## Consumer Defensive

The consumer Defensive sector comprises companies that sell foods, beverages, household goods, hygiene products, alcohol and tobacco.

This sector is also referred to as "Consumer Staples". It is more or less the opposite of the "Consumer Cyclical" sector as it comprises companies that provide essential products to retail customers. Those essential products are things that people will always demand no matter the economic cycle – no matter if there is a depression or if the economy is booming. Economists call these products "products with low price elasticity". This means that people will always buy them no matter the price.

Some companies fare better during economic depressions. Typically, Alcohol and Tobacco companies. This makes them a very interesting investment.

Stocks in this sector are not too volatile. Companies pay regular dividends and have quite consistent growth which is not dependent on the economic cycle. Those are the reasons why I like investing in this sector.

An interesting fact is that this sector is the 2$^{nd}$ best performing sector in the long run (from 1962 until 2021). The average annual return was 8.20%. Slow and steady wins the race 😊

### Sector Weighting

- Tobacco Products: 8.2 %
- Beverages – Alcoholic: 3.0 %
- Beverages – Non-Alcoholic: 18.6 %
- Retail – Defensive: 30.7 %
- Education: 1.7 %
- Consumer Packaged Goods: 37.8 %

**Industries**

- Beverages (Alcoholic, Non-alcoholic, Brewers)
- Confectioners
- Discount Stores

- Education & Training Services
- Farm Products
- Food distribution
- Grocery Stores
- Household & Personal Products
- Packaged Foods
- Tobacco

**Leading companies**

- Walmart (WMT) – Discount Stores, USA
- The Procter & Gamble Company (PG) – Household & Personal Products, USA
- The Coca-Cola Company (KO) – Beverages, USA
- PepsiCo (PEP) - Beverages, USA
- Costco Wholesale Corporation (COST) – Discount Stores, USA
- Philip Morris (PM) – Tobacco, USA
- Unilever (UL) - Household & Personal Products, United Kingdom
- Target Corporation (TGT) – Discount Stores, USA

**P/B (Price to Book ratio)**

The P/B ratio has been moving in a range from 2 to 3 in the last 20 years. Currently, it is at the lower end of this range which could be a sign of a good investment opportunity. We cannot judge just by P/B itself as it is only one piece of the puzzle to the whole picture. Still, P/B close to 2 is a good value.

Keep in mind that it is not given that the P/B needs to stay in the 2-3 range. Banks are now raising the interest rates and that could bring the P/B even lower - if the P (stock price) in the P/B equation of stocks falls.

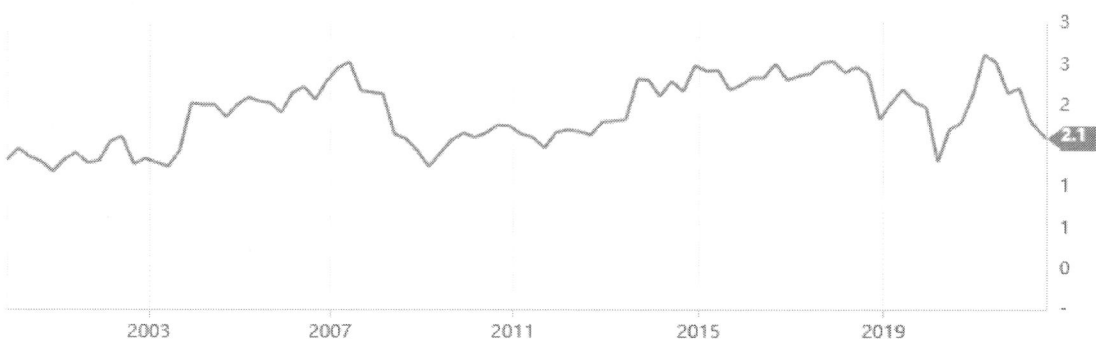

## P/E Ratio (Price to Earnings ratio)

The P/E ratio for the Consumer Defensive sector was quite high a couple of months back (it was almost 25). But now there has been a correction in the market and that brought the current average to around 20. The 25 indicated that an average company was a bit expensive. P/E = 20 is way more favorable for investment.

Generally speaking, if a company has P/E = 20 and below, then I don't consider it overpriced.

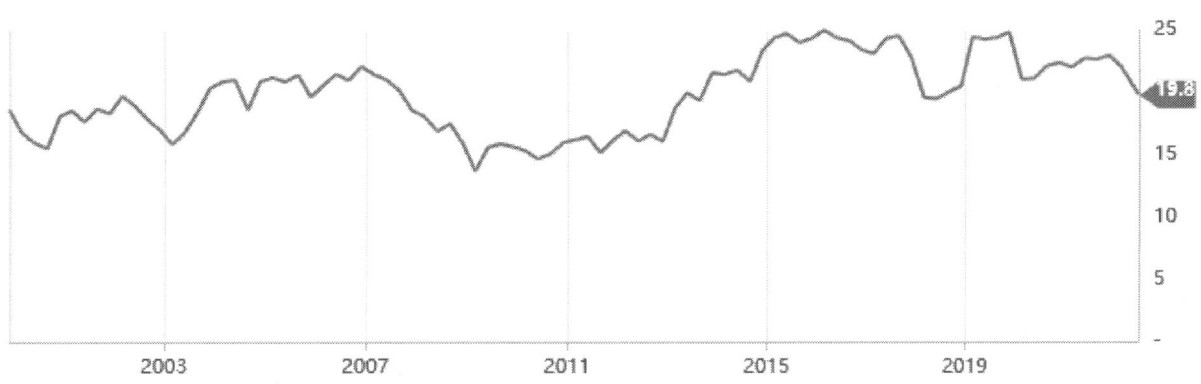

## Dividend Yield

When talking about dividends, it's not only important to look at the % yield, but also at the company's ability to pay dividends if the economic situation is not good.

A BIG advantage the Consumer Defensive companies have is that they don't rely on the business cycle. This makes them able to pay stable dividends no matter what happens with the economy. I consider this a huge advantage to other sectors!

The current average dividend yield is 2.5%. Tobacco companies pay the biggest dividend, which is an astonishing 5.6%!

The important thing here is that companies pay stable dividends and that they continue to pay them even if the economy is not doing good.

# Energy

This sector includes companies that take any part in the long chain from exploration, through drilling, refining and finally supplying us with energy. The majority of companies in the Energy sector deal with Oil and Gas.

## Sector Specifics

Prices of energy are largely driven by demand – thus by the economic cycle. If the economy is growing, then there is a strong demand for energy because without energy there would be no growth. Energy is needed to run factories, build facilities, and fuel airplanes and cars, …

Because of this, companies from the Energy sector are closely bound to the economic cycle - they hugely depend on how the economy is doing. If the economy is doing good, then the Energy sector thrives. If the economy is in a recession, then the company's business goes bad and their stock prices fall.

What I dislike about this sector is its sensitivity to political events. Energy prices, restrictions, and manipulations become standard political tools. The problem is that political events and their impact on stock prices are unpredictable. This is also one of the reasons companies from this sector are not usually among my preferred picks.

The energy sector also includes companies that focus on alternative energy sources (solar, wind, hydropower, biofuels, …). However, if you look at the chart below, you can see that their market share is only marginal. At least for now as there is a tendency to use those renewables more and more.

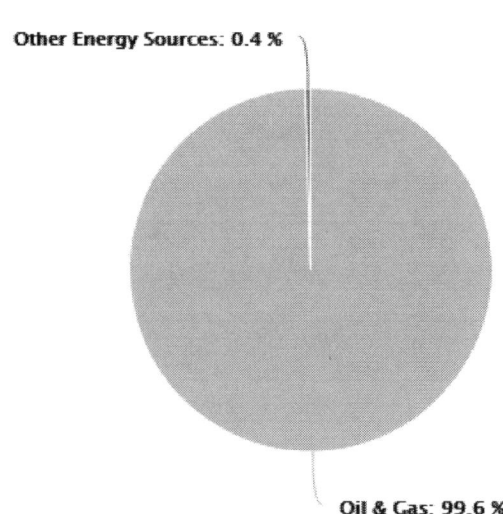

## Industries

- Oil & Gas Drilling, Equipment, Services, Refining, Marketing
- Thermal Coal
- Uranium

## Leading Companies

- Exxon Mobil Corporation (XOM) – Oil & Gas, USA
- Chevron Corporation (CVX) – Oil & Gas, USA
- Royal Dutch Shell (RDS-A, RDS-B) – Oil & Gas, Netherlands
- PetroChina Company – Oil & Gas, China

## The energy sector is very expensive to get into

Leading companies in the Energy sector have a very strong market position and market share. The reason is that it is very expensive to start a new company here as huge amounts of capital and time investment are needed for that. It's the current big companies that are fighting for their market share. The risk of a new company joining in and threatening the giants that control this sector is minimal.

This is a good thing for us investors because we know that (at least from this point of view) there probably won't be any major changes in this sector.

## P/B (Price to Book ratio)

High costs that those companies need for their facilities and equipment cause the P/B to be a nice low number (currently 2). This is a thing I like about this sector. If for some reason a company from this sector went bankrupt, then you would still be able to get quite a lot of your money back (after they have sold all their assets). Below is a chart of the historical P/B ratio since 2000.

**PB Ratio**

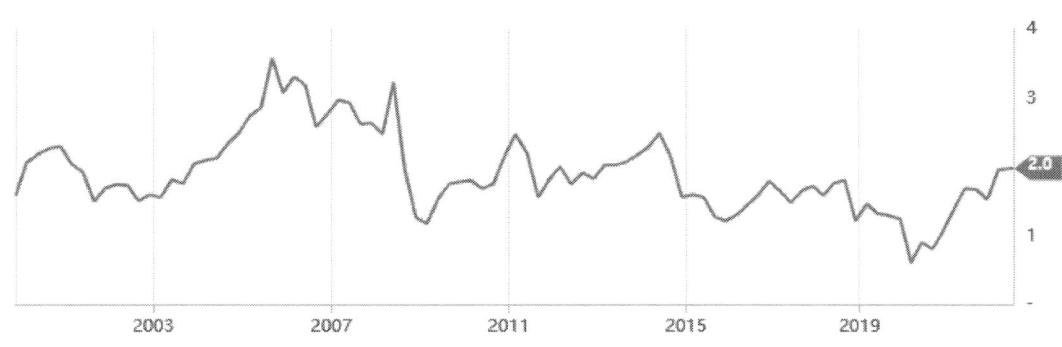

## P/E (Price to Earnings ratio)

The average P/E ratio is around 15 which is pretty good - I consider everything below 20 good.

As you can see the P/E is quite volatile and it reacts to the economic cycle and political events quite strongly.

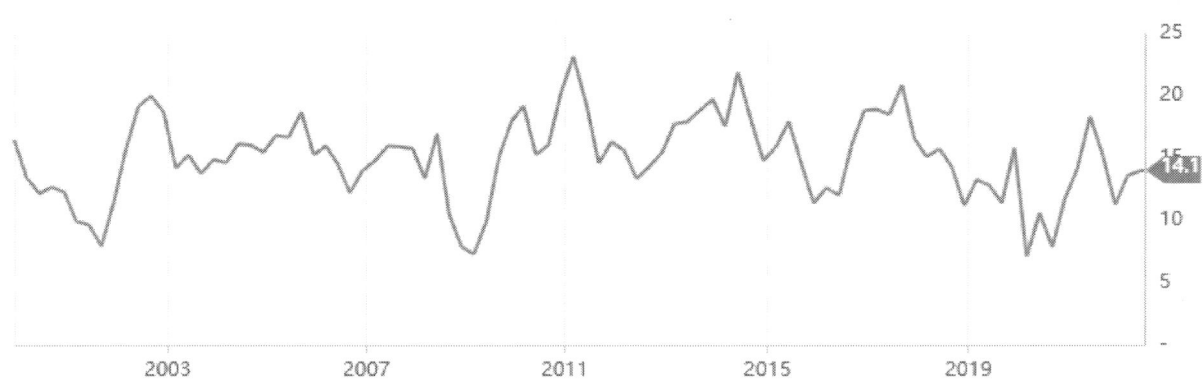

## Dividend Yield

A huge advantage of the Energy sector is the big dividend. Currently, the sector average is 3.6%, which is about twice as much as a dividend of an average US company listed in the S&P 500 index. The high dividend in this sector is also quite stable - there have always been high dividends in the Energy sector.

# Financial

Companies in this sector provide financial services both to corporations and retailers. There are many different kinds of subjects in this sector like banks, insurance companies, investment companies, and asset management companies, ...

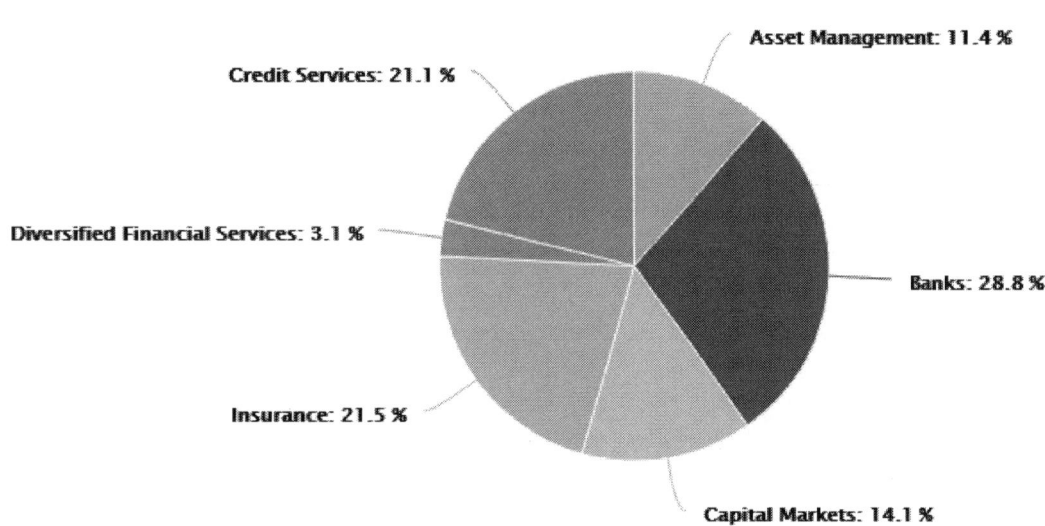

The business of the financial sector companies depends hugely on the main interest rate. The lower the rate is, the more those companies thrive. The reason is that when interest rates are low, people and companies tend to borrow more money (money is cheap to borrow). Mortgages and loans bring a lot of money to banks and other companies in the financial sector.

Also, a low-interest rate policy helps companies grow, people have extra money and everybody is looking for ways to invest (invest through financial institutions). All this helps the financial sector thrive.

If on the other hand, the rates are high then the financial sector doesn't thrive because people simply don't want to borrow money with the high interest. They are also hesitant to invest as stocks in high-interest rate environments don't usually perform well.

There are two reasons I dislike investing in this sector:

The 1st reason is that the sector is very complicated. Yes, even for me. There are so many different products and different ways how things can get sour and if they do, it's hard to tell and predict the outcome. There is another thing that is hard to gauge here, and that thing is regulation and external factors that are unpredictable.

The 2nd reason is that the financial sector is very vulnerable. The most vulnerable sector. If something bad happens, it's always this sector that starts to fall first and hardest.

I will say it bluntly - I find this sector one of the riskiest sectors and I don't recommend investing in it. Not unless you know what you are doing.

Below is a chart that compares S&P 500 with the Financials sector. Notice two things – 1st how closely correlated they are. 2nd – and that's important – reactions to a major crisis in 2007-2008 (financial crisis) and 2020 (COVID-19). In both cases, the financial sector took a serious blow. What has always saved it was low (almost zero) interest rates. If there wasn't for that, then this sector (and many others) would be in BIG trouble.

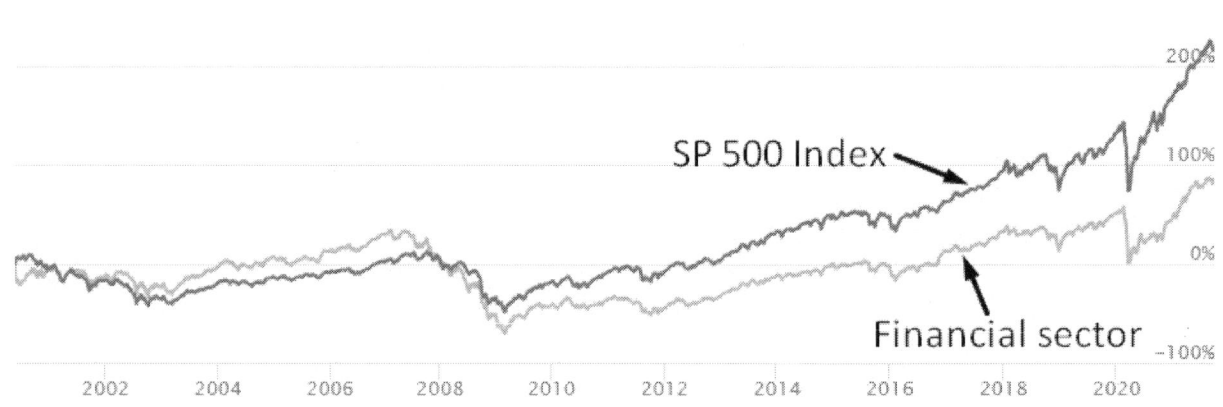

**Industries**

- ETFs
- Asset Management
- Banks
- Funds
- Credit Services
- Financial Conglomerates
- Financial Data & Stock Exchanges
- Insurance companies
- Mortgage Finance

**Leading companies**

- Berkshire Hathaway (BRK-A, BRK-B) – Insurance Diversified, USA
- Visa (V) – Credit Services, USA
- JPMorgan Chase & Co. (JMP) – Bank, USA
- Mastercard (MA) – Credit Services, USA

- Bank Of America (BAC) – Bank, USA
- PayPal (PYPL) – Credit Services, USA
- Wells Fargo (WFC) – Bank, USA

**P/B (Price to Book ratio)**

Banks and other financial sector companies usually have very low P/B (which would normally be great – if this wasn't the Financials sector). In this case, it doesn't mean banks own a lot of tangible property though. It only means they have a "healthy" balance sheet and that they utilize effectively the funds or assets they manage (this is a regulatory requirement they need to meet).

A low P/B in this particular sector doesn't indicate a good or safe investment.

With Financials, I only recommend using the P/B ratio to compare stocks within the same sector - for example, two banks.

As you can see from the chart below, the average P/B ratio in the financial sector is fluctuating mostly from 1 to 1.5.

## P/E (Price to Earnings ratio)

The Financial sector as a whole has a very low P/E ratio (averaging around 10-15). It has always been like that. If this sector wasn't as risky as it is, then such low P/E would be fantastic. In this case, though, the reason for the low P/E is because of how risky this sector is. That's why P (Price) is lower in the P/E equation. Those companies are riskier because they utilize big debt (big leverage). And their business heavily relies on interest rates.

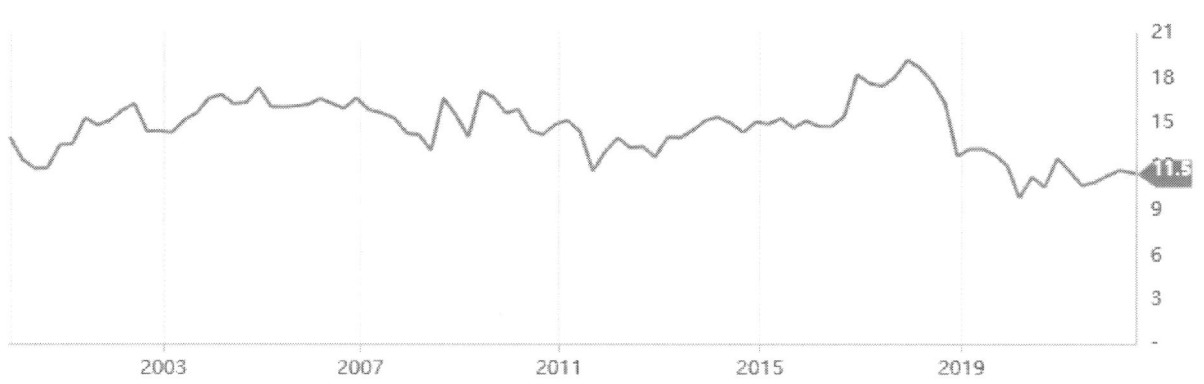

Financials are a very nice example that not everything that has good numbers (like low P/E and P/B ratios) is a good company. You should always consider the sector specifications and potential risks.

So, even though Financials have the lowest P/E and P/B I still consider them a very risky sector to invest in.

## **Dividend Yield**

The average dividend yield in the financial sector is currently 3% which is a bit above the average US company. If you are looking for a dividend stock here, then I recommend getting one of the bigger companies. Those pay dividends even when the economy is not performing well (recession) and they are also more likely to withstand a potential crisis (they are "too big to fall").

To name at least one – JP Morgan. A giant in this sector, with a consistent dividend of around 2.5%. The picture below shows the dividend payout history of JP Morgan since 1995.

Notice the drop after the 2007-2008 crisis. That's what you can expect when the next crisis hits.

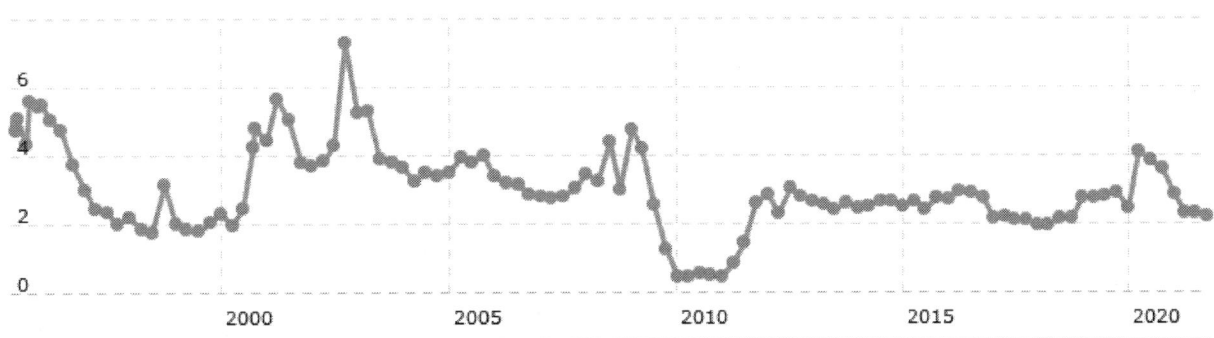

## Healthcare

This sector includes companies that Manufacture drugs, provide medical devices and instruments, do medical diagnostics and research, provide healthcare and services, etc.

It is one of the largest sectors in the US economy, making up 18% of the Gross Domestic Product (GDP).

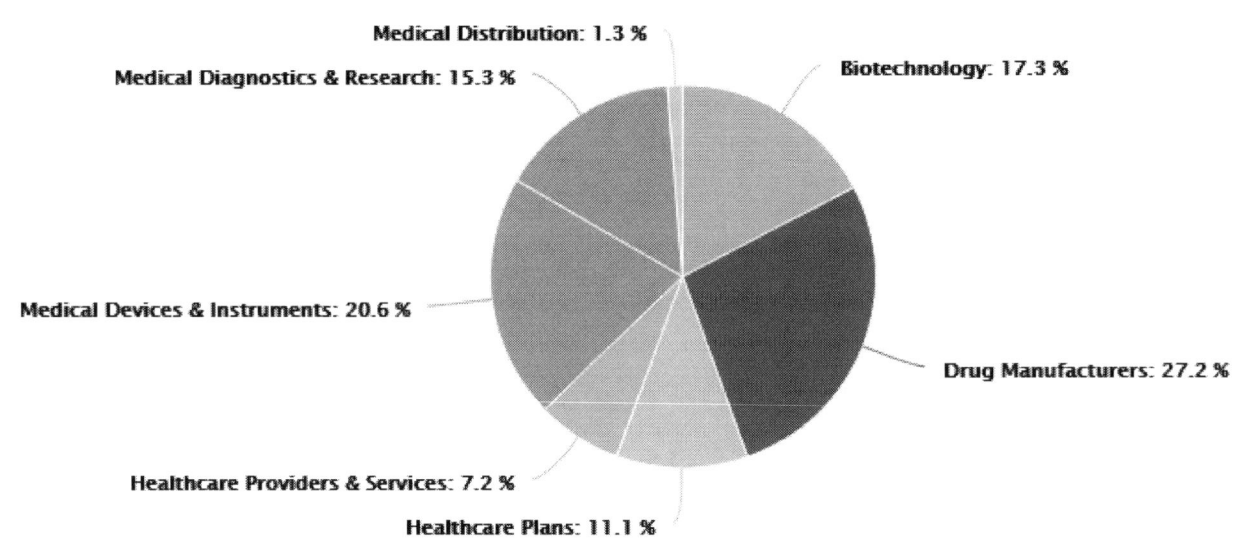

## Sector Specifics
### Long-term trend

A lot of things in the economy, especially in the long run, are very hard to predict. What is not so hard to predict though is population growth and increasing length of life expectancy. Simply put – there are more and more people, who grow older and older, and they die later. Those are "mega trends" that most likely won't change anytime soon. Why am I talking about this? Because it is closely linked to the Healthcare sector. It's mostly older people who buy drugs, use medical services, or otherwise feed the Healthcare related companies. With more and more older people around, the healthcare sector grows and thrives. There is ever-rising demand.

Here is a chart showing life expectancy in the US since 1860. I think the trend is clear, isn't it?

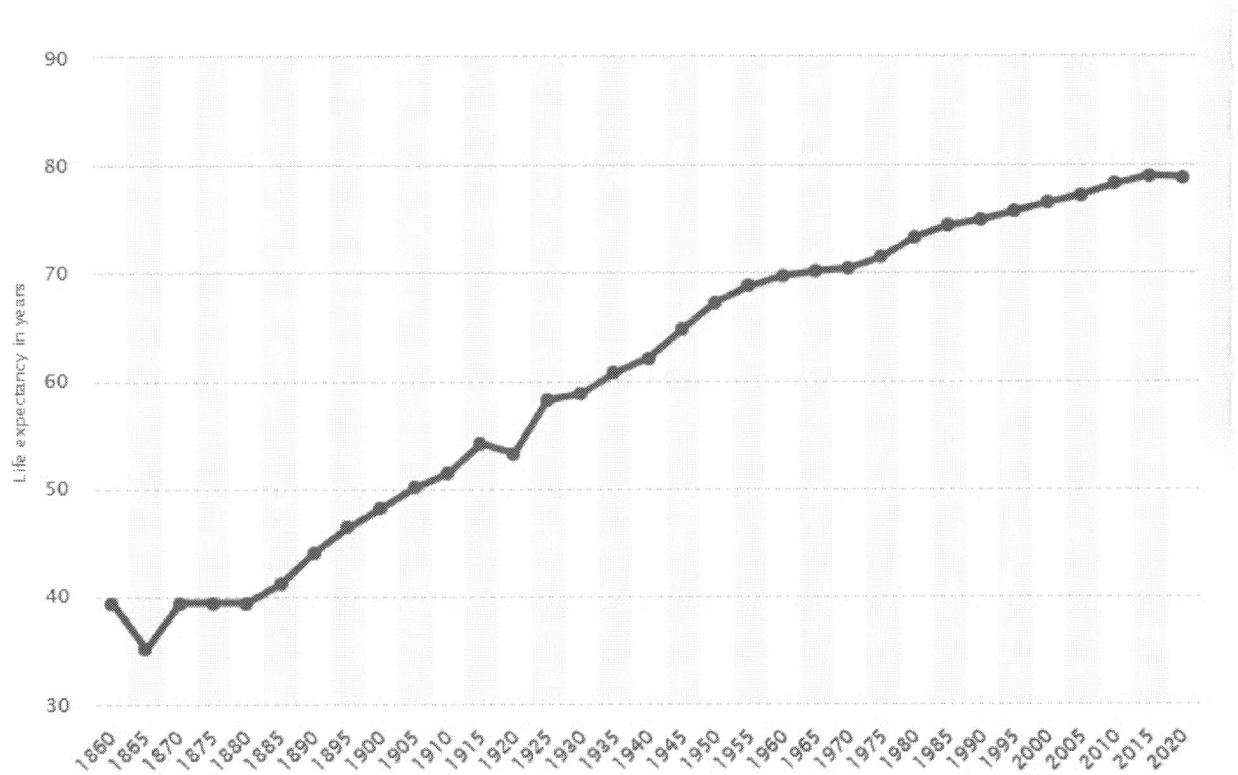

This is the whole world since 1950:

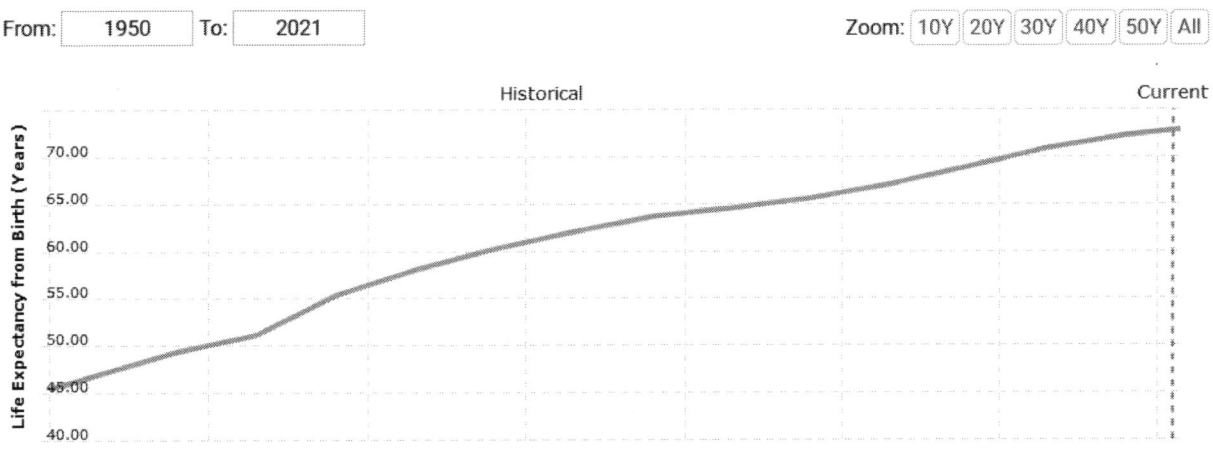

I think this overall trend of a strong and growing Healthcare sector will continue and become even stronger after the COVID-19 pandemic. I think there will be even more emphasis on new drug development, vaccines and prevention, and the healthcare companies will thrive. And I doubt this long-term trend will change anytime soon. Maybe not even within our lifetime. That's why I think that companies in the Healthcare sector could prove a very good investment.

**Government intervention**

One of the important things to keep in mind is that the Healthcare sector is intervened by the Government (regulations, rules, licenses, patents, …). This is also one of the things that makes it hard for new companies to enter this sector (not to mention research and development costs) – leaving the current strong ones without the risk of a new strong competitor rising and taking part of their market share.

**Patents**

Biotechnology companies and companies that develop new drugs rely heavily on patents and laws that protect them from getting their intellectual property stolen. However, patents only last so long and a company might benefit from its new invention only for a limited time. When the patent expires, the edge that the company had is over. For this reason, I think it is safer to invest in bigger companies that have more things and projects going on, rather than one small company that has just come up with a magic pill for curing cancer or whatever other illness.

Big swings in stock prices are often seen in biotechnology companies that are developing new products. Investing in those seems a bit risky to me because their game is all about developing a cure and getting a patent. In the extreme, it's like they either make it – develop a new drug/treatment, or they don't, and they go bankrupt. If they make it, then you can earn a lot of money as their shareholder. If they don't, then you can say goodbye to your investment.

What I prefer more is investing in bigger companies with a wide variety in their business. Companies that not only focus on new drug development, but also on drug manufacturing, marketing and on getting their current "drug portfolio" to as many customers as possible. Such businesses are generally more stable.

**Price inelastic demand**

What I like about the Healthcare sector is that demand for the products here is inelastic. This means that people will always spend their money there no matter what. No matter whether the economy is doing good or bad, or whether people are losing jobs or have excess money, people will always buy drugs when they fall sick. For this reason, the Healthcare sector is not related to the economic cycle. That's the beauty of it.

## Industries

- Biotechnology
- Diagnostics & research
- Drug Manufacturers
- Healthcare Plans
- Health Information Services
- Medical Care Facilities
- Medical Devices, Instruments, Supplies
- Medical Distribution
- Pharmaceutical Retailers

## Leading companies

- Johnson & Johnson (JNJ) – Drug Manufacturers, USA
- UnitedHealth Group (UNH) - Healthcare plans, USA
- Pfizer (PFE) – Drug Manufacturers, USA
- Danaher Corporation (DHR) – Diagnostics & Research, USA
- Abbott Laboratories (ABT) – Medical Devices, USA
- Eli Lilly and Company (LLY) – Drug Manufacturers, USA
- Novartis (NVS) – Drug Manufacturers, Switzerland

## P/E (Price to Earnings ratio)

The average P/E is currently around 25 which is quite a lot. Investors are anticipating rising earnings in this industry and they might as well be right! Still, this makes the average company a bit expensive and for that reason, I recommend waiting for a market correction - for the prices of healthcare stocks to drop. This would at least temporarily bring the P/E down making investments in this sector way more appealing.

**PE Ratio**
* Healthcare

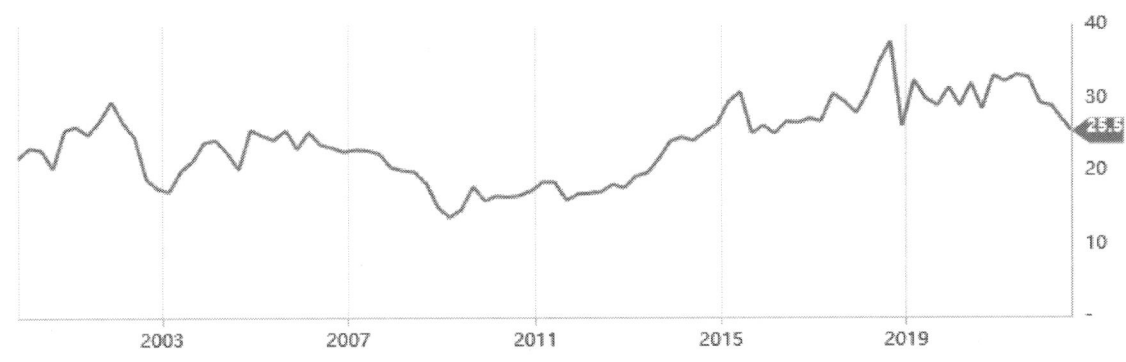

## P/B (Price to Book ratio)

The P/B ratio in the Healthcare sector has been moving between 3-4 most of the time since 2000. Now, there has been a change and the average P/B dropped dramatically. Currently, it's at 2 making an investment here way more appealing than when it was in the 3-4 range. 3-4 was too much, but P/B = 2 in the Healthcare sector is in my opinion great.

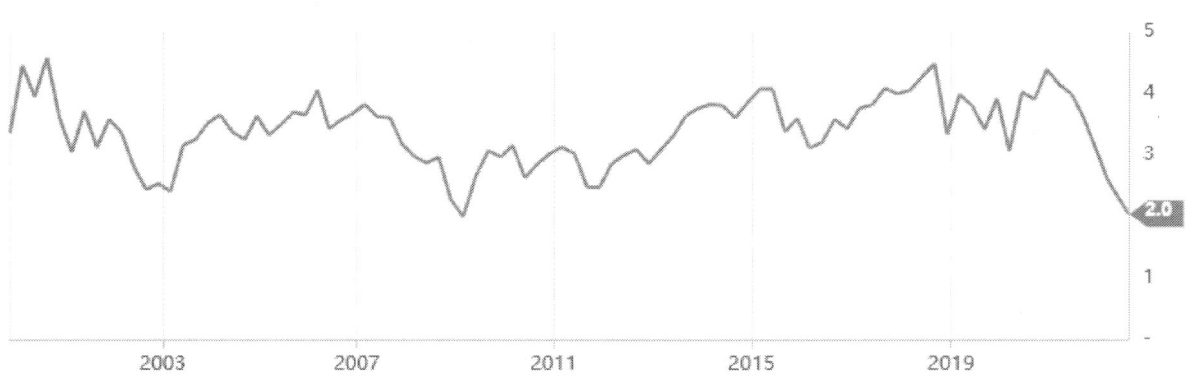

## Dividend

If you are looking for a good dividend yield, then I don't consider the Healthcare sector a good choice. On average it pays one of the lowest dividends of 1.4%. Is this bad? Not! Those companies can be great investments even if they don't pay dividends. What they do is they re-invest the money back into their business and this helps them to grow faster. I was talking about this earlier, remember?

What I am saying is if you want stocks with high dividend yield, then don't look here. The strength of the Healthcare sector lies in other areas, not in dividends.

# Industrials

The Industrial sector includes companies that sell machinery, equipment, and supplies to companies that extract resources, do construction, manufacture, and transportation, and also companies that deal with Aerospace & Defense. Those companies usually don't sell stuff directly to customers like you or me.

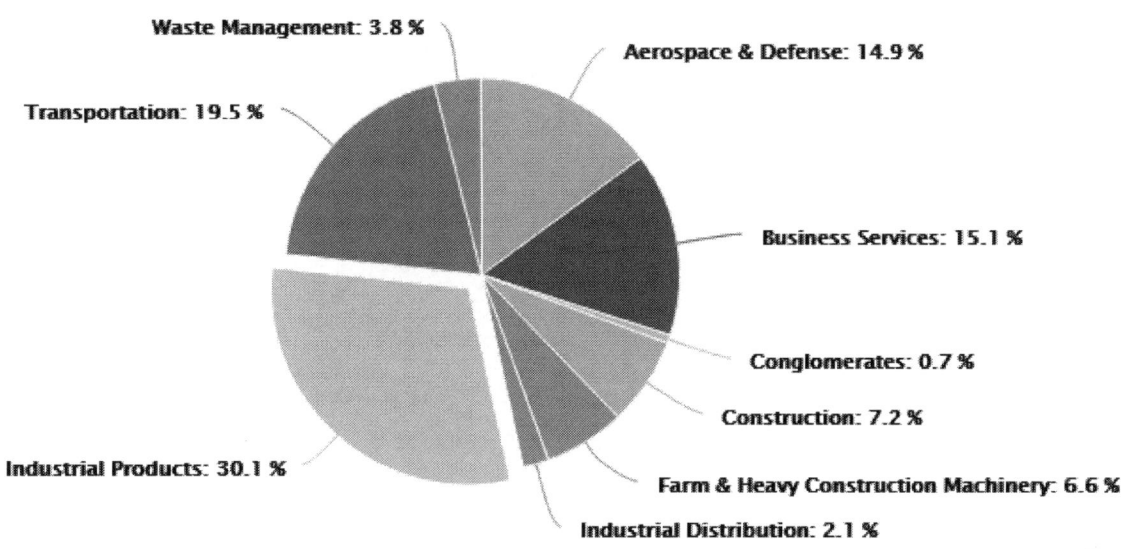

This sector is quite closely linked to the business cycle and the overall health of the economy. If the economy is doing good, then companies that manufacture, construct (building houses, ...), extract resources or build planes need the machinery and goods that the Industrials sector provides.

So, if the economy is doing good, then there is a high demand and stock prices of such companies grow.

If the economy is not doing well (recession) then the demand falls. The reason is that companies produce fewer goods, and postpone expansion, ... and this causes the demand for industrials to drop (negatively affecting stock prices).

Below is a chart that compares the Industrials sector and S&P 500 sector. Notice how closely linked they are. It is visible especially if you look at the dips after 2000, 2008, and 2020.

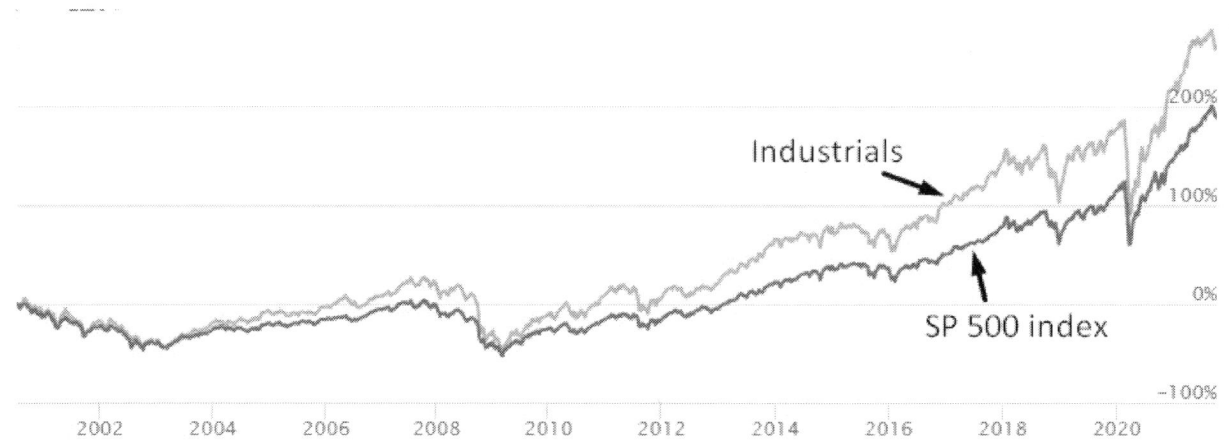

**Industries**

- Aerospace & Defense
- Airlines
- Building Products, Equipment, Supplies
- Electrical Equipment & Parts
- Engineering & Construction
- Farm & Heavy Construction Machinery
- Industrial Distribution
- Infrastructure Operations
- Integrated Freight & Logistics
- Marine Shipping
- Metal Fabrication
- Pollution & Treatment Controls
- Railroads
- Security & Protection Services
- Tools & Accessories
- Trucking
- Waste Management

## Leading Companies

- United Parcel Service (UPS) – Logistics, USA
- Honeywell (HON) – Industrial Machinery, USA
- Union Pacific Corporation (UNP) – Railroads, USA
- The Boeing Company (BA) – Aerospace & Defense, USA
- General Electric Company (GE) – Industrial Machinery, USA
- Caterpillar (CAT) – Heavy Construction Machinery, USA

## P/B (Price to Book ratio)

The Price to Book ratio in this sector was quite high a couple of months ago (when it was around 3). This was way above the long-term average in this sector.

The reasons were low rates (cheap money), optimism, and a lot of investors pumping cheap money into stocks. This led to rising stock prices (rising "P" in the P/B formula). When stock prices rise but companies still owe the same facilities, machines, and materials, … (in other words "book" value of the company stays the same), then the P/B ratio grows. Currently, the FED started to raise the rates and this brought the book value (and P/B) back to the long-term average.

**PB Ratio**
- Industrials

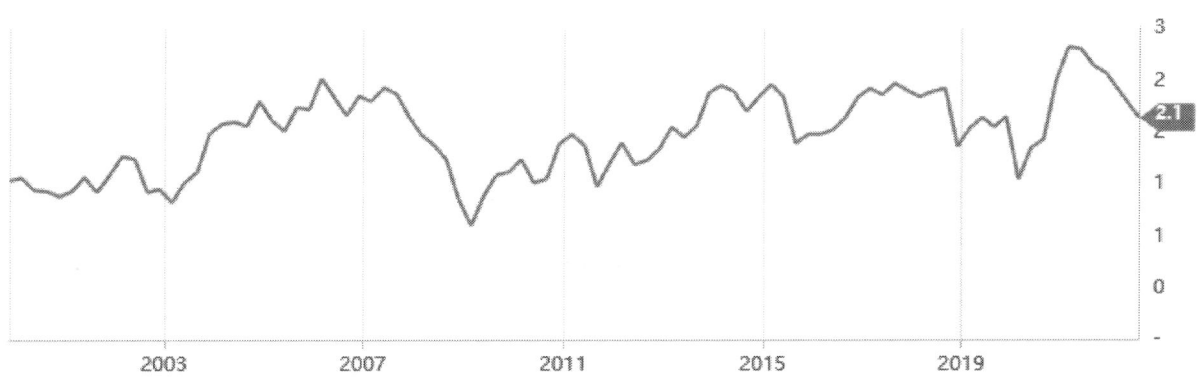

## P/E (Price to Earnings ratio)

P/E ratio is currently averaging around 17.5 but a couple of months ago it was way higher (around 25). The reason is more or less the same as I said about the P/B: cheap money drove prices (P) high.

As usual, my advice is to invest in the Industrial sector companies if the P/E is below 20.

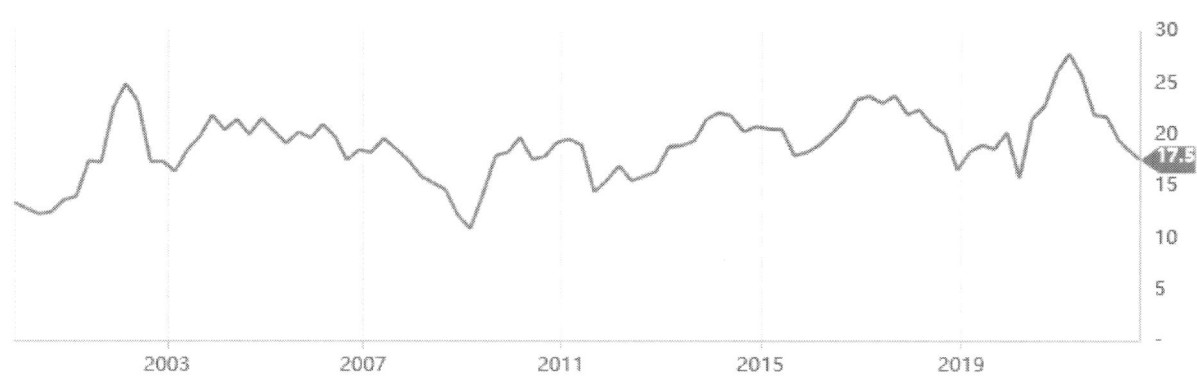

## Dividend Yield

An average dividend in this sector is around 1.9% which is roughly around the S&P 500 average. Historically speaking, the Dividend Yield in the Industrials sector has never really been outperforming the average stock in the S&P 500 index. So, if you are looking for good dividends, then you should look in a different sector. The Industrials sector is not sought after for large dividends.

# Real Estate

This sector consists of companies that are real estate developers, or companies that manage and operate real estate.

**The main types of real estate are:**

- **Residential real estate:** family houses, apartments, condominiums.
- **Commercial real estate:** property used for business – for example, hotels, shopping centers, stores, theaters, offices and grocery stores.
- **Industrial real estate:** Property used by companies for manufacture, production, storage and research.
- **Land.**

You can invest in any type of real estate through Real Estate Investment Trusts (REIT). Those companies hold a portfolio of Real Estate properties. They rent those and it generates an income. This income is by a large part paid to shareholders as a Dividend. No wonder those stocks are one of the highest dividend-paying ones around.

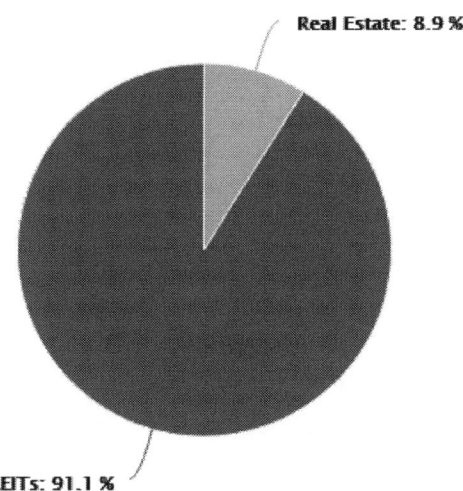

The Real Estate sector is not very volatile as stock prices here are quite stable. REITs are not much about stock price growth, rather than getting a steady and high-yielding dividend (not without risk, though).

Sector Specifics
**Reaction to recessions/crisis**

The risk with those companies is that their stocks tend to crash hard when there is an economic recession or a crisis. You can see it in the chart below which compares the Real Estate sector with the S&P 500 index. Notice the dips after the 2007-2008 crisis and also during the COVID–19 crisis in 2020. Simply put, when there is a problem, Real Estate companies crash hard along with the economy.

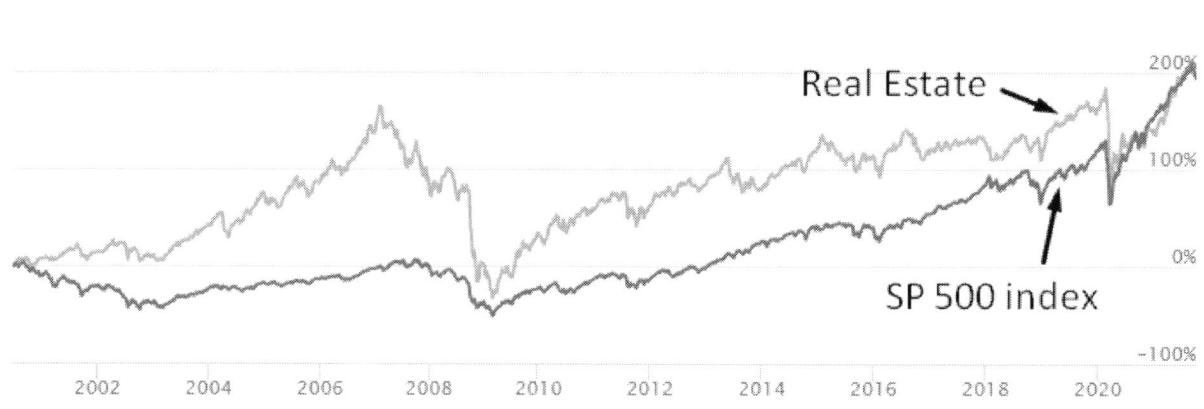

**REIT and their sensitivity to Interest rate**

REIT stock prices are very sensitive to the main interest rate. If the interest rate is low, then people put their money into REITs because they provide a stable and high-yielding dividend. REITs represent a good alternative to bonds (which are not very popular in a low-interest rate economy).

If interest rates rise, then people can get good returns from less risky investments (like bonds) and REITs become less popular which results in a decline in their stock prices.

**High leverage (big debt)**

When interest rates are low, then REITs can borrow money cheaply and leverage their business – enabling them to make more money. For this reason, it's quite common that those companies usually have huge debts. This is fine as long as the interest rates are low.

However, if the rates rise, then REITs need to borrow money for a bigger cost (higher interest rate). This hurts their business, and their income and also lowers the dividend they can pay to the shareholders.

If you are going to use the stock screener to look for REITs, then you need to lower your expectations and criteria for the company debt. The average debt/equity in this sector is around 3.5 (350% debt). This is a standard in this industry and it's what makes the dividend yields so high and the sector so fragile.

## Industries

- Real Estate – Development & Services
- REITs (Healthcare Facilities, Hotels, Industrial, Mortgage, Office, Residential, Retail, …)

## Leading companies

- American Tower Corporation (AMT) – REIT, USA
- Prologis (PLD) – REIT, USA
- Crown Castle International (CCI) – REIT, USA
- Equinix (EQIX) – REIT, USA
- Public Storage (PSA) - REIT, USA

## P/E (Price to Earnings ratio)

I don't think using the P/E ratio in the Real Estate sector makes much sense. The reason lies in accounting. The thing is that accounting companies "depreciate" the value of assets they own over time. For example, a car - depreciation is a way of saying that the car is being used, it's getting old and its condition is getting worse. This makes sense with many companies and their assets but not with Real Estate.

**Example:** A company owns some houses and the rent brought them $10 mil. The company had expenses of $2 mil and their houses depreciated (on paper) by $5 mil. In accounting, this looks like the company only made $3 mil. Income (10-2-5=3). However, the houses only depreciated on paper! In reality, they are still the same houses (which quite possibly gained in their market value).

Such a thing drives the P/E ratio higher than it should be. It is the reason I don't recommend using the P/E with Real Estate companies.

To make this complete, here is a historical P/E chart of the Real Estate sector:

**PE Ratio**
* Real Estate

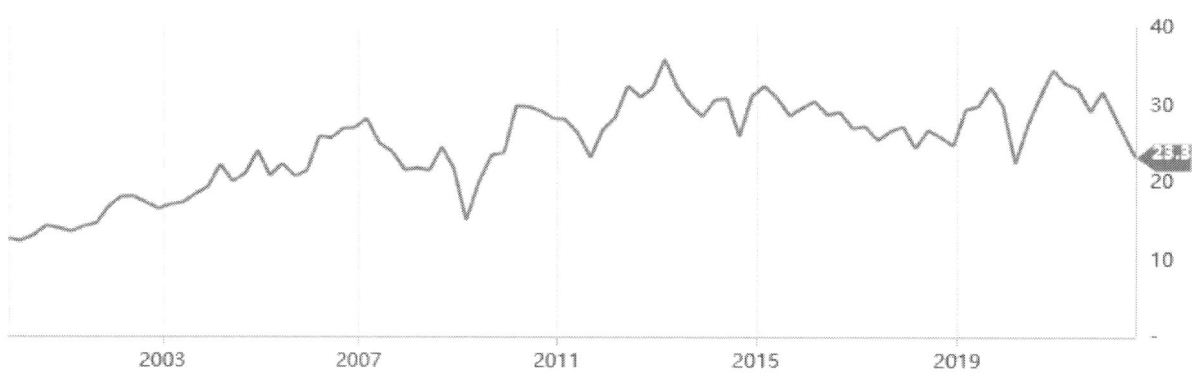

## P/B (Price to Book ratio)

Price to Book ratio is not a good way to evaluate REITs because it is calculated using the Book value which in this case, is often misleading. The book value of a house can vary so much from reality! What is important is the actual price of the house somebody would be willing to buy today. Not a value the company has in its accounting books.

I am not saying P/B is useless with Real Estates, but it's not much use either.

**PB Ratio**
* Real Estate

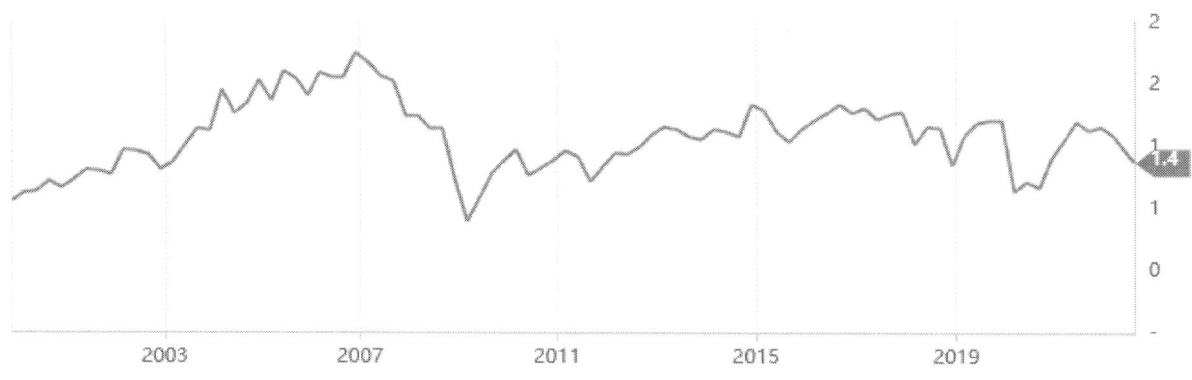

If you want something similar to the P/B ratio, but applicable to REITs, then I recommend using P/NAV. This ratio is similar to the P/B ratio, but instead of using Book value it works with the "actual value" of the asset. Not the book value.

## Dividend Yield

The majority of the Real Estate sector is represented by REIT companies. There applies a law that says that to qualify as a REIT, the company must pay 90% (or more) of profits as a dividend (btw if the company does that, then it can avoid paying corporate income tax – which is a huge motivation, of course). This is why this sector is the one with the highest dividend yield by far! No wonder dividend-oriented investors love REITs!

The average dividend in the American REIT sector is around 4%. However, some REITs pay way more than this.

The dividend yield here is so high for two reasons:

1. 90% or more of the income goes to shareholders as a dividend.
2. REITs don't pay corporate taxes.

## Example

Let's compare two companies – one standard company (that pays taxes), and the other a REIT. They both earn $100 mil but there is a 21% tax (so it's $79 mil after taxes) for the non-REIT company.

- If REIT makes $100 mil and pays 90% to shareholders, then they distribute $90 mil in dividends.
- If a standard company makes $100 mil, pays $21 mil in taxes and pays 90% to shareholders (not very likely, but let's keep it this way), then they distribute $71 mil in dividends.

It is a huge difference between $90 mil and $71 mil, isn't it?

## Mortgage REITs (mREIT)

If you look for investments in this sector you will find companies with enormous dividends. Those will most likely be mREITS. mREITs take on around 10% of the Real Estate sector.

The difference between REIT and mREIT is:

**REITs** purchase properties. This property can increase its value over time. In other words - as the costs of the real property increase, you might as well see the price of REIT stocks appreciate.

**mREITs** deal only with mortgage-backed securities. For example, they lend money to real estate developers. They don't own any property. They are here only for the monthly/quarterly income (which is generated through interest on the loan they provided). Nothing else. That's why their dividend is usually higher.

mREITs are in my opinion more complicated, more unpredictable and riskier investments than REITs. The dividend they pay is great, but so is the risk. They are very sensitive to interest rate changes.

## Technology

The technology sector consists mostly of companies that develop software and make computers, mobiles, televisions, other electronics, and semiconductors.

One of the main features is that this sector moves forward fast as new technologies are being constantly developed. New iPhone every year – that's what I am talking about.

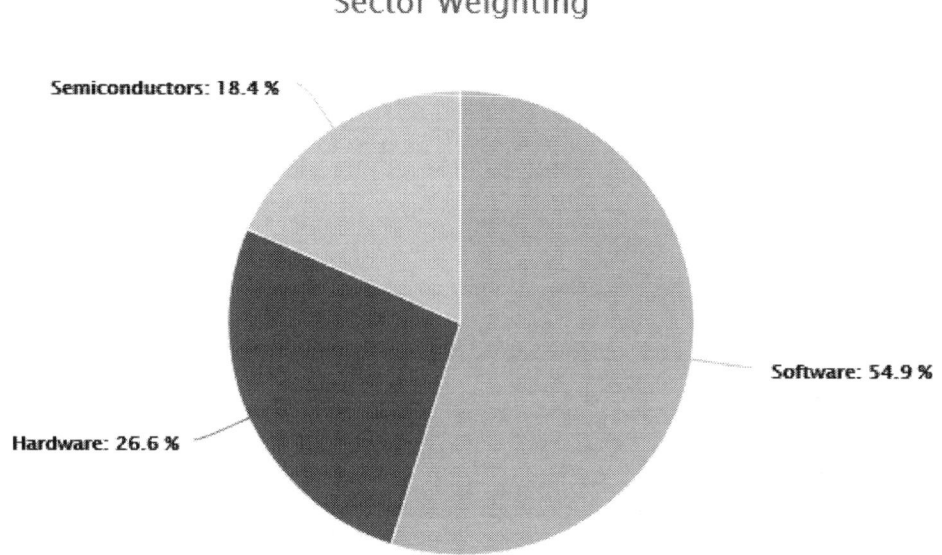

There are always new technologies, new companies, new products and dire competition. This sector is ever-changing, it develops rapidly, and this makes it difficult for investors to keep up.

On top of that, it's very popular and fast-growing, and as a result, the stock prices tend to shoot high. In my opinion, it's already quite overpriced but in this case, the sky is the limit. There is no telling how much people can inflate those stock prices.

## Sector Specifics
**Sensitive to Economic Cycle**

Technology companies are very sensitive to the economic cycle. The reason is that if there is trouble and people start losing their jobs, then one of the first expenses they cut is new technology products. If you are short on cash, you won't buy a new iPhone, Apple Watch, laptop, or television. You will keep your old ones as those are non-essential products.

When there is an economic recession, the demand for technologies is significantly weakened. This results in dropping stock prices.

If the economy is doing well and people have a lot of free cash to spend, then they like to spend it on new technology products. That's why technology companies tend to outperform other companies when the economy is booming.

The big sensitivity to the economic cycle makes the Technology sector a risky one.


**Risky stocks**

If there is any economic problem, recession or crisis, then Technology stocks crash down fast and hard. The reason is that those stocks are often overpriced, they are closely bound to the economic cycle, and the companies sell non-essential stuff. This makes them very fragile and sensitive to any kind of problem. Also, if they crash, then very little remains (they often own very little tangible goods).

All those are reasons why I consider investing in this sector quite risky.


**Industries**

- Communication Equipment
- Computer Hardware
- Consumer Electronics
- Electronic Components
- Electronics & Computer distribution
- Information Technology Services
- Semiconductors
- Software


**Leading Companies**

- Apple (AAPL) – Consumer Electronics, USA

- Microsoft (MSFT) – Software, USA
- NVIDIA (NVDA) – Semiconductors, USA
- Adobe (ADBE) - Software, USA
- Oracle (ORCL) - Software, USA
- Cisco (CSCO) - Communication Equipment, USA
- Sony (SONY) – Consumer Electronics, Japan

**P/B (Price to Book ratio)**

One of the reasons I don't recommend investing in the Technology sector is that companies in this sector often lack solid book value. This makes their prices look inflated. At least in my opinion.

The Price to Book ratio of an average firm in this sector is around 3 now. If we take into consideration only tangible stuff, then the P/Book-Tangible is now at 4.3. P/B at 3 is quite high but it was even more than that a couple of months ago when prices of those stocks got inflated and caused the P/B to climb to 4-5.

The reason the P/B is generally so high here is that those companies don't own many tangible assets. Their prices are inflated and if they go under, then very little will remain.

You need to be very optimistic to invest in stocks like these in my opinion.

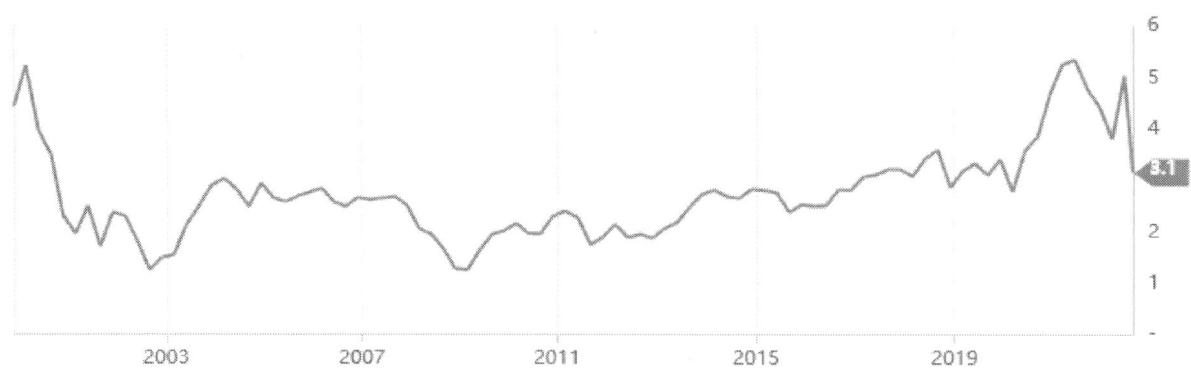

## P/E (Price to Earnings ratio)

The average P/E ratio is around 24 now, which – similarly to the P/B ratio tells us that those stocks are overpriced (not as much as they were a couple of months ago, but still …). If I were to consider investing here (I am not, but if yes), then I would need to see the P/E below 20. There would probably need to be some crash for this to happen. Something like in 2000 when the dot-com bubble burst. Now the reason for such a crash could be rising interest rates.

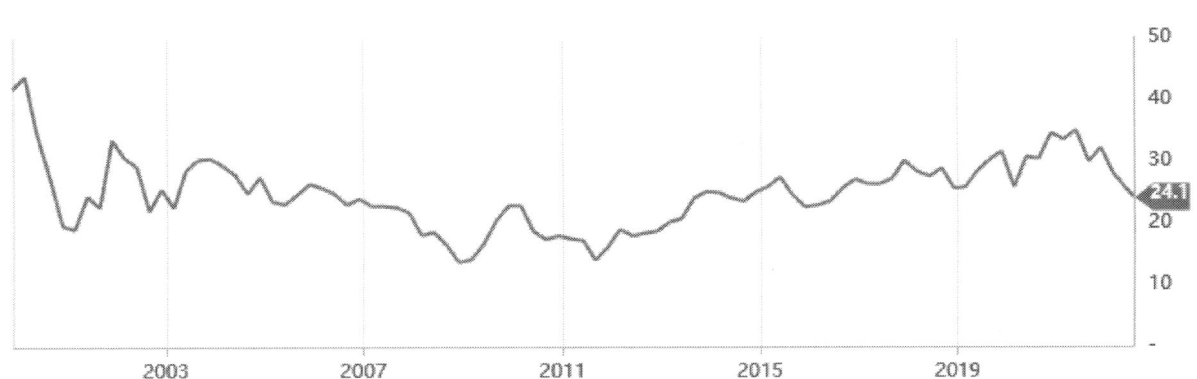

## Dividend Yield

An average dividend of a technological company listed in the S&P 500 is 1.4%. This is a bit below the average. If you are thinking about investing in this sector, then dividends should not be the reason. If anything, then it should be the potential growth of the technology companies.

## Utilities

Utilities are one of my favorite sectors to invest in. It is a large sector that provides people with essentials like water, electricity, natural gas, and sewage, ...

These companies are private but since they provide public service, they need to be heavily regulated. Over-regulation might not seem to be a good thing, but it gives those companies a certain advantage. The advantage is that it's almost impossible for new companies/competition to enter the market. This gives the current companies a very good and solid advantage of working more or less on a monopolistic basis.

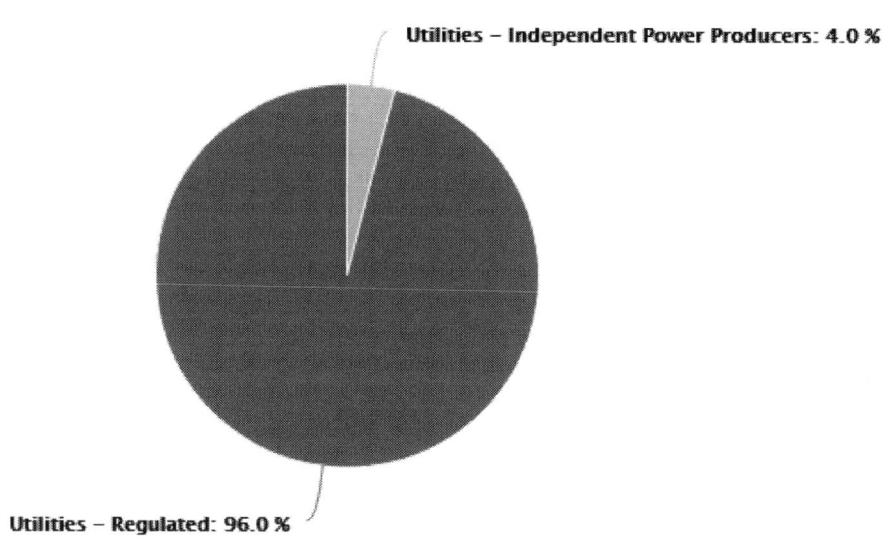

## Sector Specifics
**Non-cyclical**

The Utilities sector is considered "defensive" because it is not bound to the economic cycle and stock prices here are quite stable (less volatile). It is because these companies provide essentials = products that people necessarily need no matter what.

No matter what, people will always need electricity, water, or gas. That's the beauty of it. Also, the demand does not change too much. There is only so much water, electricity, or gas you can use every day. This is the reason that demand and stock prices in this sector are quite stable.

Below is a chart that compares the Utilities sector and S&P 500 index. The thing to notice here is that the Utilities sector is calmer and steadier than the index.

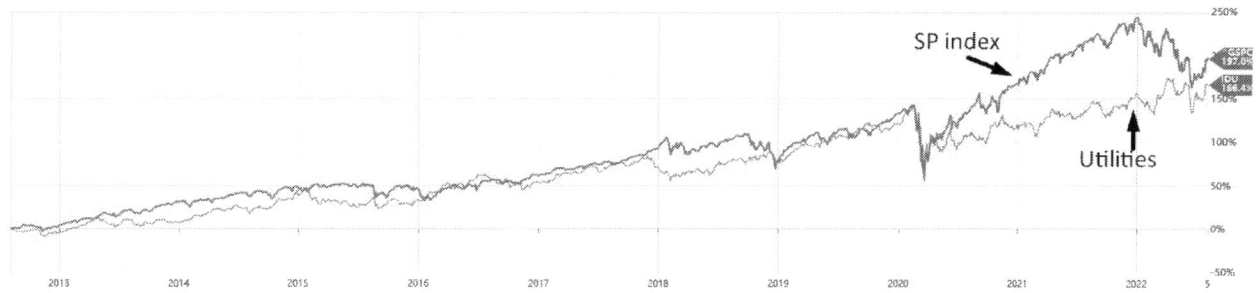

Utilities perform relatively well during economic recessions or downturns. On the other hand, if the economy is booming, then you can't expect Utilities to skyrocket like for example Technologies or the Financial sector.

## Simple to understand

What I like about Utilities is the simplicity. The business is not too innovative, it's quite stable and it is easy to understand. Company A provides water to people's homes, company B provides gas, etc. the core of it is simple, and there are no constant changes like, for example, in the Technology sector.

## Industries

- Power Producers
- Electric
- Gas
- Water
- Renewable

## Leading Companies

NextEra energy (NEE) – Regulated Electric, USA

Duke Energy Corporation (DUK) – Regulated Electric, USA

The Southern Company (SO) – Regulated Electric, USA

Dominion Energy (D) – Utilities – Diversified, USA

Exelon Corporation (EXC) – Utilities – Diversified, USA

## P/B (Price to Book ratio)

Even though the average P/B has been growing steadily for the last ten years it still hasn't reached any extreme values. Currently, it moves around P/B = 2 which is one of the lowest P/B ratios among other sectors.

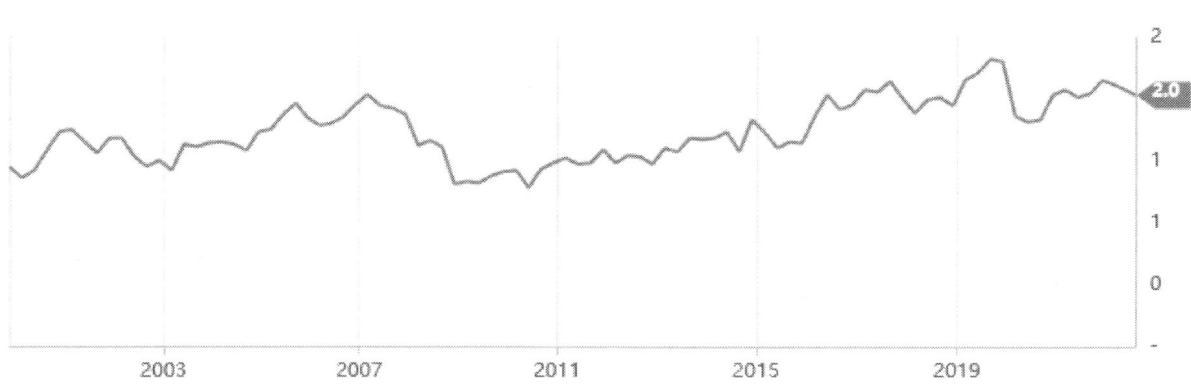

## P/E (Price to Earnings ratio)

Price to Earnings ratio here is currently at 22.6. This tells us that stocks in this sector are not too overpriced and could prove to be a good investment. That is if the P/E ratio holds around 20.

Still, a little drop below 20, maybe towards 15 would be a nice investment opportunity. Generally speaking, that's what we always want - a price drop to allow us to buy for a discount. But more on that later.

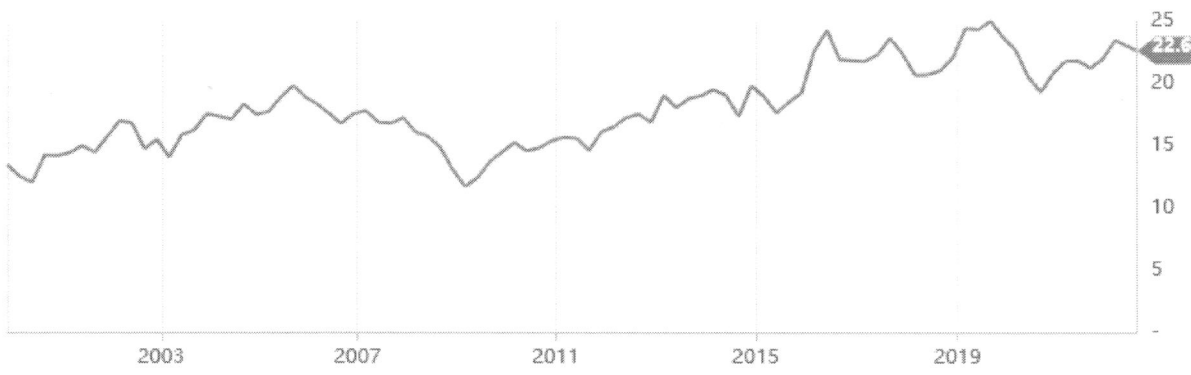

## Dividend Yield

One of the things I like about Utility stocks is that they pay out a very nice dividend. The average is currently 3.3% which is almost double the average stock from the S&P 500 index. You can get a better average dividend only in the Financial or Real Estate sectors, but I consider both riskier than Utilities (especially the Financials).

Steady growth, stable and high dividend, what more could you want? It is also a good choice if you are into the buy-and-hold type of investing.

## Debt

The average Debt to Equity in the Utilities sector is around 1.3 (130%).

Doing business in the Utilities sector is very expensive because of the infrastructure the companies need to maintain, upgrade, and operate. For this reason, Utility companies very often have a big debt. This is sort of a standard in this sector, nothing unusual. So, if you are going to look for Utilities stocks using a stock screening filter, then you need to lower your expectations and criteria regarding the company's debt.

# FINVIZ: Fundamental Tab

The Fundamental tab focuses on the company's details. Those details are taken from quarterly statements.

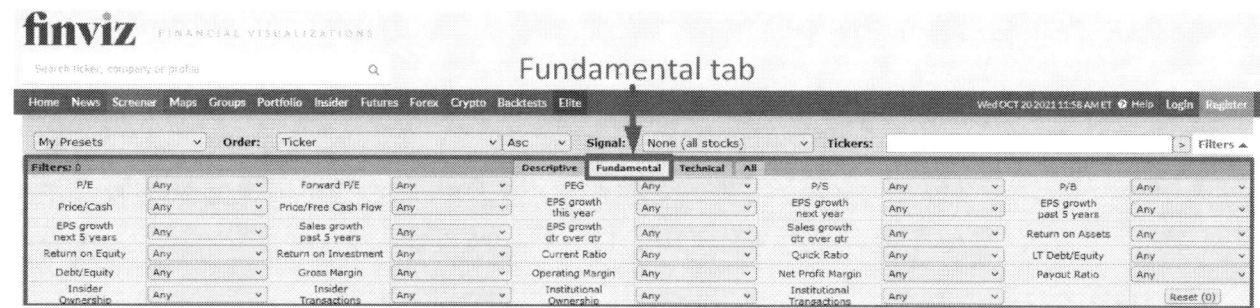

### All the parameters you can set up here are:

P/E, Forward P/E, PEG, P/S, P/B, Price/Cash, Price/Free Cash Flow, EPS growth this year, EPS growth next year, EPS growth past 5 years, EPS growth next 5 years, Sales growth past 5 years, EPS growth quarter over quarter, Sales growth quarter over quarter, Return on Assets, Return on Equity, Return on Investment, Current Ratio, Quick Ratio, LT Debt/Equity, Debt/Equity, Gross Margin, Operating Margin, Net Profit Margin, Payout Ratio, Insider Ownership, Insider Transactions, Institutional Ownership, Institutional Transactions.

As you can see, there are quite a lot of them. But don't feel overwhelmed. We won't need all of them. Just the most important ones.

### We will focus on:

P/E, P/B, EPS past 5 years, Return on Assets, Return on Equity, Debt/Equity and Net Profit Margin.

# P/E (Price to Earnings Ratio)

## Calculation

Current Stock Price / Earnings per share (EPS)

*EPS is calculated as (Net Income – Dividends)/Number of stocks. It tells you how much the company made (per share) after deducting all expenses.

## About P/E

**The P/E ratio tells us how much you pay now to receive $1 of the company earnings.**

When it comes to stocks, the P/E ratio is probably the most widely used. It tells us very important information which is – how much money is the company making related to how much you paid for it.

You can also look at it this way: P/E ratio tells you how many years it will take the company to earn you the money you paid for your stocks.

The smaller the P/E the better. Because the smaller the value, the faster the company will make your invested money back.

**Example**: Stock price is $100. Having one stock of the company makes you $10/per year. In this case, it will take 10 years to cover the investment. In 10 years, the company will earn you the money you invested in it ($100/$10) = 10 years.

The P/E Ratio is a very good indication of how good your stock is, and whether it is currently overpriced or not. BUT it is not a Holy Grail! Many factors can distort the P/E ratio so the stock can look either very good or very bad. You always need to consider more information about the company to get the complete picture. Not just the P/E. That would be a common mistake that beginner investors make (and which we won't make).

Currently, the average P/E ratio for US stocks in the S&P 500 index is around 16. However, the standard P/E differs between sectors.

## Typical companies with high P/E

The highest P/E is usually in the most popular and fast-growing sectors like the Technology sector. The reason is that the prices ("P" in the P/E formula) of these stocks are inflated with no earnings to back them up. Investors simply believe that those companies will have way bigger Earnings in the future than they have now.

A typical example of a company with huge P/E could be, for example, Tesla. The current P/E is 111 which is insane. Investors who are willing to buy Tesla for this crazy high price believe that the company will make significantly more money in the future.

Are those investors completely bananas? Does it make sense to buy Tesla now? Truth be told, Tesla is very popular and fast-growing, and its earnings may grow rapidly. So, even with P/E = 111, Tesla could potentially be a good investment (only the "E" in the P/E formula would need to rise dramatically). I don't think their earnings will ever rise as much to justify the high price, but that's not the point here.

What I am trying to show you with this example is that P/E is not a Holy Grail. It does not show us the whole picture. It only shows us the current situation, but not the future. When picking stocks, we need to look at more than just P/E.

### **Typical companies with low P/E**

Companies with typically low P/E are often in sectors or industries that are not too popular, stable (some people could say boring), and lack surprises. Typical examples are sectors like Utilities or Basic Materials.

If you see a company with extremely low P/E (for example, P/E below 5) then you should be careful. It usually doesn't mean you found a Holy Grail, but that you found a company that investors don't believe in. A company that has been able to make some money now, but investors don't see any bright future here.

### **Recommended P/E values for a stock screener**

So, what is the universal rule? Which P/E value is good and which is too high? I recommend looking for stocks that have their P/E below 20.

Yes, you will miss many good stocks with good growth potential, but you will also filter out stocks that are just too expensive and that don't have the results or bright future to back their high prices up. Under current circumstances, P/E below 20 is in my opinion a reasonable value.

*If you don't want to filter out stocks from some sectors that have naturally higher P/E values, then you may consider setting the filter even to 25. But in most cases, I would recommend sticking to the P/E < 20 rule.

### **P/E is changing over time**

Keep in mind that P/E is changing over time. It depends on the current market price ("P") and the last company's earnings ("E"). Both those variables change over time. If you would like to invest in a company with too high a P/E, then you can simply wait for your chance and purchase that stock when the market price drops (which lowers the P/E).

# P/B (Price to Book Ratio)

P/B = Current Stock Price/Book Value

*Book Value = Total Assets (what the company has) – total Liabilities (what the company owes)

### About P/B

Every company needs to own some assets to operate its business. It could be land, offices, computers, cars, factories, machines, licenses, ... All those things are called assets. The Book value represents the total value of all those assets after deduction of what the company owes (to banks, creditors, ...).

If in a critical scenario a company goes bankrupt, then investors won't lose all their investment. What will happen is that all the assets of the company will get sold (machines, buildings, land, other properties...), the company debt will be paid, and then the rest of the money will go back to the investors (shareholders). The bigger the Book value, the more money will go back to investors. That's why a good investor should be aware of the company's Book value.

The smaller the P/B ratio the better (because the higher the Book value, the smaller the P/B ratio).

**Simplified example:** Company's market value is $10 bln. It owns machines, factories, buildings and land with a total value of $5 bln. It also has a debt of $1 bln. If this company went bankrupt, then shareholders would get $4 bln. back from their investment ($5 bln. – $1bln. = $ 4bln).

What does this mean for you as a shareholder? It means you would get your cut as well as the other shareholders. How big your cut would be is depending on how many stocks you own (how big a portion of the company you own). If you own 1% of the company, then you would get $40 mil.

You can look at the Book value as a sort of catastrophic scenario Stop Loss. It is what you are going to get in the worst-case scenario.

As you can imagine, different companies in different sectors vary a lot in how many assets they need to operate and in their typical P/E values.

### Typical companies with a high Book value (and low P/B ratio)

Companies with high Book value are typically companies that need to invest significant amounts of money into tangible stuff to operate their business.

Typical examples of companies that hold expensive assets are companies from the Energy sector, Industrials sector, and Utilities sector. All those companies have one thing in common – they need expensive, tangible stuff to operate their businesses. They need factories, heavy machinery, land, and infrastructure, … all of those are expensive assets those companies need to operate their businesses.

This is why they typically have high Book value (and low P/B ratio).

### Typical companies with a low Book value (and high P/B ratio)

Those are companies that don't need a lot of tangible assets to operate their business. It's typically companies from the Technology or Healthcare sector.

Such companies often have high margins on their products.

Take for example a Healthcare company that focuses on devising new pills or vaccines. They need some offices, labs, cars, computers, and some fancy equipment in their labs, … but that's about it, right? They don't need to own super expensive assets to operate the business. This is why their Book value is low (and P/B ratio high).

### Recommended P/B values for a stock screener

Typical P/B values vary across different sectors. To give you at least some starting point, search for stocks with P/B below 3. This should give you plenty of good companies with solid assets and Book value.

If you search through sectors with typically high P/B, then you need to go for a higher P/B limit. I suggest around 3.5.

If, on the other hand, you search in sectors with typically low P/B (like Energy, Industrials, Utilities) then you may want to set the filter to 2 – 2.5.

The important thing to note is that none of this is set in stone. Conditions change and typical P/B values can also change over time. What is normal now may not be the norm in 5 years …

Here is a page where you can check out the current P/B average in all the sectors and industries:

https://www.gurufocus.com/industry_overview.php

When using the screener to filter out stocks, I recommend searching for companies that have P/B below the sector average.

## P/B conclusion

Similarly, like the P/E ratio, the P/B is also not a Holy Grail. You may find fantastic companies that have very high P/B value. Those companies may be able to generate huge earnings without owning expensive assets. There are also companies with a high Book value (low P/B ratio) but without being able to generate any decent earnings.

P/B is simply yet another piece of the puzzle you need to consider. Just on its own, P/B does not give us any special edge. A company needs more than just a low P/B ratio. The low P/B is good, but a solid company needs more than just that.

# Earnings Per Share (EPS) Growth

Earnings per Share (EPS) gives us direct information about the company's profitability. If it is positive, then the company is profitable. If negative, then the company is losing money. The bigger EPS the better.

What it says is pretty straightforward – it tells us the annual growth of the company's earnings in the last x years (percentwise). Simply put: Have the earnings grown – YES/NO, and how much? It's as simple as that.

EPS is calculated using the "Net income" which means that all costs the company had have already been deducted and we are working with the final – clear result of their business.

There are three types of EPS parameters in the Finviz screener: EPS growth this year, EPS growth next year, and EPS growth for the past 5 years. I recommend using the last one: EPS growth past 5 years because it gives you the bigger picture.

I recommend setting the filter to "Positive". That means the Earnings grew more than 0% in the last 5 years.

# Return On Assets (ROA)

## Calculation

$$ROA = \frac{Annual\ Earnings}{Total\ Assets}$$

ROA tells us how effective the company is in generating profit with the assets they have.

With stocks, it's not only about how much money a company can make but also about the number of resources they need to make that money. It's easy to make $100 with $1.000.000 worth of assets, but it's not so easy to make $100 with $1.000 assets.

**Example**

Company A has total assets = $1 mil. With those assets, it earned $100.000.

Company B has total assets = of $10 mil. With those assets, it earned $800.000.

Which company is more efficient?

ROA of Company A is 100.000/1.000.000 = 10%

ROA of Company B is 800.000/10.000.000 = 8%

Even though company B made way more money, it is not as effective as Company A. Company A can use its assets more effectively.

This is what the ROA is all about. The bigger the ROA, the better.

**ROA comparison between sectors**

ROA varies significantly across different sectors and industries. If you are comparing companies based on ROA, then it is best to compare only similar companies from the same industry or sector.

It is quite typical that for example companies from the Technology or Consumer-cyclical sector have very high ROA numbers. On the other hand, asset-heavy industries that need to invest heavily into their assets – like Energies or Utilities have typically low ROA. I recommend comparing stocks from the same industry or sector only.

You can check the average ROA by Sector here: https://csimarket.com/screening/index.php?s=roa

**Example**

McDonalds has a ROA of 13%. YUM! One of its competitors has a ROA of 26%. This means that YUM! Is twice as effective as McDonalds.

McDonalds is huge though. Its market capitalization is over $180 bln, whereas YUM has only $37 bln. Generally speaking, the smaller the company, the easier it is to be effective.

### Recommended ROA values for a stock screener

Because typical ROA differs so much across the equity sectors, it's hard to tell you one universal value to use with the screener. I can give you some pointers though:

Firstly, search for companies that have positive ROA. That's a rule you should always stick to. A company simply needs to make money. That means it needs to have a ROA bigger than 0%.

Secondly, I recommend narrowing your search down to companies with ROA over 5%. This will filter out some of the less-effective companies but also some huge companies that struggle with their effectiveness because of their size (for example Disney).

If you want to narrow down your search even further, then you can go as far as looking for companies with ROA over 10%.

# Return On Equity (ROE)

### Calculation

ROE = Annual Earnings/Equity

ROE is very similar to ROA as it tells us how the company is efficient in generating profit.

The difference between ROA and ROE is that ROE has a different denominator.

ROA tells us how the company is efficient concerning its Assets, whereas ROE tells us how the company is efficient concerning its total Equity.

You get the total Equity if you take all the Assets and deduct the company's liabilities:

Equity = Assets - Liabilities

The ROE is telling us how efficient the company is without borrowed money - using only its equity.

The biggest difference between ROA and ROE is in companies with high debts. Otherwise, ROA and ROE tell us pretty much the same thing – how effective the company is in making money.

Both are important metrics you need to consider when planning your stock investment.

### ROE comparison between sectors

ROE differs quite a lot between sectors and industries. Typical sectors with high ROE are Technologies and Consumer-cyclical, and typical sectors with low ROE are asset-heavy industries like Energies or Utilities.

Average ROE by Sectors: https://csimarket.com/screening/index.php?s=roe

### Recommended ROE values for a stock screener

ROE values will always be higher than ROA because ROE shows how effective the company is only with their Equity without liabilities. I suggest you search for companies that have an ROE over 10%. If you want to narrow down your search more, then go for 15% - 20%, or even a bit higher (depending on the sector and industry).

## Debt/Equity

Debt/Equity is a ratio that compares the company's Debt to its Equity – in other words, it tells us how much leverage the company is using. It tells us whether the company is financing its operations through Debt or with its funds.

### Example

A company's equity is $10bln, and they borrowed $5bln. Debt/Equity will be $5bln/$10bln = 0.5 (= 50%).

### No Debt = good Debt?

Our common sense tells us that it is better if a company is not in debt and it's able to finance its business with only its funds, right? Well, in this case, being without debt may not be the best way to go.

What is positive about Debt is that it allows companies to grow faster.

Imagine you run a good business, and you want to scale it to make more money. To scale a business, you typically need a lot of capital. Sure, you can save bit by bit, but if you want to expand quickly, then you need to borrow money – you need Debt. In such a case Debt is good.

However, too much Debt could prove to be risky. You need to find the sweet spot between a healthy portion of Debt and Debt that could ruin your business. The thing is, that if you borrow money, you need to pay interest. If the economy is booming and you are doing fine, then paying interest may not be a problem. But if the economy starts to slow down, goes into a recession, and your company is making less and less, then too big Debt could endanger your business as you may not be able to pay the interest anymore.

The bottom line is that debt can help the company grow, especially if the economy is booming. However, when the economy is slowing down and your business is not performing as expected then too much Debt can be dangerous.

## Recommended Debt/Equity values for a stock screener

If you want a simple rule-of-thumb, then search for companies that have Debt around, or below 60-70%. When a company's Debt is over 100%, then I consider the investment riskier.

As always, this is not as super-simple because the average Debt varies between sectors. Some sectors naturally need more investments (and therefore are more indebted), whereas some sectors don't need the Debt so much and their Debt levels are lower overall.

Some of the **higher-debt sectors** are Utilities, Energy (because large investments are needed there), Financials (because banks borrow money to lend money), and Real Estate.

**A smaller Debt** is generally in sectors like Healthcare, or Technology.

Also, keep in mind that too small Debt may not be a good thing, because it could indicate that the company is not using its full potential. In other words - it could be growing faster. For this reason, I recommend avoiding companies with too low debt. Typically, below 10-20%.

## What if Debt/Equity is negative?

If Debt/Equity is negative, then it means the company has more liabilities than assets. This is a sign of a company in trouble. You should avoid investing in such companies.

# Net Profit Margin

Net Profit Margin tells us how much a company keeps from every $1 made in sales.

The reason I like to use "Net" Profit Margin over some of the other Margin metrics (like gross, or operating margin) is that Net Margin calculates with all expenses already deducted. In other words – this is what the company earned and got after all expenses got covered. That's why it's called "Net".

## Calculation

If a company makes a Net profit (this means all expenses are already deducted) = $50.000 and the total Revenue (money the company collected for their products & services) = $200.000, then the Net Profit Margin is $50.000/$200.000 = 0.25. That's 25%. This means that if this company sells you a beer for $5, then what they get after the deduction of all costs is $1.25 (25% from $5).

Quite obviously, the higher the Margin, the better.

Each sector has its specifics and therefore it's not a good idea to compare margins between different sectors.

Sectors and industries with typically **high margins** are for example the Financial, Real Estate or Utilities sector.

Sectors with typically **low margins** are Healthcare (drug manufacturers) and Energy.

*Note: Are you confused about why drug manufacturers have low margins when drugs are so expensive? It's because the high margins are added later in the long distribution chain that starts with drug manufacturers and ends in your local pharmacy.

### Recommended Net Profit Margin values for a stock screener

When it comes to screener values, I am usually not too strict with my Net Profit Margin requirements. The reason is that for me, this metric is not among the most important ones. And also, as I already pointed out, each sector has different typical margins.

What I recommend though is using this tab to filter out companies that have negative margins = and companies that lose money. You don't want those. So, don't be too strict here and only set the parameter to "**Positive**". That means margins above 0%.

# Picking Stocks with Stock Screener: Step-By-Step Examples

In this part, I will show you how to look for good stocks using the Finviz filter step-by-step.

To filter out the stocks we are going to use the parameters we discussed before. This is a little recap of those parameters and what they tell us:

- **Market Capitalization:** How big a company is.
- **Dividend Yield:** How much dividend a company pays out.
- **P/E ratio:** How much a company makes and whether it is worth it compared to its market price.
- **P/B Ratio:** How much a company owns compared to its market price.
- **EPS growth past 5 years:** How much the company's earnings have risen in the last 5 years.
- **ROA:** How efficient the company is in making money.
- **ROE:** How efficient the company is in making money.
- **Debt/Equity:** How much the company owes.
- **Net Profit Margin:** How big the company's margins are.

With those parameters, we cover pretty much all the important "measurable" aspects of stocks.

Now, I am going to show you how to use the Finviz screener to find fundamentally good stocks. I am going to do this sector by sector. So, we will go through each sector and look for good stocks in that sector. As you have already learned, each sector is a bit specific. For this reason, we cannot use the same parameters and filters for each one of them.

Here is a table with recommended values to use in your stock screening. You can use it as sort of a starting point. Save it or print it. You will need it.

| | Descriptive Tab | | Fundamental Tab | | | | | | |
|---|---|---|---|---|---|---|---|---|---|
| Sector | Market Cap | Dividend Yield | P/E | P/B | EPS past 5 yrs | ROA | ROE | Debt/Equity | Net Profit Margin |
| Basic Materials | over $2bl | over 2% | Under 20 | Under 3 | Positive | Positive or Over 5% | Over 10% | Under 0.7 | Positive |
| Communication Services | over $2bl | over 2% | Under 20 | Under 3 | Positive | Positive or Over 5% | Over 10% | Under 1 | Positive |
| Consumer Cyclical | over $2bl | over 1% | Under 20 | Under 3 | Positive | Positive or Over 5% | Over 10% | Under 70% | Positive |
| Consumer Defensive | over $2bl | over 2% | Under 20 | Under 3 | Positive | Positive or Over 5% | Over 10% | Under 70% | Positive |
| Energy | over $2bl | over 2% | Under 20 | Under 3 | Positive | Positive or Over 5% | Over 10% | Under 70% | Positive |
| Financial | over $2bl | over 2% | Under 20 | Under 3 | Positive | Positive or Over 5% | Over 10% | Under 70% | Positive |
| Healthcare | over $2bl | Any | Under 20 | Under 3 | Positive | Positive or Over 5% | Over 10% | Under 70% | Positive |
| Industrials | over $2bl | over 1% | Under 20 | Under 3 | Positive | Positive or Over 5% | Over 10% | Under 70% | Positive |
| Real Estate | over $2bl | over 3% | Any | Any | Positive | Positive or Over 5% | Over 10% | Any | Positive |
| Technology | over $2bl | over 1% | Under 20 | Under 3 | Positive | Positive or Over 5% | Over 10% | Under 70% | Positive |
| Utilities | over $2bl | over 3% | Under 20 | Under 3 | Positive | Positive or Over 5% | Over 10% | Any | Positive |

Let's now go to the Finviz screener and use the table above to find some good stocks.

Go to: https://finviz.com/screener.ashx

This is the screener. We are going to use the Descriptive and Fundamental tabs only.

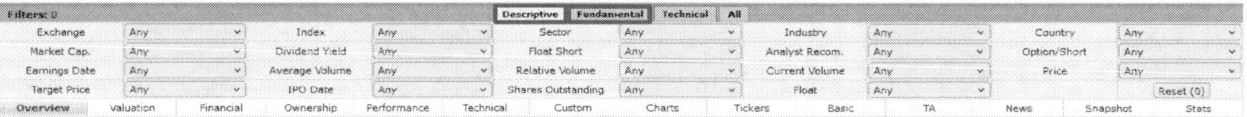

# Companies from the Basic Materials Sector

Let's start in the Descriptive tab and select the Basic Materials sector.

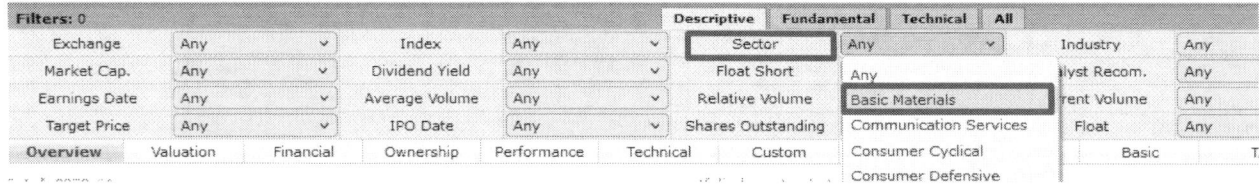

Then adjust the column saying, "Market Capitalization" and "Dividend Yield" according to the table I gave you. In this case, you will set the Market Cap to "over $2bln" and the "Dividend Yield" to "over 2%". That's all we are going to do in the Descriptive tab.

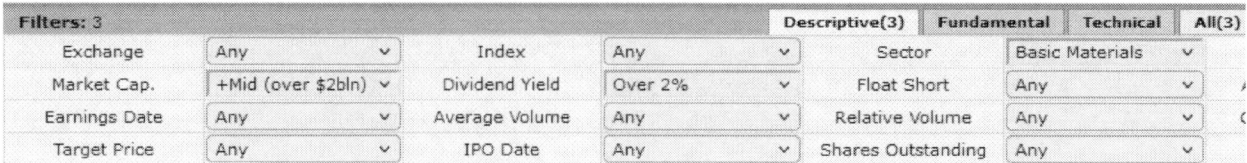

Now, switch over to the **Fundamental tab** and adjust all the parameters according to the table above. For the **Basic Materials** sector, it will be like this:

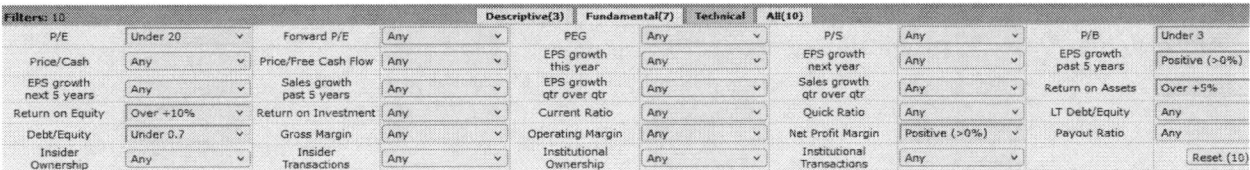

Doing this will filter out stocks from the Basic Materials sector. When I did this (November 2021), ten stocks suited all the parameters. They were these:

| No. | Ticker | Company | Sector | Industry | Country |
| --- | --- | --- | --- | --- | --- |
| 1 | AU | AngloGold Ashanti Limited | Basic Materials | Gold | South Africa |
| 2 | BBL | BHP Group | Basic Materials | Other Industrial Metals & Mining | Australia |
| 3 | BHP | BHP Group | Basic Materials | Other Industrial Metals & Mining | Australia |
| 4 | GFI | Gold Fields Limited | Basic Materials | Gold | South Africa |
| 5 | GGB | Gerdau S.A. | Basic Materials | Steel | Brazil |
| 6 | HMY | Harmony Gold Mining Company Limited | Basic Materials | Gold | South Africa |
| 7 | RIO | Rio Tinto Group | Basic Materials | Other Industrial Metals & Mining | United Kingdom |
| 8 | SBSW | Sibanye Stillwater Limited | Basic Materials | Gold | South Africa |
| 9 | TX | Ternium S.A. | Basic Materials | Steel | Luxembourg |
| 10 | VALE | Vale S.A. | Basic Materials | Other Industrial Metals & Mining | Brazil |

Based on our parameters, those should be relatively good stocks we can work with further.

It's best to save the list so you can get back to it later. You can take a screenshot, write down the companies, or preferably save them to your Finviz portfolio. To do this, you need to be Registered (free).

This is what the portfolio I have just created looks like. It is interactive, so you can click the stock Ticker and it will take you straight to the company details and chart.

*NOTE: The stocks the Finviz found as suitable according to my parameters will differ from the stocks you get. I was doing this screening at the end of 2021 and things changed since then. Don't worry about that though. This is not supposed to be about me picking ideal stocks for you, but about teaching you the method on a concrete example.*

What I am going to do now is look more in-depth into two companies from this "viable stocks" list. I recommend you do this with all the companies from your list.

Let's start with the first company – Anglo Gold Ashanti Limited.

### (AU) Anglo Gold Ashanti Limited – Company Details

If you click the 1st ticker from the list above (AU), then it will take you to a page with a company profile.

**Company description (info from Finviz):** AngloGold Ashanti Limited operates as a gold mining company. It also produces gold, silver, uranium, sulphuric acid; and dore bars. The company operates ten operations and three projects in eight countries in South Africa, Continental Africa, the Americas, and Australia. AngloGold Ashanti Limited was incorporated in 1944 and is headquartered in Johannesburg, South Africa.

At the top of the page, you can see the AngloGold Ashanti stock chart. Below that it says that the company is from the Basic Materials sector, that they deal in Gold and that they are from South Africa.

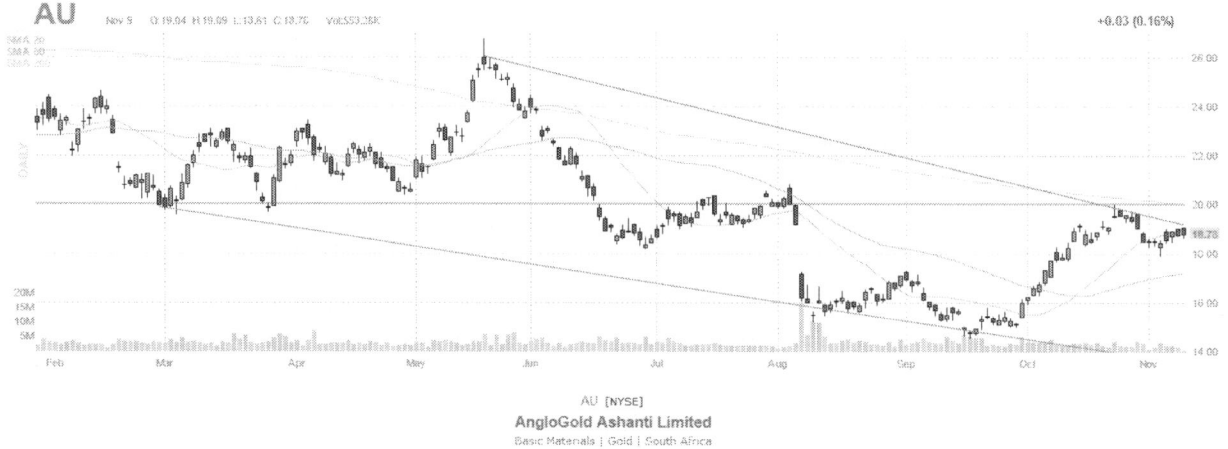

Below that there is a table with various company details:

| Index | - | P/E | 8.50 | EPS (ttm) | 2.21 | Insider Own | 3.10% | Shs Outstand | 419.14M | Perf Week | 1.35% |
|---|---|---|---|---|---|---|---|---|---|---|---|
| Market Cap | 7.71B | Forward P/E | 9.01 | EPS next Y | 2.08 | Insider Trans | 0.00% | Shs Float | 412.47M | Perf Month | 5.51% |
| Income | 926.00M | PEG | 0.24 | EPS next Q | 0.79 | Inst Own | 31.80% | Short Float | 1.81% | Perf Quarter | 20.97% |
| Sales | 4.43B | P/S | 1.74 | EPS this Y | 159.20% | Inst Trans | -0.17% | Short Ratio | 2.12 | Perf Half Y | -17.58% |
| Book/sh | 9.10 | P/B | 2.06 | EPS next Y | 24.92% | ROA | 11.70% | Target Price | 21.50 | Perf Year | -31.97% |
| Cash/sh | - | P/C | - | EPS next 5Y | 34.89% | ROE | 25.30% | 52W Range | 14.57 - 26.77 | Perf YTD | -17.11% |
| Dividend | 0.53 | P/FCF | 15.93 | EPS past 5Y | 97.20% | ROI | 14.40% | 52W High | -29.96% | Beta | 0.59 |
| Dividend % | 2.83% | Quick Ratio | 1.60 | Sales past 5Y | 2.00% | Gross Margin | 36.50% | 52W Low | 28.69% | ATR | 0.50 |
| Employees | 36952 | Current Ratio | 2.40 | Sales Q/Q | 9.00% | Oper. Margin | 30.80% | RSI (14) | 57.83 | Volatility | 2.54% 2.41% |
| Optionable | Yes | Debt/Eq | 0.55 | EPS Q/Q | 18.50% | Profit Margin | 20.20% | Rel Volume | 0.67 | Prev Close | 18.75 |
| Shortable | Yes | LT Debt/Eq | 0.48 | Earnings | - | Payout | 21.90% | Avg Volume | 3.51M | Price | 18.75 |
| Recom | 2.80 | SMA20 | -0.65% | SMA50 | 9.12% | SMA200 | -6.40% | Volume | 537,538 | Change | 0.00% |

As you can see, there is quite a lot of info and most of it has little real value (at least for us).

The most important parameters are the ones we talked about in the previous part of the book. Those parameters are **Dividend %, P/E, P/B, EPS past 5 years, Return on Assets, Return on Equity, Debt/Equity and Net Profit Margin**.

- **Market Capitalization:** 8.00 B
- **Dividend Yield:** 2.83%
- **P/E ratio:** 8.50
- **P/B Ratio:** 2.06
- **EPS past 5 years:** 97.20%
- **ROA:** 11.70%
- **ROE:** 25.30%
- **Debt/Equity:** 0.55
- **Net Profit Margin:** 20.20%

AngloGold Ashanti is quite a big company, with a nice Dividend and a very good P/E ratio. It can generate positive income (ROA, ROE) and its debt is also quite okay.

See? It's not rocket science to do a quick company overview and tell if the company is fundamentally good or bad!

Our next step would be chart analysis where we look for a viable price level to invest in this company. I won't do this here as we will cover it later in the book.

Let's now move to the next stock from the list!

## (BHP) BHP Group – Company Details
**Company description (from Finviz):** BHP Group engages in the natural resources business in Australia, Europe, China, Japan, India, South Korea, the rest of Asia, North America, South America, and internationally. It operates through Petroleum, Copper, Iron Ore, and Coal segments. The company engages in the exploration, development, and production of oil and gas properties; and mining of copper, silver, zinc, molybdenum, uranium, gold, iron ore, and metallurgical and energy coal. It is also involved in mining, smelting, and refining of nickel; the

provision of towing, freight, marketing and trading, marketing support, finance, administrative, and other services; and potash development activities. The company was founded in 1851 and is headquartered in Melbourne, Australia.

As you can see from the company's description, this is quite the giant!

Below is a weekly chart (one candle = 1 week):

## Company details

| Index | - | P/E | 12.82 | EPS (ttm) | 4.46 | Insider Own | 5.40% | Shs Outstand | 2.53B | Perf Week | 4.93% |
|---|---|---|---|---|---|---|---|---|---|---|---|
| Market Cap | 149.10B | Forward P/E | 12.41 | EPS next Y | 4.61 | Insider Trans | 0.00% | Shs Float | 1.48B | Perf Month | 9.33% |
| Income | 11.30B | PEG | - | EPS next Q | - | Inst Own | 7.10% | Short Float | 1.92% | Perf Quarter | -6.37% |
| Sales | 60.82B | P/S | 2.45 | EPS this Y | 42.10% | Inst Trans | 3.27% | Short Ratio | 7.73 | Perf Half Y | -24.23% |
| Book/sh | 20.27 | P/B | 2.82 | EPS next Y | -16.21% | ROA | 10.80% | Target Price | 59.90 | Perf Year | -11.66% |
| Cash/sh | 5.94 | P/C | 9.63 | EPS next 5Y | -5.00% | ROE | 23.00% | 52W Range | 51.88 - 82.07 | Perf YTD | -12.46% |
| Dividend | 3.12 | P/FCF | 7.92 | EPS past 5Y | 92.20% | ROI | 20.40% | 52W High | -30.30% | Beta | 1.00 |
| Dividend % | 5.45% | Quick Ratio | 1.40 | Sales past 5Y | 16.30% | Gross Margin | - | 52W Low | 10.25% | ATR | 1.51 |
| Employees | 34478 | Current Ratio | 1.60 | Sales Q/Q | 49.40% | Oper. Margin | 42.60% | RSI (14) | 55.87 | Volatility | 1.35% 1.92% |
| Optionable | Yes | Debt/Eq | 0.41 | EPS Q/Q | 62.10% | Profit Margin | 18.60% | Rel Volume | 0.70 | Prev Close | 57.06 |
| Shortable | Yes | LT Debt/Eq | 0.36 | Earnings | - | Payout | 0.00% | Avg Volume | 3.67M | Price | 57.20 |
| Recom | 1.00 | SMA20 | 3.96% | SMA50 | 3.77% | SMA200 | -15.27% | Volume | 2,574,086 | Change | 0.25% |

Again, we are going to look only at the most important ones:

- **Market Capitalization:** 149.10B
- **Dividend Yield:** 5.45%
- **P/E ratio:** 12.82
- **P/B Ratio:** 2.82
- **EPS past 5 years:** 92.20%
- **ROA:** 10.80%
- **ROE:** 23.00%
- **Debt/Equity:** 0.41
- **Net Profit Margin:** 18.60

BHP is a huge company, with a fantastic dividend, and a really good P/E ratio. It also has quite a low Debt - especially if you consider how big the company is!

# Companies from Communication Services Sector

Let's use the screener again to look for viable stocks in the Communication Services sector.

Again, I will set it according to the table I gave you. Just to remind you – this is the table:

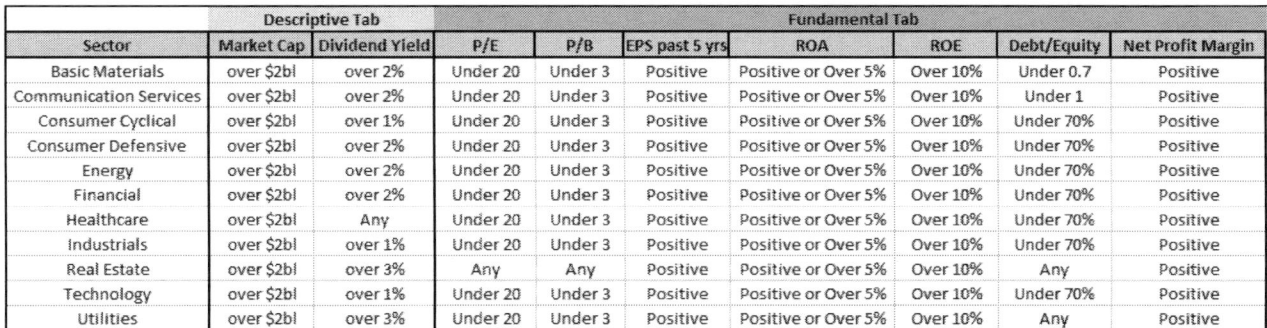

I will use the Finviz screener with the parameters from the table. It will look like this:

## Descriptive tab

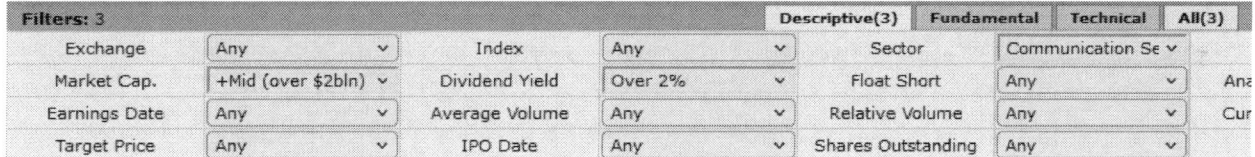

## Fundamental Tab

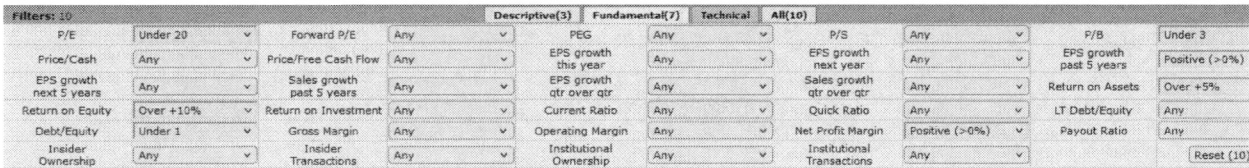

With the filter set like this, I am currently getting only 2 companies that meet the criteria. It's Autohome (ATHM), and ViacomCBS (VIAC).

To get more results, we will need to lower our criteria a bit. I suggest lowering our requirements on Dividends and Debt. The reason is that overall, this sector does not offer too high dividends, and the companies here often utilize a higher debt. With Dividend criteria lowered to "over 1%" and Debt to "any" we will get these companies:

| Ticker | Company | Sector | Industry | Country |
|---|---|---|---|---|
| ATHM | Autohome Inc. | Communication Services | Internet Content & Information | China |
| CMCSA | Comcast Corporation | Communication Services | Entertainment | USA |
| FOXA | Fox Corporation | Communication Services | Broadcasting | USA |
| NXST | Nexstar Media Group, Inc. | Communication Services | Broadcasting | USA |
| TEF | Telefonica, S.A. | Communication Services | Telecom Services | Spain |
| TGNA | TEGNA Inc. | Communication Services | Broadcasting | USA |
| TKC | Turkcell Iletisim Hizmetleri A.S. | Communication Services | Telecom Services | Turkey |
| VIAC | ViacomCBS Inc. | Communication Services | Entertainment | USA |

At this point, I recommend saving the list as a new portfolio so you can get back to it easily in the future. You want to do this with each sector.

## (CMCSA) Comcast Corporation

**Company description (from Finviz):** Comcast Corporation operates as a media and technology company worldwide. It operates through Cable Communications, Cable Networks, Broadcast Television, Filmed Entertainment, Theme Parks, and Sky segments. The Cable Communications segment offers cable services, including high-speed Internet, video, voice, wireless, and security and automation services to residential and business customers under the Xfinity brand, as well as sells advertising. The Cable Networks segment operates national cable networks that provide various entertainment, news and information, and sports content; regional sports and news networks; international cable networks; and various digital properties, including brand-aligned Websites; and engages in the cable television studio production operations. The Broadcast Television segment operates NBC and Telemundo broadcast networks, NBC and Telemundo local broadcast television stations, broadcast television studio production operations, and various digital properties. The Filmed Entertainment segment produces, acquires, markets, and distributes filmed entertainment under the Universal Pictures, Illumination, DreamWorks Animation, and Focus Features names. It also develops, produces, and licenses stage plays, and distributes filmed entertainment produced by third parties. The Theme Parks segment operates Universal theme parks in Orlando, Florida; Hollywood, California; and Osaka, Japan. The Sky segment offers direct-to-consumer services, such as video, high-speed Internet, voice, and wireless phone services; and content services comprising operating entertainment networks, the Sky News broadcast network, and Sky Sports networks. The company also owns the Philadelphia Flyers, as well as the Wells Fargo Center arena in Philadelphia, Pennsylvania; and provides streaming services, such as Peacock. Comcast Corporation was founded in 1963 and is headquartered in Philadelphia, Pennsylvania.

Below is a weekly chart (one candle = 1 week):

## Company details

The most important ones are:

- **Market Capitalization:** 220.17B
- **Dividend Yield:** 2.06%
- **P/E ratio:** 15.60
- **P/B Ratio:** 2.32
- **EPS past 5 years:** 7.00%
- **ROA:** 5.20%
- **ROE:** 15.50%
- **Debt/Equity:** 1.07
- **Net Profit Margin:** 12.70%

As you can see, Comcast is a huge company. Despite this and its huge popularity, it currently has a P/E ratio quite small. Not as much as the other companies on the list but P/E = 15.60 is still good! The other parameters are also acceptable and this makes the Comcast company a viable candidate for further Price Action & Volume Profile analysis, and possibly even for an investment.

## (FOXA) Fox Corporation

**Company description (from Finviz):** Fox Corporation operates as a news, sports, and entertainment company in the United States. The company operates through three segments: Cable Network Programming; Television; and Other, Corporate and Eliminations. The Cable Network Programming segment produces and licenses news, business news, and sports content for distribution primarily through cable television systems, direct broadcast satellite operators, telecommunications companies, and online multichannel video programming distributors. It operates FOX News, a national cable news channel; FOX Business, a business news national cable channel; FS1 and FS2 multi-sport national networks; FOX Sports Racing, a video programming service that comprises motor sports programming; and FOX Soccer Plus, a video programming network for live soccer and rugby competitions; FOX Deportes, a Spanish-language sports programming service; and Big Ten Network, a national video programming service. The Television segment acquires, produces, markets, and distributes broadcast network programming. It operates The FOX Network, a national television broadcast network that broadcasts sports programming and entertainment; MyNetworkTV, a programming distribution service; Fox Alternative Entertainment, a full-service production studio that develops and produces unscripted and alternative programming; Bento Box, which develops and produces animated programing; and Tubi, a free advertising-supported video-on-demand service. This segment owns and operates 29 broadcast television stations. The Other, Corporate and Eliminations segment owns the FOX Studios lot that provides production and post-production services, including 15 sound stages, 2 broadcast studios, theaters and screening rooms, editing bays, and television and film production facilities in Los Angeles, California. The company was incorporated in 2018 and is based in New York, New York.

Below is a weekly chart (one candle = 1 week):

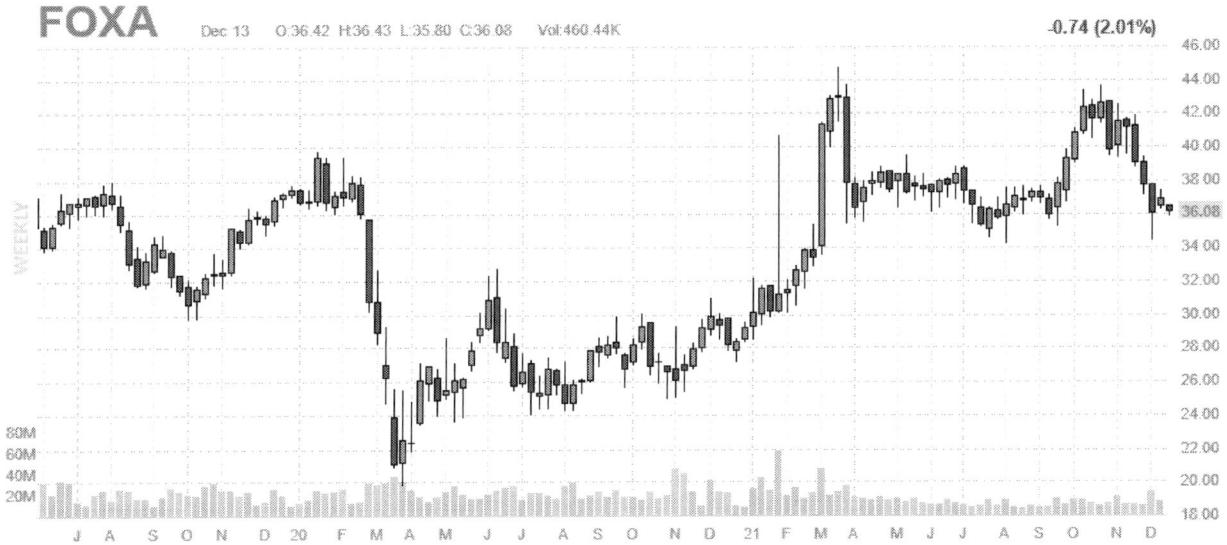

## Company details

| Index | S&P 500 | P/E | 12.38 | EPS (ttm) | 2.98 | Insider Own | 0.10% | Shs Outstand | 575.00M | Perf Week | 2.16% |
|---|---|---|---|---|---|---|---|---|---|---|---|
| Market Cap | 20.01B | Forward P/E | 10.35 | EPS next Y | 3.56 | Insider Trans | 0.00% | Shs Float | 463.50M | Perf Month | -9.51% |
| Income | 1.75B | PEG | 1.31 | EPS next Q | 1.02 | Inst Own | 99.90% | Short Float | 3.40% | Perf Quarter | 1.32% |
| Sales | 13.24B | P/S | 1.51 | EPS this Y | 122.80% | Inst Trans | 0.38% | Short Ratio | 5.23 | Perf Half Y | -2.28% |
| Book/sh | 19.88 | P/B | 1.85 | EPS next Y | 25.32% | ROA | 7.60% | Target Price | 45.29 | Perf Year | 26.49% |
| Cash/sh | 9.95 | P/C | 3.70 | EPS next 5Y | 9.47% | ROE | 15.70% | 52W Range | 27.12 - 44.80 | Perf YTD | 26.44% |
| Dividend | 0.48 | P/FCF | 13.20 | EPS past 5Y | 15.90% | ROI | 12.40% | 52W High | -19.46% | Beta | - |
| Dividend % | 1.30% | Quick Ratio | 2.70 | Sales past 5Y | 7.70% | Gross Margin | 36.20% | 52W Low | 33.04% | ATR | 1.06 |
| Employees | 9000 | Current Ratio | 3.10 | Sales Q/Q | 12.10% | Oper. Margin | 19.30% | RSI (14) | 36.48 | Volatility | 2.31% 2.57% |
| Optionable | Yes | Debt/Eq | 0.70 | EPS Q/Q | -33.70% | Profit Margin | 13.20% | Rel Volume | 1.02 | Prev Close | 36.82 |
| Shortable | Yes | LT Debt/Eq | 0.63 | Earnings | Nov 03 AMC | Payout | 15.40% | Avg Volume | 3.02M | Price | 36.08 |
| Recom | 2.40 | SMA20 | -4.70% | SMA50 | -10.03% | SMA200 | -5.76% | Volume | 460,444 | Change | -2.01% |

The most important are:

- **Market Capitalization:** 20.01b
- **Dividend Yield:** 1.30%
- **P/E ratio:** 12.38
- **P/B Ratio:** 1.85
- **EPS past 5 years:** 15.90%
- **ROA:** 7.60%
- **ROE:** 15.70%
- **Debt/Equity:** 0.70
- **Net Profit Margin:** 13.20

FOX is a huge and well—known company. Despite this, the P/E ratio remains quite low, which is great! Their debt isn't too bad either, given how big they are, and given the industry standards. Other important fundamentals are fine as well.

# Companies from Consumer Cyclical Sector

Let's use the table I gave you again to set the stock filter. For Consumer Cyclical sector the screener settings will look like this:

**Descriptive tab**

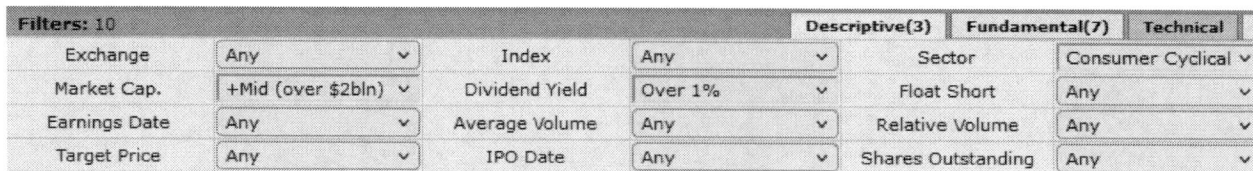

**Fundamental tab**

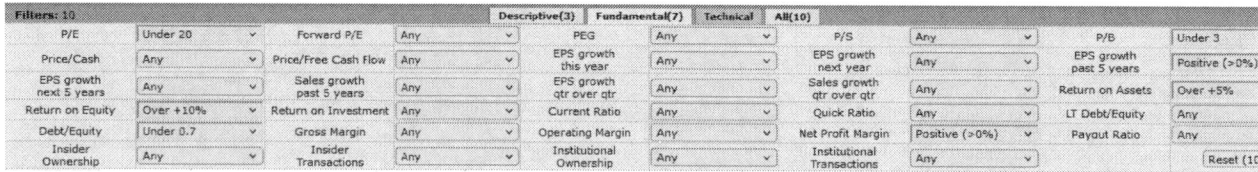

Those are the five companies that met the criteria. Again, I recommend saving the list as a portfolio:

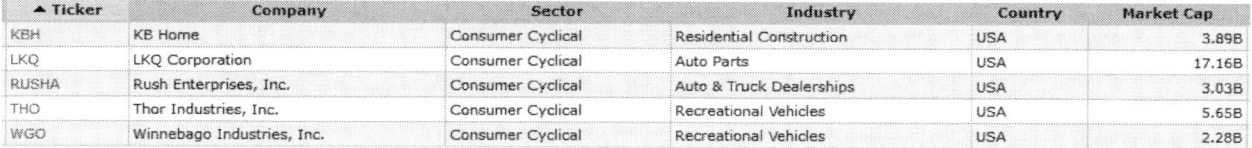

The biggest companies on the list are LKQ and THO so let's check them out! Again, I recommend you go over all of the companies from the list.

## (LKQ) LKQ Corporation

**Company description (from Finviz):** LKQ Corporation distributes replacement parts, components, and systems used in the repair and maintenance of vehicles. It operates through three segments: North America, Europe, and Specialty. The company distributes bumper covers, automotive body panels, and lights, as well as automotive glass products, such as windshields; salvage products, including mechanical and collision parts comprising engines; transmissions; door assemblies; sheet metal products, such as trunk lids, fenders, and hoods; lights and bumper assemblies; scrap metal and other materials to metals recyclers; and brake pads, discs and sensors, clutches, steering and suspension products, filters, and oil and automotive fluids, as well as electrical products, including spark plugs and batteries. It also operates self-service retail operations under the LKQ Pick Your Part name; and designs, manufactures and markets vehicle equipment and accessories. In addition, the company distributes recreational vehicle appliances and air conditioners, towing hitches, truck bed covers, vehicle protection products, cargo management products, wheels, tires, and suspension products. It serves collision and mechanical repair shops, new and used car dealerships, as well as retail customers. The company operates in the United States, Canada, the United Kingdom, Germany, Belgium, the Netherlands, Luxembourg, Italy, Poland, Slovakia, Austria, Taiwan, and various other European countries. LKQ Corporation was incorporated in 1998 and is headquartered in Chicago, Illinois.

Below is a weekly chart (one candle = 1 week)

I would like you to notice the dip at the beginning of 2020 when the COVID-19 crisis hit the world. This company – as a part of the Consumer Cyclical sector was hit hard and the price fell sharply from $35 to $15. The Consumer Cyclical sector is very sensitive to the economic cycle, and significant events that affect the economy. If there is a problem, then this sector gets hit hard. This time it was saved and recovered quickly thanks to the central bank and its stimulus (money printing).

## Company details

| Index | S&P 500 | P/E | 16.84 | EPS (ttm) | 3.44 | Insider Own | 0.30% | Shs Outstand | 294.03M | Perf Week | 2.51% |
|---|---|---|---|---|---|---|---|---|---|---|---|
| Market Cap | 17.16B | Forward P/E | 14.54 | EPS next Y | 3.99 | Insider Trans | -0.20% | Shs Float | 289.67M | Perf Month | 2.01% |
| Income | 1.04B | PEG | 0.50 | EPS next Q | 1.13 | Inst Own | 99.80% | Short Float | 1.99% | Perf Quarter | 13.76% |
| Sales | 12.86B | P/S | 1.33 | EPS this Y | 20.40% | Inst Trans | -0.91% | Short Ratio | 3.40 | Perf Half Y | 19.06% |
| Book/sh | 20.07 | P/B | 2.89 | EPS next Y | 3.16% | ROA | 8.30% | Target Price | 65.89 | Perf Year | 58.52% |
| Cash/sh | 1.36 | P/C | 42.61 | EPS next 5Y | 33.50% | ROE | 17.80% | 52W Range | 34.11 - 60.05 | Perf YTD | 64.50% |
| Dividend | 1.00 | P/FCF | 11.63 | EPS past 5Y | 8.80% | ROI | 8.50% | 52W High | -5.90% | Beta | 1.61 |
| Dividend % | 1.73% | Quick Ratio | 0.80 | Sales past 5Y | 10.10% | Gross Margin | 40.60% | 52W Low | 65.67% | ATR | 1.29 |
| Employees | 44000 | Current Ratio | 1.80 | Sales Q/Q | 8.20% | Oper. Margin | 11.20% | RSI (14) | 46.65 | Volatility | 1.89% 2.06% |
| Optionable | Yes | Debt/Eq | 0.40 | EPS Q/Q | 51.60% | Profit Margin | 8.10% | Rel Volume | 1.01 | Prev Close | 57.97 |
| Shortable | Yes | LT Debt/Eq | 0.40 | Earnings | Oct 28 BMO | Payout | 7.20% | Avg Volume | 1.69M | Price | 56.51 |
| Recom | 1.50 | SMA20 | -2.66% | SMA50 | 0.68% | SMA200 | 12.52% | Volume | 1,493,387 | Change | -2.52% |

The most important are:

- **Market Capitalization:** 17.16B
- **Dividend Yield:** 1.73%
- **P/E ratio:** 16.84
- **P/B Ratio:** 2.89
- **EPS past 5 years:** 8.80%
- **ROA:** 8.30%
- **ROE:** 17.80%
- **Debt/Equity:** 0.40
- **Net Profit Margin:** 8.10%

## (THO) Thor Industries

**Company description (from Finviz):** Thor Industries, Inc. designs, manufactures and sells recreational vehicles (RVs), and related parts and accessories in the United States, Canada, and Europe. The company offers travel trailers; gasoline and diesel Class A, Class B, and Class C motorhomes; conventional travel trailers and fifth wheels; luxury fifth wheels; and motor caravans, caravans, campervans, and urban vehicles. It also provides aluminum extrusion and specialized component products to RV and other manufacturers, and digital products and services for RVs. The company provides its products through independent and non-franchise dealers. The company was founded in 1980 and is based in Elkhart, Indiana.

Below is a weekly chart (one candle = 1 week)

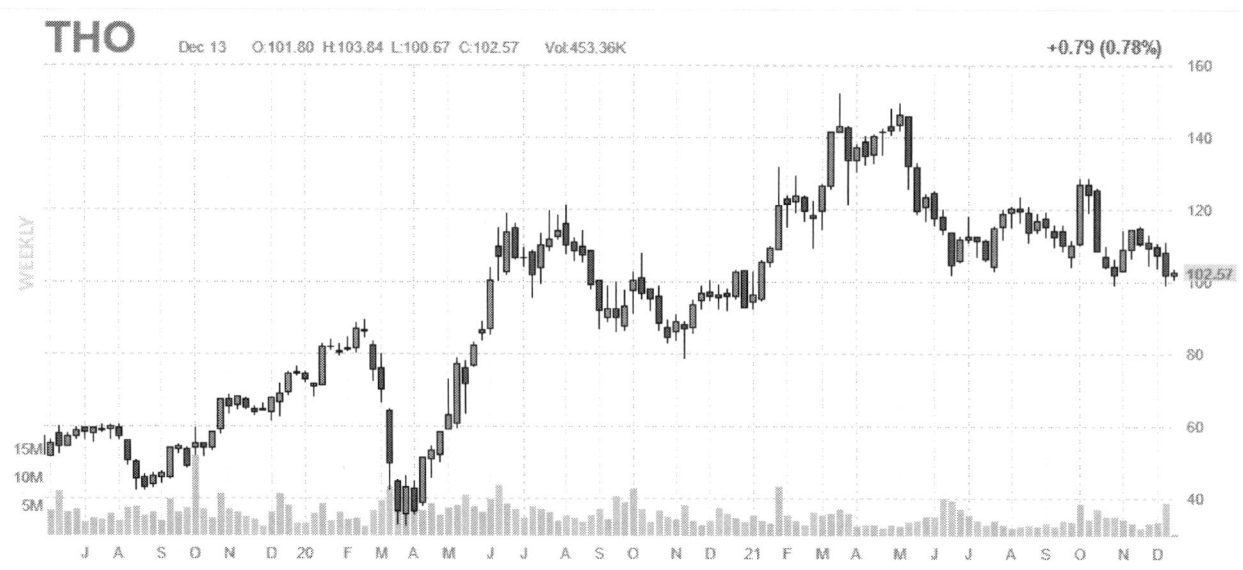

Very similar to the previous case (LKQ), there was a crazy sell-off as a reaction to the COVID-19 pandemic in 2020. The price plummeted from $90 to almost $30. The reason for such a sell-off is that if there is a pandemic with all the restrictions and risks involved, then people are not likely to buy a new recreational RV and drive on a vacation with it, right? This is exactly the kind of thing people stop buying first when a crisis hits. If the banks didn't print insane amounts of money to boost the economy, and if the peak of the crisis lasted longer, then the price of THO and similar stocks wouldn't recover so easily. This is the risk involved in the Consumer Cyclical sector. Keep it in mind.

## Company details

| Index | - | P/E | 8.60 | EPS (ttm) | 11.84 | Insider Own | 2.50% | Shs Outstand | 55.37M | Perf Week | -5.11% |
|---|---|---|---|---|---|---|---|---|---|---|---|
| Market Cap | 5.65B | Forward P/E | 7.73 | EPS next Y | 13.17 | Insider Trans | 0.00% | Shs Float | 53.12M | Perf Month | -8.50% |
| Income | 659.90M | PEG | 1.46 | EPS next Q | 3.56 | Inst Own | 92.80% | Short Float | 9.10% | Perf Quarter | -11.26% |
| Sales | 12.32B | P/S | 0.46 | EPS this Y | 194.40% | Inst Trans | 0.41% | Short Ratio | 7.17 | Perf Half Y | -6.15% |
| Book/sh | 52.77 | P/B | 1.93 | EPS next Y | 1.30% | ROA | 10.30% | Target Price | 144.29 | Perf Year | 9.24% |
| Cash/sh | 8.03 | P/C | 12.68 | EPS next 5Y | 5.90% | ROE | 24.90% | 52W Range | 91.58 - 152.20 | Perf YTD | 9.45% |
| Dividend | 1.72 | P/FCF | 16.05 | EPS past 5Y | 19.30% | ROI | 14.50% | 52W High | -32.70% | Beta | 2.04 |
| Dividend % | 1.69% | Quick Ratio | 0.80 | Sales past 5Y | 21.90% | Gross Margin | 15.40% | 52W Low | 11.85% | ATR | 4.02 |
| Employees | 31000 | Current Ratio | 1.60 | Sales Q/Q | 54.60% | Oper. Margin | 6.90% | RSI (14) | 38.32 | Volatility | 4.49% 3.44% |
| Optionable | Yes | Debt/Eq | 0.56 | EPS Q/Q | 92.10% | Profit Margin | 5.40% | Rel Volume | 0.66 | Prev Close | 101.78 |
| Shortable | Yes | LT Debt/Eq | 0.55 | Earnings | Dec 08 BMO | Payout | 13.70% | Avg Volume | 673.43K | Price | 102.43 |
| Recom | 2.40 | SMA20 | -5.65% | SMA50 | -7.52% | SMA200 | -14.40% | Volume | 389,019 | Change | 0.64% |

The most important are:

- **Market Capitalization:** 5.65B
- **Dividend Yield:** 1.69%
- **P/E ratio:** 8.60
- **P/B Ratio:** 1.93
- **EPS past 5 years:** 19.30%
- **ROA:** 10.30%
- **ROE:** 24.90%
- **Debt/Equity:** 0.56%
- **Net Profit Margin:** 5.40%

If you compare the most important company details of LKQ and THO, then the most significant difference is in their P/E ratios. The reason for this is a big part caused by the fact that LKQ is currently at its all-time high price and THO dipped from $150 to $100 (when "P" – Price in the P/E formula drops, then the P/E ratio drops). Such a dip might be a nice trading opportunity to buy cheap (with lower P/E). On the other hand, buying LKQ when it's at its historical highs is not too clever in my opinion.

# Companies from Consumer Defensive Sector

If you set the Descriptive and Fundamentals tab according to the table I gave you, then you should have it like this:

**Descriptive tab**

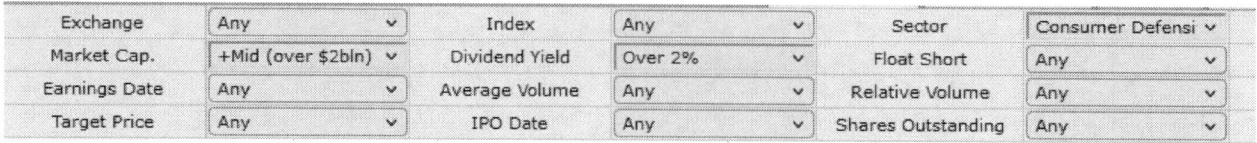

**Fundamental tab**

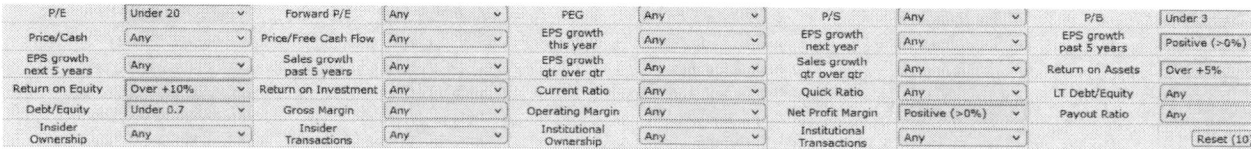

Setting it like this, the filter gave me four companies that all met the criteria. Again, I recommend saving the company list as a portfolio.

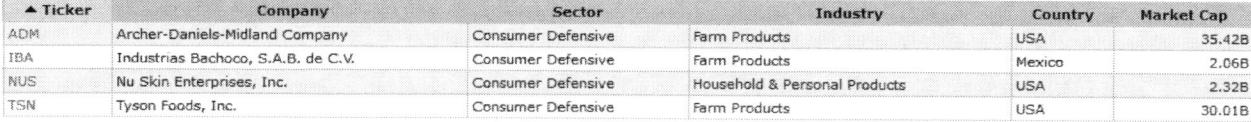

| ▲ Ticker | Company | Sector | Industry | Country | Market Cap |
|---|---|---|---|---|---|
| ADM | Archer-Daniels-Midland Company | Consumer Defensive | Farm Products | USA | 35.42B |
| IBA | Industrias Bachoco, S.A.B. de C.V. | Consumer Defensive | Farm Products | Mexico | 2.06B |
| NUS | Nu Skin Enterprises, Inc. | Consumer Defensive | Household & Personal Products | USA | 2.32B |
| TSN | Tyson Foods, Inc. | Consumer Defensive | Farm Products | USA | 30.01B |

Let's now have a closer look at ADM and TSN, as those are the biggest companies on this list.

## (ADM) Archer-Daniels-Midland Company

**Company description (from Finviz):** Archer-Daniels-Midland Company procures, transports, stores, processes, and merchandises agricultural commodities, products, and ingredients in the United States and internationally. The company operates through three segments: Ag Services and Oilseeds, Carbohydrate Solutions, and Nutrition. It procures, stores, cleans and transports agricultural raw materials, such as oilseeds, corn, wheat, milo, oats, and barley. The company also engages in agricultural commodity and feed product import, export and distribution; and structured trade finance activities. In addition, it offers vegetable oils and protein meals; ingredients for food, feed, energy, and industrial customers; crude vegetable oils, salad oils, margarine, shortening, and other food products; and partially refined oils to produce biodiesel and glycols for use in chemicals, paints, and other industrial products. Further, the company provides peanuts, peanut-derived ingredients, and cotton cellulose pulp; sweeteners, corn and wheat starches, syrup, glucose, wheat flour, and dextrose; alcohol and other food and animal feed ingredients; ethyl alcohol and ethanol; corn gluten feed and meal, as well as distillers' grains; and citric acids. Additionally, the company provides natural flavor ingredients, flavor systems, natural colors, proteins, emulsifiers, soluble fiber, polyols, hydrocolloids, and natural health and nutrition products, including probiotics, prebiotics, enzymes, botanical extracts; and other specialty food and feed ingredients; edible beans; formula feeds, and animal health and nutrition products; and contract and private label pet treats and foods. It also offers futures commission merchant and insurance services. The company was founded in 1902 and is headquartered in Chicago, Illinois.

Below is a weekly chart (one candle = 1 week)

A thing to notice on the chart is how much the price dropped during the COVID-19 pandemic at the start of 2020. The drop was there, it was everywhere. But here it wasn't as severe as in the Consumer Cyclical sector we covered before. Also, if there wasn't the money-printing stimulus from the central bank, I think that this company would still have survived and fared way better than companies in the Consumer Cyclical sector, or other sectors that are more sensitive to the economic cycle.

## Company details

| | | | | | | | | | | | | |
|---|---|---|---|---|---|---|---|---|---|---|---|---|
| Index | S&P 500 | P/E | 13.73 | EPS (ttm) | 4.62 | Insider Own | 0.10% | Shs Outstand | 564.00M | Perf Week | 1.47% |
| Market Cap | 35.42B | Forward P/E | 13.39 | EPS next Y | 4.74 | Insider Trans | -12.90% | Shs Float | 556.85M | Perf Month | -2.97% |
| Income | 2.61B | PEG | 1.37 | EPS next Q | 1.14 | Inst Own | 81.10% | Short Float | 0.97% | Perf Quarter | 3.76% |
| Sales | 80.14B | P/S | 0.44 | EPS this Y | 24.80% | Inst Trans | 1.16% | Short Ratio | 2.11 | Perf Half Y | -2.71% |
| Book/sh | 38.95 | P/B | 1.63 | EPS next Y | -2.71% | ROA | 5.10% | Target Price | 69.93 | Perf Year | 28.96% |
| Cash/sh | 1.94 | P/C | 32.71 | EPS next 5Y | 10.00% | ROE | 12.40% | 52W Range | 48.56 - 69.30 | Perf YTD | 25.87% |
| Dividend | 1.48 | P/FCF | 11.15 | EPS past 5Y | 1.00% | ROI | 3.90% | 52W High | -6.72% | Beta | 0.88 |
| Dividend % | 2.33% | Quick Ratio | 1.00 | Sales past 5Y | -1.00% | Gross Margin | 7.10% | 52W Low | 33.10% | ATR | 1.29 |
| Employees | 39000 | Current Ratio | 1.60 | Sales Q/Q | 34.50% | Oper. Margin | 3.10% | RSI (14) | 52.53 | Volatility | 1.40% 1.84% |
| Optionable | Yes | Debt/Eq | 0.41 | EPS Q/Q | 130.80% | Profit Margin | 3.30% | Rel Volume | 1.02 | Prev Close | 63.45 |
| Shortable | Yes | LT Debt/Eq | 0.37 | Earnings | Oct 26 BMO | Payout | 31.70% | Avg Volume | 2.54M | Price | 64.64 |
| Recom | 1.80 | SMA20 | 0.01% | SMA50 | 0.56% | SMA200 | 4.52% | Volume | 2,591,994 | Change | 1.88% |

The most important are:

- **Market Capitalization:** 35.42B
- **Dividend Yield:** 2.33%
- **P/E ratio:** 13.73
- **P/B Ratio:** 1.63
- **EPS past 5 years:** 1.00%
- **ROA:** 5.10%
- **ROE:** 12.40%
- **Debt/Equity:** 0.41
- **Net Profit Margin:** 3.30%

## (TSN) Tyson Foods

**Company Description (from Finviz):** Tyson Foods, Inc., together with its subsidiaries, operates as a food company worldwide. It operates through four segments: Beef, Pork, Chicken, and Prepared Foods. The company processes live-fed cattle and live market hogs; fabricates dressed beef and pork carcasses into primal and subprimal meat cuts, as well as case-ready beef and pork, and fully-cooked meats; raises and processes chickens into fresh, frozen, and value-added chicken products; and supplies poultry breeding stock; sells specialty products, such as hides and meats. It also manufactures and markets frozen and refrigerated food products, including ready-to-eat sandwiches, flame-grilled hamburgers, Philly steaks, pepperoni, bacon, breakfast sausage, turkey, lunchmeat, hot dogs, flour and corn tortilla products, appetizers, snacks, prepared meals, ethnic foods, side dishes, meat dishes, breadsticks, and processed meats under the Jimmy Dean, Hillshire Farm, Ball Park, Wright, State Fair, Aidells, and Gallo Salame brands. The company also offers its products under Tyson and ibp brands. It sells its products through its sales staff to grocery retailers, grocery wholesalers, meat distributors, warehouse club stores, military commissaries, industrial food processing companies, chain restaurants or their distributors, live markets, international export companies, and domestic distributors who serve restaurants and foodservice operations, such as plant and school cafeterias, convenience stores, hospitals, and other vendors, as well as through independent brokers and trading companies. The company was founded in 1935 and is headquartered in Springdale, Arkansas.

Below is a weekly chart (one candle = 1 week)

The 2020 dip looks quite drastic on the weekly chart, but when it is compared to Consumer Cyclical stocks that we covered, it isn't that bad. The price dropped "only" around -50%, whereas companies in the Consumer Cyclical often dropped way more than that.

## Company details

| Index | S&P 500 | P/E | 10.02 | EPS (ttm) | 8.39 | Insider Own | 1.20% | Shs Outstand | 363.00M | Perf Week | 1.83% |
|---|---|---|---|---|---|---|---|---|---|---|---|
| Market Cap | 30.01B | Forward P/E | 10.93 | EPS next Y | 7.70 | Insider Trans | -1.67% | Shs Float | 287.21M | Perf Month | 1.90% |
| Income | 3.05B | PEG | 0.92 | EPS next Q | 2.02 | Inst Own | 85.00% | Short Float | 1.32% | Perf Quarter | 10.05% |
| Sales | 47.05B | P/S | 0.64 | EPS this Y | 48.00% | Inst Trans | 0.86% | Short Ratio | 2.16 | Perf Half Y | 8.74% |
| Book/sh | 48.82 | P/B | 1.72 | EPS next Y | 3.97% | ROA | 8.60% | Target Price | 91.17 | Perf Year | 21.18% |
| Cash/sh | 7.03 | P/C | 11.97 | EPS next 5Y | 10.85% | ROE | 18.50% | 52W Range | 62.47 - 85.61 | Perf YTD | 30.52% |
| Dividend | 1.78 | P/FCF | 15.04 | EPS past 5Y | 13.00% | ROI | 12.60% | 52W High | -0.80% | Beta | 0.81 |
| Dividend % | 2.12% | Quick Ratio | 0.90 | Sales past 5Y | 5.00% | Gross Margin | 14.60% | 52W Low | 35.95% | ATR | 1.80 |
| Employees | 137000 | Current Ratio | 1.60 | Sales Q/Q | 11.80% | Oper. Margin | 9.30% | RSI (14) | 61.14 | Volatility | 1.78% 2.30% |
| Optionable | Yes | Debt/Eq | 0.53 | EPS Q/Q | 121.00% | Profit Margin | 6.50% | Rel Volume | 1.46 | Prev Close | 84.11 |
| Shortable | Yes | LT Debt/Eq | 0.47 | Earnings | Nov 15 BMO | Payout | 21.20% | Avg Volume | 1.75M | Price | 84.93 |
| Recom | 2.20 | SMA20 | 3.08% | SMA50 | 4.55% | SMA200 | 9.69% | Volume | 2,559,753 | Change | 0.97% |

The most important are:

- **Market Capitalization:** 30.01B
- **Dividend Yield:** 2.12%
- **P/E ratio:** 10.02
- **P/B Ratio:** 1.72
- **EPS past 5 years:** 13.00%
- **ROA:** 8.60%
- **ROE:** 18.50%
- **Debt/Equity:** 0.53
- **Net Profit Margin:** 6.50%

# Companies from Energy Sector

According to the table I gave you at the beginning of this chapter, the Descriptive and Fundamentals tab for the Energy sector should look like this:

**Descriptive tab**

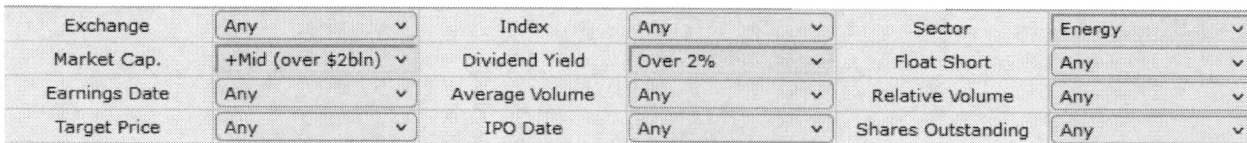

**Fundamentals tab**

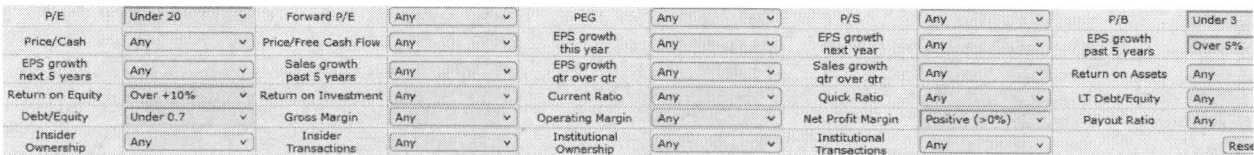

Setting the filter like this now (November 2021), I only got one result. If you want more companies to choose from, then you will need to lower your criteria a bit. I recommend lowering the criteria regarding Debt/Equity to "Under 1" and then if the screener still doesn't give you the desired number of results you can try lowering some other criteria a bit as well.

Let's now have a closer look at the only company that met the criteria. The company is (CNQ) Canadian Natural Resources.

## (CNQ) Canadian Natural Resources

**Company Description (from Finviz):** Canadian Natural Resources Limited acquires, explores for, develops, produces, markets, and sells crude oil, natural gas, and natural gas liquids (NGLs). The company offers synthetic crude oil (SCO), light and medium crude oil, bitumen (thermal oil), primary heavy crude oil, and Pelican Lake heavy crude oil. Its midstream assets include two crude oil pipeline systems; and a 50% working interest in an 84-megawatt cogeneration plant at Primrose. It operates primarily in Western Canada; the United Kingdom portion of the North Sea; and Offshore Africa. Canadian Natural Resources Limited was incorporated in 1973 and is headquartered in Calgary, Canada.

Below is a weekly chart (one candle = 1 week)

## Company details

| | | | | | | | | | | | | | |
|---|---|---|---|---|---|---|---|---|---|---|---|---|---|
| Index | - | P/E | 10.30 | EPS (ttm) | 3.87 | Insider Own | 3.30% | Shs Outstand | 1.18B | Perf Week | -5.30% |
| Market Cap | 46.81B | Forward P/E | 21.42 | EPS next Y | 1.86 | Insider Trans | 0.00% | Shs Float | 1.15B | Perf Month | -4.51% |
| Income | 4.59B | PEG | 2.64 | EPS next Q | 0.49 | Inst Own | 66.60% | Short Float | 1.21% | Perf Quarter | 17.14% |
| Sales | 20.19B | P/S | 2.32 | EPS this Y | -108.10% | Inst Trans | -2.80% | Short Ratio | 4.33 | Perf Half Y | 5.01% |
| Book/sh | 23.51 | P/B | 1.70 | EPS next Y | 7.50% | ROA | 7.80% | Target Price | 40.74 | Perf Year | 59.08% |
| Cash/sh | 0.80 | P/C | 49.96 | EPS next 5Y | 3.90% | ROE | 17.40% | 52W Range | 22.40 - 44.33 | Perf YTD | 65.70% |
| Dividend | 1.47 | P/FCF | 5.58 | EPS past 5Y | 8.80% | ROI | 0.40% | 52W High | -10.11% | Beta | 1.84 |
| Dividend % | 3.69% | Quick Ratio | 0.70 | Sales past 5Y | 6.40% | Gross Margin | 50.60% | 52W Low | 77.90% | ATR | 1.55 |
| Employees | 9993 | Current Ratio | 0.90 | Sales Q/Q | 71.20% | Oper. Margin | 28.30% | RSI (14) | 43.13 | Volatility | 2.63% 3.18% |
| Optionable | Yes | Debt/Eq | 0.52 | EPS Q/Q | 438.10% | Profit Margin | 22.70% | Rel Volume | 1.02 | Prev Close | 41.62 |
| Shortable | Yes | LT Debt/Eq | 0.48 | Earnings | Nov 04 BMO | Payout | 47.30% | Avg Volume | 3.22M | Price | 39.85 |
| Recom | 1.90 | SMA20 | -4.14% | SMA50 | -4.10% | SMA200 | 13.06% | Volume | 3,277,533 | Change | -4.25% |

The most important are:

- **Market Capitalization:** 46.81B
- **Dividend Yield:** 3.69%
- **P/E ratio:** 10.30
- **P/B Ratio:** 1.70
- **EPS past 5 years:** 8.80%
- **ROA:** 7.80%
- **ROE:** 17.40%
- **Debt/Equity:** 0.52
- **Net Profit Margin:** 22.70%

I have to say that this company looks good to me. It has a long history, huge dividends, a very low P/E ratio and doesn't have a huge amount of debt. The only thing I dislike here is that the price is at its historical highs. This company surely would be appealing if there was a little drop (discount) in its price.

# Companies from Financial Sector

This is a sector I don't recommend because of the reasons I have already mentioned. Still, to make this complete, I will go through it and show you how to use the filter here. Set the Finviz screener like this:

**Descriptive tab**

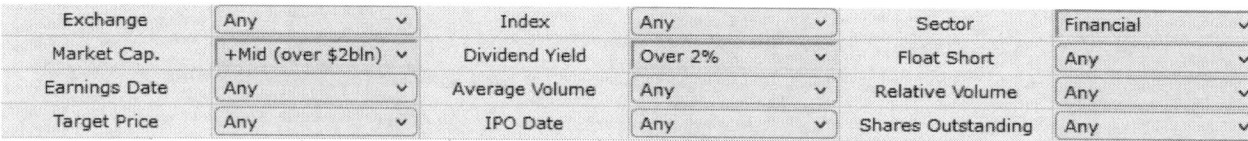

**Fundamental Tab**

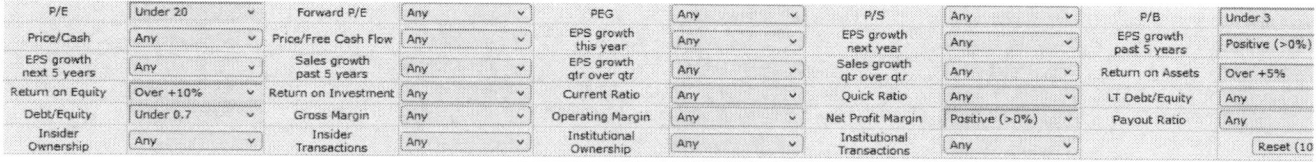

Those are the companies that meet the criteria:

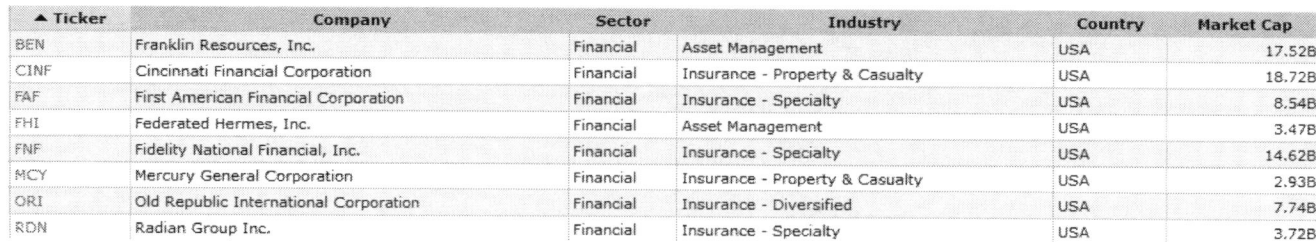

The biggest one is (CINF) Cincinnati Financial Corporation. Let's check it out!

## (CINF) Cincinnati Financial Corporation

Cincinnati Financial Corporation, together with its subsidiary, provides property casualty insurance products in the United States. The company operates through five segments:

Commercial Lines Insurance, Personal Lines Insurance, Excess and Surplus Lines Insurance, Life Insurance, and Investments. Cincinnati Financial Corporation was founded in 1950 and is headquartered in Fairfield, Ohio.

Below is a weekly chart (one candle = 1 week)

Let me show you one more chart to demonstrate how this company made it through the 2008 Financial crisis and the 2020 COVID-19 pandemic.

Below is a monthly chart (one candle = 1 month)

Not too good, right? If there wasn't the central bank to save the day (in both cases), then the recovery wouldn't be so fast and the company might even have gone under.

Note that CINF focuses on insurance, so the situation wasn't as bad as it could have been if the company was dealing with other, more risky financial products.

## Company details

| Index | S&P 500 | P/E | 7.36 | EPS (ttm) | 15.54 | Insider Own | 0.40% | Shs Outstand | 161.10M | Perf Week | -1.65% |
|---|---|---|---|---|---|---|---|---|---|---|---|
| Market Cap | 18.72B | Forward P/E | 22.13 | EPS next Y | 5.17 | Insider Trans | 0.19% | Shs Float | 149.16M | Perf Month | -6.85% |
| Income | 2.52B | PEG | 0.51 | EPS next Q | 1.73 | Inst Own | 70.00% | Short Float | 2.81% | Perf Quarter | -2.61% |
| Sales | 9.00B | P/S | 2.08 | EPS this Y | -38.10% | Inst Trans | -0.41% | Short Ratio | 8.43 | Perf Half Y | -6.02% |
| Book/sh | 73.50 | P/B | 1.56 | EPS next Y | -11.95% | ROA | 8.70% | Target Price | 134.80 | Perf Year | 42.66% |
| Cash/sh | 6.63 | P/C | 17.26 | EPS next 5Y | 14.39% | ROE | 22.10% | 52W Range | 78.56 - 127.25 | Perf YTD | 30.90% |
| Dividend | 2.52 | P/FCF | 12.62 | EPS past 5Y | 14.40% | ROI | 10.90% | 52W High | -10.12% | Beta | 0.69 |
| Dividend % | 2.20% | Quick Ratio | - | Sales past 5Y | 7.90% | Gross Margin | - | 52W Low | 45.59% | ATR | 2.78 |
| Employees | 5266 | Current Ratio | - | Sales Q/Q | -19.80% | Oper. Margin | 35.50% | RSI (14) | 41.08 | Volatility | 1.71% 2.21% |
| Optionable | Yes | Debt/Eq | 0.08 | EPS Q/Q | -68.60% | Profit Margin | 28.10% | Rel Volume | 0.97 | Prev Close | 116.38 |
| Shortable | Yes | LT Debt/Eq | 0.07 | Earnings | Oct 27 AMC | Payout | 15.70% | Avg Volume | 498.22K | Price | 114.37 |
| Recom | 2.40 | SMA20 | -3.08% | SMA50 | -4.31% | SMA200 | -1.66% | Volume | 483,495 | Change | -1.73% |

The most important are:

- **Market Capitalization:** 18.72B
- **Dividend Yield:** 2.52%
- **P/E ratio:** 7.36
- **P/B Ratio:** 1.56
- **EPS past 5 years:** 14.40%
- **ROA:** 8.70%
- **ROE:** 22.10%
- **Debt/Equity:** 0.08
- **Net Profit Margin:** 28.10%

Since this is the Financials sector, we cannot compare those fundamentals to other sectors as that could be quite misleading.

# Companies from Healthcare Sector

In the Healthcare sector, the filter I recommend starting with looks like this:

## Descriptive tab

| Exchange | Any | Index | Any | Sector | Healthcare |
|---|---|---|---|---|---|
| Market Cap. | +Mid (over $2bln) | Dividend Yield | Any | Float Short | Any |
| Earnings Date | Any | Average Volume | Any | Relative Volume | Any |
| Target Price | Any | IPO Date | Any | Shares Outstanding | Any |

Note that I did not set any filter for Dividends. The reason is that Dividends are not so common in this sector.

## Fundamental tab

| P/E | Under 20 | Forward P/E | Any | PEG | Any | P/S | Any | P/B | Under 3 |
|---|---|---|---|---|---|---|---|---|---|
| Price/Cash | Any | Price/Free Cash Flow | Any | EPS growth this year | Any | EPS growth next year | Any | EPS growth past 5 years | Positive (>0%) |
| EPS growth next 5 years | Any | Sales growth past 5 years | Any | EPS growth qtr over qtr | Any | Sales growth qtr over qtr | Any | Return on Assets | Over +5% |
| Return on Equity | Over +10% | Return on Investment | Any | Current Ratio | Any | Quick Ratio | Any | LT Debt/Equity | Any |
| Debt/Equity | Under 0.7 | Gross Margin | Any | Operating Margin | Any | Net Profit Margin | Positive (>0%) | Payout Ratio | Any |
| Insider Ownership | Any | Insider Transactions | Any | Institutional Ownership | Any | Institutional Transactions | Any | | Reset (9) |

The companies that met the criteria (in November 2021) were:

| ▲ Ticker | Company | Sector | Industry | Country | Market Cap |
|---|---|---|---|---|---|
| ANTM | Anthem, Inc. | Healthcare | Healthcare Plans | USA | 105.63B |
| COO | The Cooper Companies, Inc. | Healthcare | Medical Instruments & Supplies | USA | 18.77B |
| EBS | Emergent BioSolutions Inc. | Healthcare | Drug Manufacturers - Specialty & Generic | USA | 2.22B |
| FLGT | Fulgent Genetics, Inc. | Healthcare | Diagnostics & Research | USA | 2.65B |
| LH | Laboratory Corporation of America Holdings | Healthcare | Diagnostics & Research | USA | 28.08B |
| SAGE | Sage Therapeutics, Inc. | Healthcare | Biotechnology | USA | 2.40B |
| UHS | Universal Health Services, Inc. | Healthcare | Medical Care Facilities | USA | 10.35B |

Let's have a closer look at two of them. The biggest ones are (ANTM) Anthem, and (LH) Laboratory Corporation of America Holdings. The third one is the COO (The Cooper Companies).

I prefer to consider an investment in a company that focuses on Medical Instruments & Supplies (COO), rather than in a company that does Diagnostics & Research (LH). The reason is that medical instruments seem like a more stable business than "research" – which could rely on research success and patents. Also, "medical instruments" means tangible stuff. This is something I prefer over research and patents. For this reason, I will look closer at ANTM (this is the biggest one on the list by far), and COO, which deals with medical instruments & supplies.

## (ANTM) Anthem

Anthem, Inc., through its subsidiaries, operates as a health benefits company in the United States. It operates through four segments: Commercial & Specialty Business, Government Business, IngenioRx, and Other. The company offers a spectrum of network-based managed care health benefit plans to large and small groups, individuals, Medicaid, and Medicare markets. Its managed care plans include preferred provider organizations; health maintenance organizations; point-of-service plans; traditional indemnity plans and other hybrid plans, including consumer-driven health plans; and hospital-only and limited benefit products. The company also provides a range of managed care services to self-funded customers, including claims processing, underwriting, stop loss insurance, actuarial services, provider network access, medical cost management, disease management, wellness programs, and other administrative services. In addition, it offers an array of specialty and other insurance products and services, such as pharmacy benefits management, dental, vision, life and disability insurance benefits, radiology benefit management, and analytics-driven personal health care. Further, the company provides services to the federal government in connection with the Federal Employee Program; and operates as a licensee of the Blue Cross and Blue Shield Association. As of December 31, 2020, it served 43 million medical members through its affiliated health plans. The company was formerly known as WellPoint, Inc. and changed its name to Anthem, Inc. in December 2014. Anthem, Inc. was founded in 1944 and is headquartered in Indianapolis, Indiana.

Below is a weekly chart (one candle = 1 week)

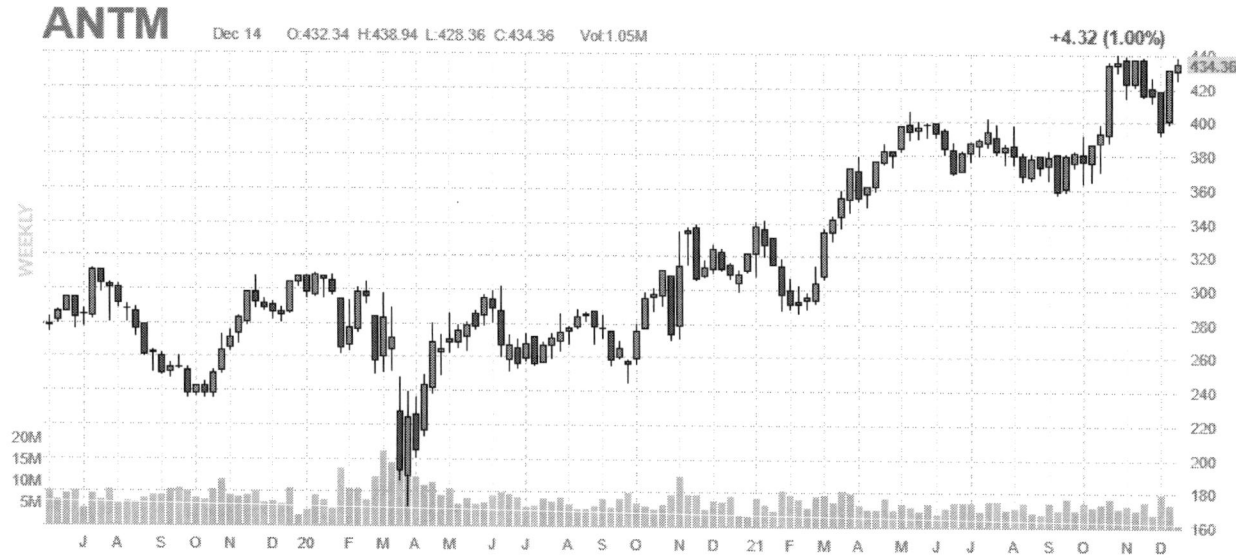

## Company details

The most important are:

- **Market Capitalization:** 101.63B
- **Dividend Yield:** 1.05%
- **P/E ratio:** 19.30
- **P/B Ratio:** 2.96
- **EPS past 5 years:** 13.90%
- **ROA:** 5.90%
- **ROE:** 16.00%
- **Debt/Equity:** 0.64
- **Net Profit Margin:** 4.10%

This company meets the criteria we set but only barely. P/E is just below 20, and P/B is just below 3. The stock price is at its historical maximum so this company would not be appealing for me to invest in unless the price dropped a bit and offered a better entry.

## (COO) The Cooper Companies

The Cooper Companies, Inc. operates as a medical device company worldwide. The company develops, manufactures, and markets a range of contact lenses, including spherical lenses, and toric and multifocal lenses that correct near- and farsightedness, as well as address various complex visual defects. It also provides a range of products and services for enhancing the health of women, babies, and families, including medical devices, fertility, genomics, and diagnostics and contraception for hospitals and surgical centers, obstetricians' and gynecologists' (OB/GYNs) medical offices, and fertility clinics. In addition, the company develops mechanical surgical solutions for skin closure; and offers PARAGARD, a contraceptive, as well as provides assisted reproductive technology products, genetic screening and testing. Cooper Companies, Inc. was founded in 1980 and is headquartered in San Ramon, California.

Below is a weekly chart (one candle = 1 week)

## Company details

| | | | | | | | | | | | | |
|---|---|---|---|---|---|---|---|---|---|---|---|---|
| Index | S&P 500 | P/E | 6.66 | EPS (ttm) | 59.22 | Insider Own | 0.10% | Shs Outstand | 49.30M | Perf Week | -1.41% |
| Market Cap | 19.88B | Forward P/E | 28.47 | EPS next Y | 13.85 | Insider Trans | -64.63% | Shs Float | 49.02M | Perf Month | -4.01% |
| Income | 2.94B | PEG | 0.67 | EPS next Q | 3.08 | Inst Own | - | Short Float | 3.56% | Perf Quarter | -10.67% |
| Sales | 2.92B | P/S | 6.80 | EPS this Y | -47.90% | Inst Trans | -0.43% | Short Ratio | 6.18 | Perf Half Y | 4.64% |
| Book/sh | 137.63 | P/B | 2.87 | EPS next Y | 3.94% | ROA | 27.50% | Target Price | 466.75 | Perf Year | 16.27% |
| Cash/sh | 2.23 | P/C | 177.14 | EPS next 5Y | 10.00% | ROE | 41.40% | 52W Range | 337.40 - 463.59 | Perf YTD | 8.54% |
| Dividend | 0.06 | P/FCF | 48.24 | EPS past 5Y | 3.00% | ROI | 3.40% | 52W High | -13.65% | Beta | 0.86 |
| Dividend % | 0.02% | Quick Ratio | 0.80 | Sales past 5Y | 6.20% | Gross Margin | 66.90% | 52W Low | 18.64% | ATR | 9.98 |
| Employees | 12000 | Current Ratio | 1.40 | Sales Q/Q | 32.00% | Oper. Margin | 15.40% | RSI (14) | 48.96 | Volatility | 2.30% 2.45% |
| Optionable | Yes | Debt/Eq | 0.24 | EPS Q/Q | 1015.60% | Profit Margin | 80.60% | Rel Volume | 1.93 | Prev Close | 394.35 |
| Shortable | Yes | LT Debt/Eq | 0.17 | Earnings | Dec 02 AMC | Payout | 0.10% | Avg Volume | 282.25K | Price | 400.30 |
| Recom | 2.30 | SMA20 | 0.74% | SMA50 | -1.74% | SMA200 | -1.40% | Volume | 165,293 | Change | 1.51% |

The most important are:

- **Market Capitalization:** 19.88B
- **Dividend Yield:** 0.02%
- **P/E ratio:** 6.66
- **P/B Ratio:** 2.87
- **EPS past 5 years:** 3.00%
- **ROA:** 27.50%
- **ROE:** 41.40%
- **Debt/Equity:** 0.24
- **Net Profit Margin:** 80.60%

A couple of things to point out here: Very low P/E (which is great), very low debt, and also quite big margins.

## Companies from Industrials Sector

With the recommended settings the Descriptive and Fundamentals tab will look like this:

### Descriptive tab

| Exchange | Any | Index | Any | Sector | Industrials |
|---|---|---|---|---|---|
| Market Cap. | +Mid (over $2bln) | Dividend Yield | Over 1% | Float Short | Any |
| Earnings Date | Any | Average Volume | Any | Relative Volume | Any |
| Target Price | Any | IPO Date | Any | Shares Outstanding | Any |

### Fundamental tab

| P/E | Under 20 | Forward P/E | Any | PEG | Any | P/S | Any | P/B | Under 3 |
|---|---|---|---|---|---|---|---|---|---|
| Price/Cash | Any | Price/Free Cash Flow | Any | EPS growth this year | Any | EPS growth next year | Any | EPS growth past 5 years | Over 5% |
| EPS growth next 5 years | Any | Sales growth past 5 years | Any | EPS growth qtr over qtr | Any | Sales growth qtr over qtr | Any | Return on Assets | Over +5% |
| Return on Equity | Over +10% | Return on Investment | Any | Current Ratio | Any | Quick Ratio | Any | LT Debt/Equity | Any |
| Debt/Equity | Under 0.7 | Gross Margin | Any | Operating Margin | Any | Net Profit Margin | Positive (>0%) | Payout Ratio | Any |
| Insider Ownership | Any | Insider Transactions | Any | Institutional Ownership | Any | Institutional Transactions | Any | | Reset |

Stocks that met the criteria above were:

| MATX | Matson, Inc. | Industrials | Marine Shipping | USA | 3.44B |
|---|---|---|---|---|---|
| OSK | Oshkosh Corporation | Industrials | Farm & Heavy Construction Machinery | USA | 7.42B |
| SNA | Snap on Incorporated | Industrials | Tools & Accessories | USA | 11.29B |
| SNDR | Schneider National, Inc. | Industrials | Trucking | USA | 4.65B |
| SWK | Stanley Black & Decker, Inc. | Industrials | Tools & Accessories | USA | 30.96B |
| TKR | The Timken Company | Industrials | Tools & Accessories | USA | 5.08B |
| WERN | Werner Enterprises, Inc. | Industrials | Trucking | USA | 3.14B |

*Again, I recommend saving your list as a portfolio.*

All companies from the list meet our criteria so they should all be good to invest in (if the price is right). The biggest two companies are (SWK) Stanley Black & Decker, and (SNA) Snap-on Incorporated. Let's check them out!

## (SWK) Stanley Black & Decker

Stanley Black & Decker, Inc. engages in the tools and storage, industrial, and security businesses worldwide. Its Tools & Storage segment offers power tools and equipment, including professional products, such as professional grade corded and cordless electric power tools and equipment, and pneumatic tools and fasteners; and consumer products comprising corded and cordless electric power tools primarily under the BLACK+DECKER brand, as well as lawn and garden products and related accessories, and home products. This segment sells its products through retailers, distributors, and a direct sales force to professional end users, distributors, retail consumers, and industrial customers in various industries. The company's Industrial segment provides engineered fastening systems and products to customers in the automotive, manufacturing, electronics, construction, aerospace, and other industries; sells and rents custom pipe handling, joint welding, and coating equipment for use in the construction of large and small diameter pipelines, as well as provides pipeline inspection services; and sells hydraulic tools, attachments, and accessories. This segment also serves the oil and natural gas pipeline industry and other industrial customers. Its Security segment designs, supplies, and installs commercial electronic security systems and provides electronic security services. Stanley Black & Decker, Inc. was founded in 1843 and is headquartered in New Britain, Connecticut.

Below is a weekly chart (one candle = 1 week)

**Company details**

| | | | | | | | | | | | | |
|---|---|---|---|---|---|---|---|---|---|---|---|---|
| Index | S&P 500 | P/E | 17.43 | EPS (ttm) | 11.04 | Insider Own | 0.30% | Shs Outstand | 159.44M | Perf Week | 4.38% | |
| Market Cap | 30.96B | Forward P/E | 16.25 | EPS next Y | 11.84 | Insider Trans | 0.00% | Shs Float | - | Perf Month | 1.12% | |
| Income | 1.81B | PEG | 1.50 | EPS next Q | 2.04 | Inst Own | 87.80% | Short Float | - | Perf Quarter | 5.51% | |
| Sales | 17.17B | P/S | 1.80 | EPS this Y | 22.30% | Inst Trans | 0.31% | Short Ratio | 1.78 | Perf Half Y | -4.86% | |
| Book/sh | 66.27 | P/B | 2.90 | EPS next Y | 8.13% | ROA | 7.60% | Target Price | 221.43 | Perf Year | 9.83% | |
| Cash/sh | 1.82 | P/C | 105.77 | EPS next 5Y | 11.64% | ROE | 18.10% | 52W Range | 167.65 - 225.00 | Perf YTD | 7.77% | |
| Dividend | 3.16 | P/FCF | - | EPS past 5Y | 5.60% | ROI | 10.40% | 52W High | -14.74% | Beta | 1.39 | |
| Dividend % | 1.64% | Quick Ratio | 0.50 | Sales past 5Y | 5.40% | Gross Margin | 35.40% | 52W Low | 14.43% | ATR | 5.25 | |
| Employees | 53100 | Current Ratio | 1.20 | Sales Q/Q | 10.70% | Oper. Margin | 13.50% | RSI (14) | 56.36 | Volatility | 2.10% | 2.54% |
| Optionable | Yes | Debt/Eq | 0.42 | EPS Q/Q | 2.80% | Profit Margin | 10.60% | Rel Volume | 0.80 | Prev Close | 192.43 | |
| Shortable | Yes | LT Debt/Eq | 0.40 | Earnings | Oct 28 BMO | Payout | 25.10% | Avg Volume | 1.21M | Price | 191.84 | |
| Recom | 2.20 | SMA20 | 2.41% | SMA50 | 3.90% | SMA200 | -2.09% | Volume | 353,275 | Change | -0.31% | |

The most important are:

- **Market Capitalization:** 30.96B
- **Dividend Yield:** 1.64%
- **P/E ratio:** 17.43
- **P/B Ratio:** 2.90
- **EPS past 5 years:** 5.60%
- **ROA:** 7.60%
- **ROE:** 18.10%
- **Debt/Equity:** 0.42
- **Net Profit Margin:** 10.60%

## Snap-on Incorporated

Snap-on Incorporated manufactures and markets tools, equipment, diagnostics, repair information and systems solutions for professional users worldwide. The company offers hand tools, including wrenches, sockets, ratchet wrenches, pliers, screwdrivers, punches and chisels, saws and cutting tools, pruning tools, torque measuring instruments, and other products; power tools, such as cordless, pneumatic, hydraulic, and corded tools; and tool storage products comprising tool chests, roll cabinets, and other products. It also provides handheld and PC-based diagnostic products, service and repair information products, diagnostic software solutions, electronic parts catalogs, business management systems and services, point-of-sale systems, integrated systems for vehicle service shops, original equipment manufacturer purchasing facilitation services, and warranty management systems and analytics. In addition, the company offers solutions for the service of vehicles and industrial equipment that include wheel alignment equipment, wheel balancers, tire changers, vehicle lifts, test lane equipment, collision repair equipment, vehicle air conditioning service equipment, brake service equipment, fluid exchange equipment, transmission troubleshooting equipment, safety testing equipment, battery chargers, and hoists. The company serves the aviation and aerospace, agriculture, construction, government and military, mining, natural resources, power generation, and technical education industries, as well as vehicle dealerships and repair centers. Snap-on Incorporated was founded in 1920 and is based in Kenosha, Wisconsin.

Below is a weekly chart (one candle = 1 week)

## Company details

| Index | S&P 500 | P/E | 14.54 | EPS (ttm) | 14.66 | Insider Own | 1.30% | Shs Outstand | 53.81M | Perf Week | 1.40% |
|---|---|---|---|---|---|---|---|---|---|---|---|
| Market Cap | 11.29B | Forward P/E | 14.20 | EPS next Y | 15.01 | Insider Trans | -5.58% | Shs Float | 52.81M | Perf Month | -3.14% |
| Income | 805.70M | PEG | 1.44 | EPS next Q | 3.65 | Inst Own | 91.30% | Short Float | 7.73% | Perf Quarter | -1.33% |
| Sales | 4.57B | P/S | 2.47 | EPS this Y | -7.80% | Inst Trans | 0.09% | Short Ratio | 9.92 | Perf Half Y | -7.75% |
| Book/sh | 75.21 | P/B | 2.83 | EPS next Y | 3.90% | ROA | 12.10% | Target Price | 236.25 | Perf Year | 17.93% |
| Cash/sh | 13.89 | P/C | 15.35 | EPS next 5Y | 10.10% | ROE | 20.50% | 52W Range | 165.56 - 259.99 | Perf YTD | 24.57% |
| Dividend | 5.68 | P/FCF | 15.79 | EPS past 5Y | 7.20% | ROI | 13.10% | 52W High | -18.79% | Beta | 1.23 |
| Dividend % | 2.66% | Quick Ratio | 2.20 | Sales past 5Y | 1.90% | Gross Margin | 53.60% | 52W Low | 27.53% | ATR | 4.66 |
| Employees | 12300 | Current Ratio | 3.00 | Sales Q/Q | 9.50% | Oper. Margin | 24.20% | RSI (14) | 46.66 | Volatility | 1.79% 2.02% |
| Optionable | Yes | Debt/Eq | 0.30 | EPS Q/Q | 9.00% | Profit Margin | 17.60% | Rel Volume | 0.62 | Prev Close | 213.19 |
| Shortable | Yes | LT Debt/Eq | 0.29 | Earnings | Oct 21 BMO | Payout | 33.00% | Avg Volume | 411.73K | Price | 211.14 |
| Recom | 2.60 | SMA20 | -1.38% | SMA50 | -1.29% | SMA200 | -6.21% | Volume | 92,687 | Change | -0.96% |

The most important are:

- **Market Capitalization:** 11.29B
- **Dividend Yield:** 2.66%
- **P/E ratio:** 14.54
- **P/B Ratio:** 2.83
- **EPS past 5 years:** 7.20
- **ROA:** 12.10%
- **ROE:** 20.50%
- **Debt/Equity:** 0.30
- **Net Profit Margin:** 17.60%

What I like about this company is the nice Dividend yield (considering the industry the company operates in), quite low P/E ratio, low Debt, and quite high Margins.

## Companies from Real Estate Sector

Set the Descriptive and Fundamental tab using the table I gave you. Those tabs should look like this:

### Descriptive tab

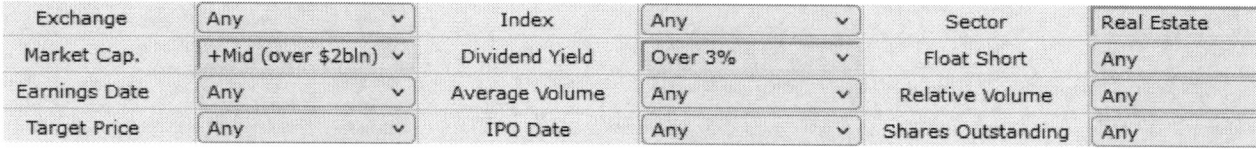

It is typical for companies in the Real Estate sector to pay out high dividends. That's why we will want to get 3% or more here.

### Fundamental tab

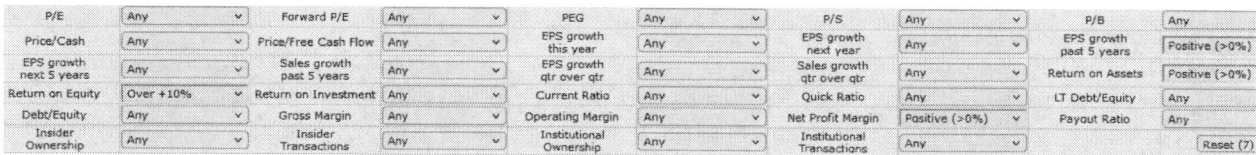

As you can see, the filter settings I used in the Fundamentals tab are a bit different from the other sectors we already went through. The main differences are that I don't use P/E, and P/B ratios, nor the Debt/Equity filter. The reason I don't use P/E and P/B ratios is that they are often misleading in this sector. The reason I don't set any filter to Debt/Equity is that it is quite common for companies in the Real Estate sector to have huge Debt. Way above 100%.

Setting the filter like this gave me the following companies:

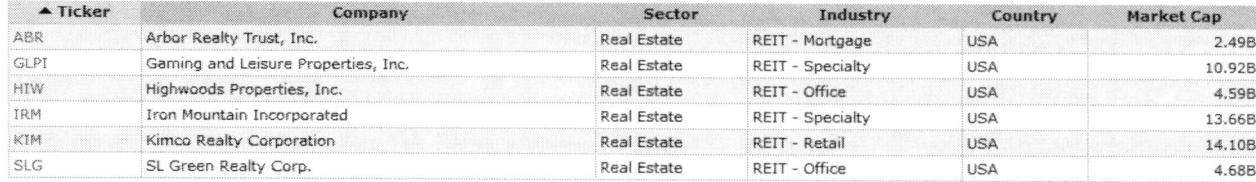

| ▲ Ticker | Company | Sector | Industry | Country | Market Cap |
|---|---|---|---|---|---|
| ABR | Arbor Realty Trust, Inc. | Real Estate | REIT - Mortgage | USA | 2.49B |
| GLPI | Gaming and Leisure Properties, Inc. | Real Estate | REIT - Specialty | USA | 10.92B |
| HIW | Highwoods Properties, Inc. | Real Estate | REIT - Office | USA | 4.59B |
| IRM | Iron Mountain Incorporated | Real Estate | REIT - Specialty | USA | 13.66B |
| KIM | Kimco Realty Corporation | Real Estate | REIT - Retail | USA | 14.10B |
| SLG | SL Green Realty Corp. | Real Estate | REIT - Office | USA | 4.68B |

The biggest ones are (KIM) Kimco Realty Corporation and (IRM) Iron Mountain Incorporated. Let's check them out!

# (KIM) Kimco Realty Corporation

Kimco Realty Corp. is a real estate investment trust (REIT) headquartered in Jericho, N.Y. that is one of North America's largest publicly traded owners and operators of open-air, grocery-anchored shopping centers and mixed-use assets. As of September 30, 2020, the company owned interests in 400 U.S. shopping centers and mixed-use assets comprising 70 million square feet of gross leasable space primarily concentrated in the top major metropolitan markets. Publicly traded on the NYSE since 1991, and included in the S&P 500 Index, the company has specialized in shopping center acquisitions, development and management for more than 60 years.

Below is a weekly chart (one candle = 1 week)

## Company details

| | | | | | | | | | | | | |
|---|---|---|---|---|---|---|---|---|---|---|---|---|
| Index | S&P 500 | P/E | 12.33 | EPS (ttm) | 1.84 | Insider Own | 2.04% | Shs Outstand | 546.84M | Perf Week | -4.11% |
| Market Cap | 14.10B | Forward P/E | 32.58 | EPS next Y | 0.69 | Insider Trans | -0.07% | Shs Float | 421.64M | Perf Month | -3.82% |
| Income | 933.50M | PEG | 2.68 | EPS next Q | 0.16 | Inst Own | 93.20% | Short Float | 4.90% | Perf Quarter | 3.47% |
| Sales | 1.21B | P/S | 11.66 | EPS this Y | 181.30% | Inst Trans | 33.30% | Short Ratio | 5.05 | Perf Half Y | 6.54% |
| Book/sh | 18.13 | P/B | 1.25 | EPS next Y | -58.46% | ROA | 6.50% | Target Price | 26.00 | Perf Year | 56.90% |
| Cash/sh | 0.78 | P/C | 29.15 | EPS next 5Y | 4.60% | ROE | 12.90% | 52W Range | 14.03 - 24.95 | Perf YTD | 50.83% |
| Dividend | 0.68 | P/FCF | 144.27 | EPS past 5Y | 2.40% | ROI | 2.90% | 52W High | -9.26% | Beta | 1.51 |
| Dividend % | 3.00% | Quick Ratio | - | Sales past 5Y | -1.90% | Gross Margin | 68.90% | 52W Low | 61.37% | ATR | 0.69 |
| Employees | 484 | Current Ratio | - | Sales Q/Q | 41.90% | Oper. Margin | 29.90% | RSI (14) | 43.91 | Volatility | 2.04% 2.53% |
| Optionable | Yes | Debt/Eq | 0.76 | EPS Q/Q | 966.00% | Profit Margin | 71.80% | Rel Volume | 0.90 | Prev Close | 22.96 |
| Shortable | Yes | LT Debt/Eq | 0.76 | Earnings | Nov 05 BMO | Payout | 39.20% | Avg Volume | 4.10M | Price | 22.64 |
| Recom | 2.30 | SMA20 | -3.38% | SMA50 | -1.80% | SMA200 | 6.12% | Volume | 4,292,772 | Change | -1.39% |

The most important are:

- **Market Capitalization:** 14.10B
- **Dividend Yield:** 3.00%
- **EPS past 5 years:** 2.40%
- **ROA:** 6.50%
- **ROE:** 12.90%

A surprising thing to notice here is the unusually low Debt/Equity ratio (unusually low in this sector). This is a big plus for the company as it's not in too big debt.

## (IRM) Iron Mountain Incorporated

Iron Mountain Incorporated, founded in 1951, is the global leader in storage and information management services. Trusted by more than 225,000 organizations around the world, and with a real estate network of more than 90 million square feet across approximately 1,450 facilities in approximately 50 countries, Iron Mountain stores and protects billions of valued assets, including critical business information, highly sensitive data, and cultural and historical artifacts. Providing solutions that include secure records storage, information management, digital transformation, secure destruction, as well as data centers, cloud services and art storage and logistics.

Below is a weekly chart (one candle = 1 week)

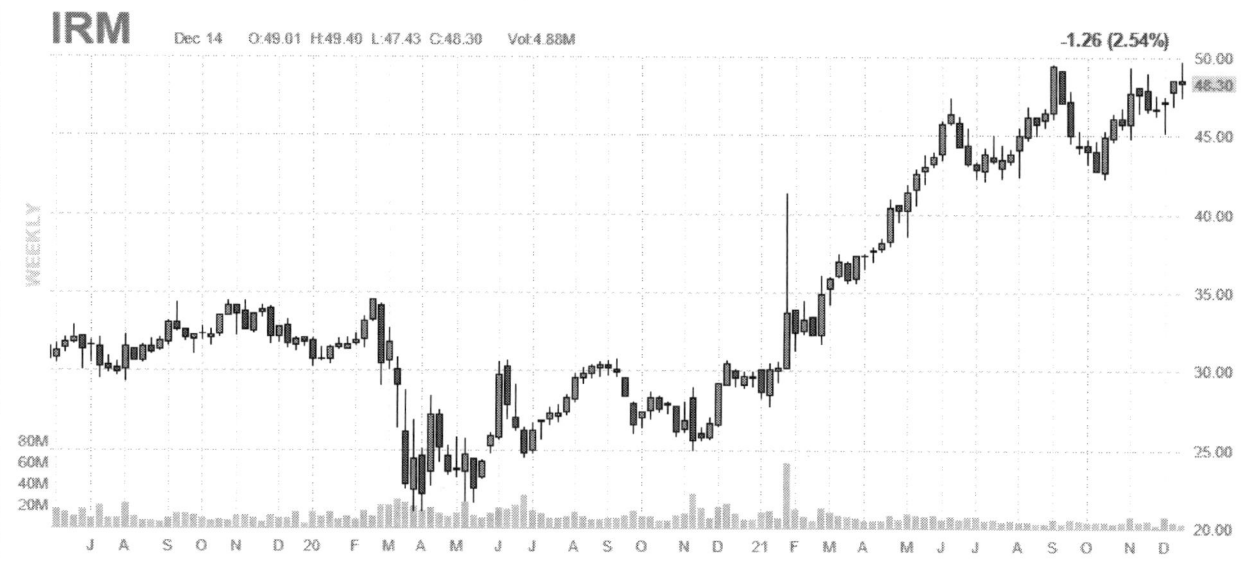

### **Company details**

| Index | S&P 500 | P/E | 22.04 | EPS (ttm) | 2.19 | Insider Own | 0.10% | Shs Outstand | 289.76M | Perf Week | 0.50% |
|---|---|---|---|---|---|---|---|---|---|---|---|
| Market Cap | 13.66B | Forward P/E | 29.69 | EPS next Y | 1.63 | Insider Trans | -12.35% | Shs Float | 285.76M | Perf Month | 1.58% |
| Income | 636.00M | PEG | 3.43 | EPS next Q | 0.40 | Inst Own | 80.90% | Short Float | 10.32% | Perf Quarter | 7.17% |
| Sales | 4.39B | P/S | 3.11 | EPS this Y | 27.80% | Inst Trans | -0.07% | Short Ratio | 18.80 | Perf Half Y | 6.48% |
| Book/sh | 3.36 | P/B | 14.37 | EPS next Y | 8.47% | ROA | 4.50% | Target Price | 43.12 | Perf Year | 65.02% |
| Cash/sh | 0.57 | P/C | 84.61 | EPS next 5Y | 6.44% | ROE | 60.30% | 52W Range | 27.72 - 49.75 | Perf YTD | 63.84% |
| Dividend | 2.47 | P/FCF | - | EPS past 5Y | 15.40% | ROI | 8.50% | 52W High | -2.91% | Beta | 0.83 |
| Dividend % | 5.11% | Quick Ratio | 0.70 | Sales past 5Y | 6.60% | Gross Margin | 73.40% | 52W Low | 74.24% | ATR | 1.32 |
| Employees | 24610 | Current Ratio | 0.70 | Sales Q/Q | 9.00% | Oper. Margin | 24.70% | RSI (14) | 55.68 | Volatility | 2.48% 2.50% |
| Optionable | Yes | Debt/Eq | 9.44 | EPS Q/Q | 74.70% | Profit Margin | 14.50% | Rel Volume | 1.65 | Prev Close | 49.56 |
| Shortable | Yes | LT Debt/Eq | 9.11 | Earnings | Nov 04 BMO | Payout | 112.40% | Avg Volume | 1.57M | Price | 48.30 |
| Recom | 2.60 | SMA20 | 2.17% | SMA50 | 4.41% | SMA200 | 11.31% | Volume | 2,576,897 | Change | -2.54% |

The most important are:

- **Market Capitalization:** 13.66B
- **Dividend Yield:** 5.11%
- **EPS past 5 years:** 15.40%
- **ROA:** 4.50%
- **ROE:** 60.30%

This company is paying a very nice 5.11% dividend. One of the reasons it can pay such a high-yielding dividend is the amount of debt the company uses to leverage its business. Its Debt/Equity is 9.44 which is huge! This is also the reason why there is such a huge difference between its ROA (4.50%) and ROE (60.30%).

The big dividend would probably be the main reason for many investors to invest in this company. What I would prefer is to wait until the price drops a bit (don't buy when the price is at its all-time high). Such a drop would enable us to buy with a "discount" and it would also increase the dividend yield (because dividend yield depends not only on the amount paid out to shareholders but also on the market price of the stock).

## Companies from Technology Sector

My filter for this sector looks like this:

### Descriptive tab

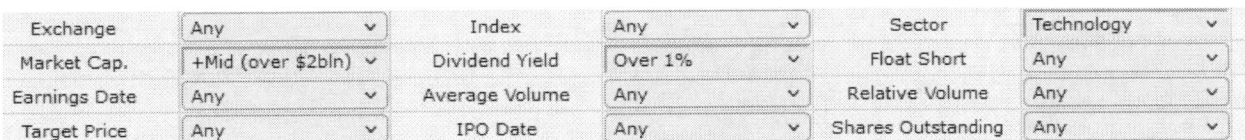

### Fundamental tab

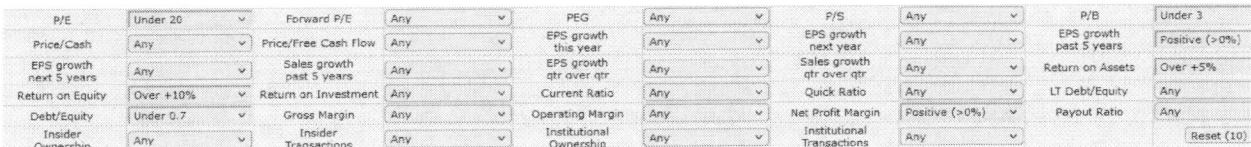

Companies that meet the criteria:

| Ticker | Company | Sector | Industry | Country | Market Cap |
|---|---|---|---|---|---|
| DOX | Amdocs Limited | Technology | Software - Infrastructure | USA | 9.42B |
| HPE | Hewlett Packard Enterprise Company | Technology | Communication Equipment | USA | 19.27B |
| INTC | Intel Corporation | Technology | Semiconductors | USA | 201.19B |
| UMC | United Microelectronics Corporation | Technology | Semiconductors | Taiwan | 28.19B |
| VSH | Vishay Intertechnology, Inc. | Technology | Semiconductors | USA | 2.94B |

The biggest two companies here are (INTC) Intel Corporation, and (UMC) United Microelectronics Corporation. Let's check them out!

## (INTC) Intel Corporation

Intel Corporation designs, manufactures and sells essential technologies for the cloud, smart, and connected devices for retail, industrial, and consumer uses worldwide. It offers platform products, such as central processing units and chipsets, system-on-chip and multichip packages; and non-platform or adjacent products comprising accelerators, boards and systems, connectivity products, and memory and storage products. The company also provides Internet of Things products, including high-performance computing solutions for targeted verticals and embedded applications; and computer vision and machine learning-based sensing, data analysis, localization, mapping, and driving policy technology. It serves original equipment manufacturers, original design manufacturers, and cloud service providers. The company was founded in 1968 and is headquartered in Santa Clara, California.

Below is a weekly chart (one candle = 1 week)

**Company details**

| Index | DJIA S&P500 | P/E | 9.65 | EPS (ttm) | 5.15 | Insider Own | 0.07% | Shs Outstand | 4.06B | Perf Week | -5.46% |
|---|---|---|---|---|---|---|---|---|---|---|---|
| Market Cap | 201.19B | Forward P/E | 13.43 | EPS next Y | 3.70 | Insider Trans | 2.86% | Shs Float | 4.04B | Perf Month | -1.21% |
| Income | 21.10B | PEG | 3.05 | EPS next Q | 0.90 | Inst Own | 65.10% | Short Float | 1.88% | Perf Quarter | -9.83% |
| Sales | 78.47B | P/S | 2.56 | EPS this Y | 4.90% | Inst Trans | -0.03% | Short Ratio | 2.50 | Perf Half Y | -13.14% |
| Book/sh | 22.18 | P/B | 2.24 | EPS next Y | -29.91% | ROA | 13.50% | Target Price | 55.02 | Perf Year | -1.53% |
| Cash/sh | 8.56 | P/C | 5.81 | EPS next 5Y | 3.16% | ROE | 25.10% | 52W Range | 43.24 - 68.49 | Perf YTD | -0.24% |
| Dividend | 1.39 | P/FCF | 5.35 | EPS past 5Y | 16.20% | ROI | 16.60% | 52W High | -27.43% | Beta | 0.52 |
| Dividend % | 2.80% | Quick Ratio | 1.70 | Sales past 5Y | 7.10% | Gross Margin | 56.30% | 52W Low | 9.86% | ATR | 1.35 |
| Employees | 110600 | Current Ratio | 2.10 | Sales Q/Q | 4.70% | Oper. Margin | 25.90% | RSI (14) | 46.18 | Volatility | 2.26% 2.66% |
| Optionable | Yes | Debt/Eq | 0.45 | EPS Q/Q | 64.40% | Profit Margin | 26.90% | Rel Volume | 1.10 | Prev Close | 50.00 |
| Shortable | Yes | LT Debt/Eq | 0.40 | Earnings | Oct 21 AMC | Payout | 26.50% | Avg Volume | 30.36M | Price | 49.70 |
| Recom | 2.80 | SMA20 | -0.68% | SMA50 | -2.74% | SMA200 | -10.93% | Volume | 34,120,384 | Change | -0.60% |

The most important are:

- **Market Capitalization:** 201.19B
- **Dividend Yield:** 2.80%
- **P/E ratio:** 9.65
- **P/B Ratio:** 2.24
- **EPS past 5 years:** 16.20%
- **ROA:** 13.50%
- **ROE:** 25.10%
- **Debt/Equity:** 0.45
- **Net Profit Margin:** 26.90%

Even though Intel is a technology company, it currently doesn't seem overpriced. Its P/E ratio shows 9.65 which is good for a company in the Technology sector. Moreover, their Debt is below 50% (Debt/Equity 0.45) and the company has high margins and ROA, ROE. The dividend yield is also above the average when compared to other companies in this sector.

## (UMC) United Microelectronics Corporation

United Microelectronics Corporation operates as a semiconductor wafer foundry in Taiwan, Singapore, China, Hong Kong, Japan, the United States, Europe, and internationally. It operates through Wafer Fabrication and New Business segments. The company provides circuit design, mask tooling, wafer fabrication, and assembly and testing services. It serves fabless design companies and integrated device manufacturers. United Microelectronics Corporation was incorporated in 1980 and is headquartered in Hsinchu City, Taiwan.

Below is a weekly chart (one candle = 1 week)

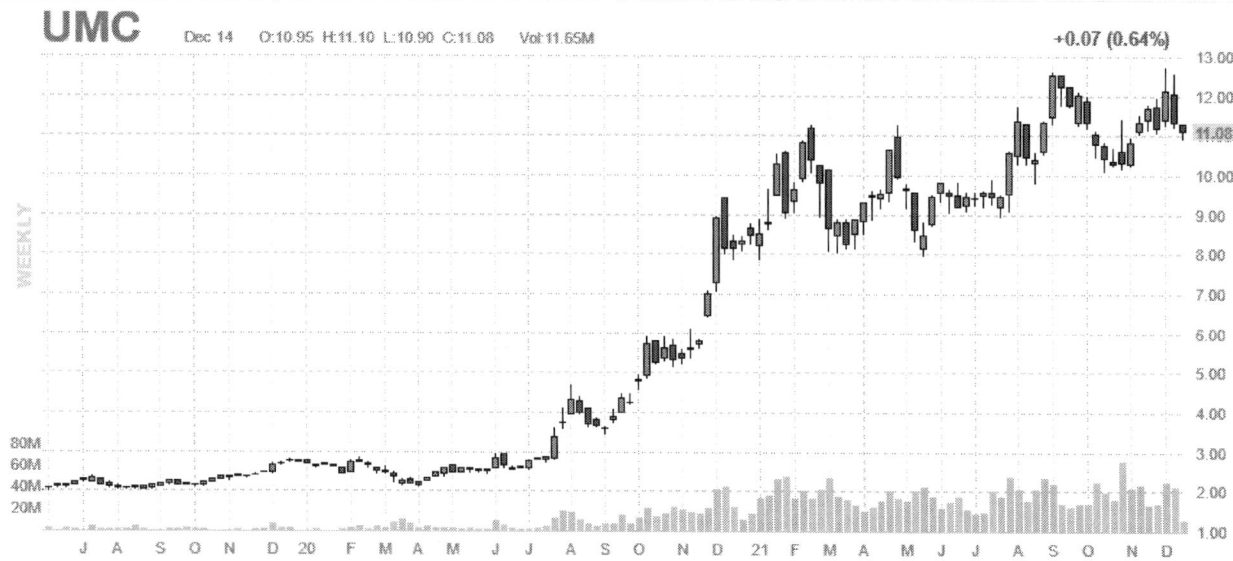

Below is a monthly chart (one candle = 1 month)

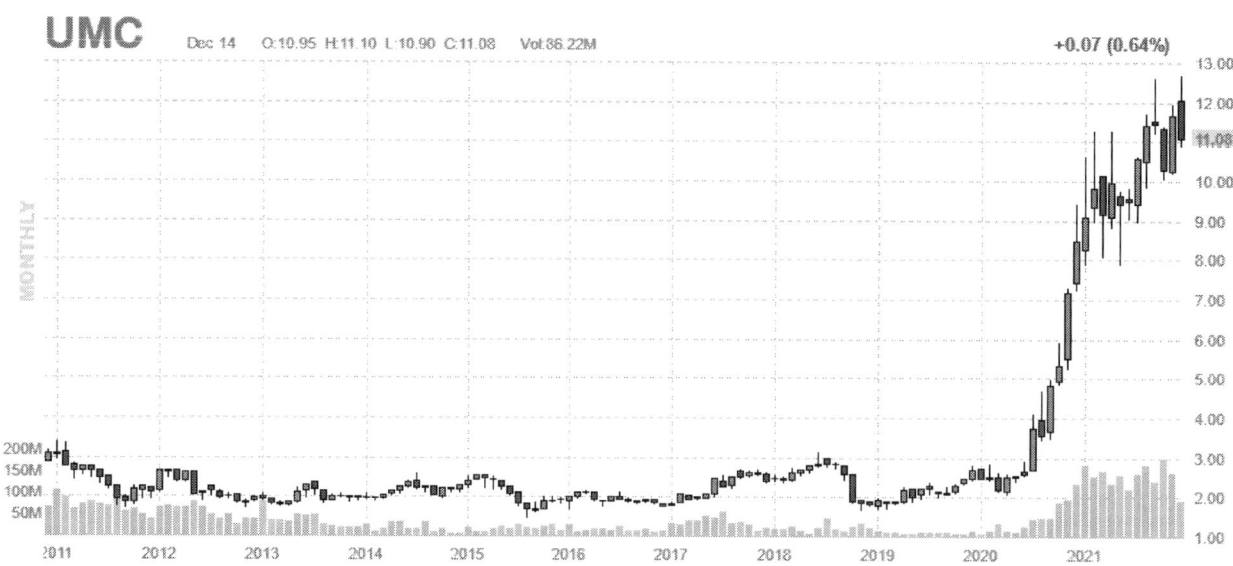

The reason I put here not just the Weekly chart but also the Monthly chart is that I want to show you that this company was selling for $2/stock for 10 years, and now it skyrocketed to $11-12/stock.

Looking just at this makes me VERY cautious. To me, it looks like the money has already been made here, and the risk/gain ratio I could get from this investment is very low (big risk of a big drop, small chance of more rocket gains).

What makes it even riskier is that this is a company from an "exotic" country (Taiwan) and that I have very little understanding of what this company is doing.

Let's now have a look at the company details:

| | | | | | | | | | | | |
|---|---|---|---|---|---|---|---|---|---|---|---|
| Index | - | P/E | 14.87 | EPS (ttm) | 0.74 | Insider Own | - | Shs Outstand | 2.44B | Perf Week | -11.64% |
| Market Cap | 28.19B | Forward P/E | 10.81 | EPS next Y | 1.02 | Insider Trans | - | Shs Float | 2.31B | Perf Month | -1.95% |
| Income | 1.84B | PEG | 0.51 | EPS next Q | 0.21 | Inst Own | 5.00% | Short Float | 1.46% | Perf Quarter | -7.44% |
| Sales | 7.18B | P/S | 3.92 | EPS this Y | 209.10% | Inst Trans | 34.04% | Short Ratio | 4.44 | Perf Half Y | 17.87% |
| Book/sh | 3.80 | P/B | 2.92 | EPS next Y | 28.93% | ROA | 12.60% | Target Price | 14.34 | Perf Year | 34.79% |
| Cash/sh | 1.71 | P/C | 6.49 | EPS next 5Y | 29.00% | ROE | 20.80% | 52W Range | 7.82 - 12.68 | Perf YTD | 31.44% |
| Dividend | 0.29 | P/FCF | 22.63 | EPS past 5Y | 18.10% | ROI | 7.00% | 52W High | -12.62% | Beta | 0.92 |
| Dividend % | 2.62% | Quick Ratio | 2.20 | Sales past 5Y | 4.10% | Gross Margin | 30.00% | 52W Low | 41.60% | ATR | 0.39 |
| Employees | 19929 | Current Ratio | 2.50 | Sales Q/Q | 24.60% | Oper. Margin | 19.90% | RSI (14) | 44.18 | Volatility | 2.67% 2.73% |
| Optionable | Yes | Debt/Eq | 0.31 | EPS Q/Q | 88.20% | Profit Margin | 25.60% | Rel Volume | 0.81 | Prev Close | 11.01 |
| Shortable | Yes | LT Debt/Eq | 0.22 | Earnings | Oct 27 BMO | Payout | - | Avg Volume | 7.61M | Price | 11.08 |
| Recom | 2.70 | SMA20 | -4.51% | SMA50 | 0.37% | SMA200 | 9.16% | Volume | 6,213,659 | Change | 0.64% |

The most important are:

- **Market Capitalization:** 28.19B
- **Dividend Yield:** 0.29
- **P/E ratio:** 14.87
- **P/B Ratio:** 2.92
- **EPS past 5 years:** 18.10%
- **ROA:** 12.60%
- **ROE:** 20.80%
- **Debt/Equity:** 0.31
- **Net Profit Margin:** 25.60%

Things to notice here are that UMC pays almost no dividend (this is not unusual for the Technology sector though) and quite a high P/B ratio. On the positive side, it's not too much in debt, having only a 0.31 Debt/Equity ratio.

# Companies from Utilities Sector

My filter for this sector looks like this:

### Descriptive tab

| | | | | | |
|---|---|---|---|---|---|
| Exchange | Any | Index | Any | Sector | Utilities |
| Market Cap. | +Mid (over $2bln) | Dividend Yield | Over 3% | Float Short | Any |
| Earnings Date | Any | Average Volume | Any | Relative Volume | Any |
| Target Price | Any | IPO Date | Any | Shares Outstanding | Any |

### Fundamental tab

| | | | | | | | |
|---|---|---|---|---|---|---|---|
| P/E | Under 20 | Forward P/E | Any | PEG | Any | P/S | Any | P/B | Under 3 |
| Price/Cash | Any | Price/Free Cash Flow | Any | EPS growth this year | Any | EPS growth next year | Any | EPS growth past 5 years | Positive (>0%) |
| EPS growth next 5 years | Any | Sales growth past 5 years | Any | EPS growth qtr over qtr | Any | Sales growth qtr over qtr | Any | Return on Assets | Over +5% |
| Return on Equity | Over +10% | Return on Investment | Any | Current Ratio | Any | Quick Ratio | Any | LT Debt/Equity | Any |
| Debt/Equity | Any | Gross Margin | Any | Operating Margin | Any | Net Profit Margin | Positive (>0%) | Payout Ratio | Any |
| Insider Ownership | Any | Insider Transactions | Any | Institutional Ownership | Any | Institutional Transactions | Any | | Reset (9) |

The reason I didn't include the Debt/Equity filter here is that companies from the Utility sector usually need to have high debt to operate in this expensive sector. Having a Debt/Equity filter would filter out too many companies from our search.

Companies that met the criteria:

| AQN | Algonquin Power & Utilities Corp. | Utilities | Utilities - Renewable | Canada | 11.67B |
|-----|-----------------------------------|-----------|------------------------|--------|--------|
| CIG | Companhia Energetica de Minas Gerais | Utilities | Utilities - Diversified | Brazil | 4.59B |
| NRG | NRG Energy, Inc. | Utilities | Utilities - Independent Power Producers | USA | 9.68B |
| UGI | UGI Corporation | Utilities | Utilities - Regulated Gas | USA | 9.11B |

The biggest two are (AQN) Algonquin Power & Utilities Corporation, and (NRG) NRG Energy, Inc. Let's check them out!

## (AQN) Algonquin Power & Utilities Corporation

Algonquin Power & Utilities Corp., through its subsidiaries, owns and operates a portfolio of regulated and non-regulated generation, distribution, and transmission utility assets in Canada, the United States, Chile, and Bermuda. It generates and sells electrical energy through non-regulated renewable and clean energy power generation facilities. The company also owns and operates hydroelectric, wind, solar, and thermal facilities with generating capacity of approximately 2.1 gigawatts; and regulated electric, natural gas, water distribution, and wastewater collection utility systems. The company was incorporated in 1988 and is headquartered in Oakville, Canada.

Below is a monthly chart (one candle = 1 month)

**Company details**

| | | | | | | | | | | | |
|---|---|---|---|---|---|---|---|---|---|---|---|
| Index | - | P/E | 9.65 | EPS (ttm) | 1.42 | Insider Own | 0.16% | Shs Outstand | 614.01M | Perf Week | -2.98% |
| Market Cap | 11.67B | Forward P/E | - | EPS next Y | - | Insider Trans | 0.00% | Shs Float | 611.49M | Perf Month | -3.80% |
| Income | 849.80M | PEG | - | EPS next Q | - | Inst Own | 53.72% | Short Float | 1.17% | Perf Quarter | -12.15% |
| Sales | 2.58B | P/S | 4.52 | EPS this Y | 32.40% | Inst Trans | - | Short Ratio | 2.88 | Perf Half Y | -14.36% |
| Book/sh | 10.33 | P/B | 1.32 | EPS next Y | - | ROA | 6.00% | Target Price | - | Perf Year | -14.41% |
| Cash/sh | 0.30 | P/C | 45.11 | EPS next 5Y | - | ROE | 17.30% | 52W Range | 13.39 - 17.86 | Perf YTD | -17.01% |
| Dividend | 0.68 | P/FCF | - | EPS past 5Y | 26.80% | ROI | 3.10% | 52W High | -23.52% | Beta | 0.19 |
| Dividend % | 4.98% | Quick Ratio | 0.50 | Sales past 5Y | 10.30% | Gross Margin | 71.00% | 52W Low | 2.05% | ATR | 0.25 |
| Employees | 3441 | Current Ratio | 0.60 | Sales Q/Q | 53.50% | Oper. Margin | 15.90% | RSI (14) | 39.57 | Volatility | 1.67% 1.61% |
| Optionable | Yes | Debt/Eq | 1.33 | EPS Q/Q | -69.40% | Profit Margin | 41.90% | Rel Volume | 2.50 | Prev Close | 13.99 |
| Shortable | Yes | LT Debt/Eq | 1.22 | Earnings | Nov 11 AMC | Payout | 32.00% | Avg Volume | 2.48M | Price | 13.66 |
| Recom | - | SMA20 | -1.70% | SMA50 | -4.79% | SMA200 | -10.64% | Volume | 6,000,963 | Change | -2.36% |

The most important are:

- **Market Capitalization:** 11.67B
- **Dividend Yield:** 4.98%
- **P/E ratio:** 9.65
- **P/B Ratio:** 1.32
- **EPS past 5 years:** 26.80%
- **ROA:** 6.00%
- **ROE:** 17.30%
- **Debt/Equity:** 1.33
- **Net Profit Margin:** 41.90%

What is nice about this company is the high dividend yield, low P/E, and P/B ratios, high ROA, and a very high margin.

## (NRG) NRG Energy, Inc.

NRG Energy, Inc., operates as an integrated power company in the United States. It operates through Texas, East, and West. The company is involved in producing, selling, and delivering electricity and related products and services to residential, industrial, and commercial consumers. It generates electricity using natural gas, coal, oil, solar, nuclear, and battery storage. The company also provides system power, distributed generation, renewable products, backup generation, storage and distributed solar, demand response, energy efficiency, advisory, and on-site energy solutions; and carbon management and specialty services. In addition, it trades in electric power, natural gas, and related commodities; environmental products; weather products; and financial products, including forwards, futures, options, and swaps. Further, the company procures fuels; provides transportation services; and directly sells energy, services, and products and services to retail. NRG Energy, Inc. was founded in 1989 and is headquartered in Princeton, New Jersey.

Below is a monthly chart (one candle = 1 month)

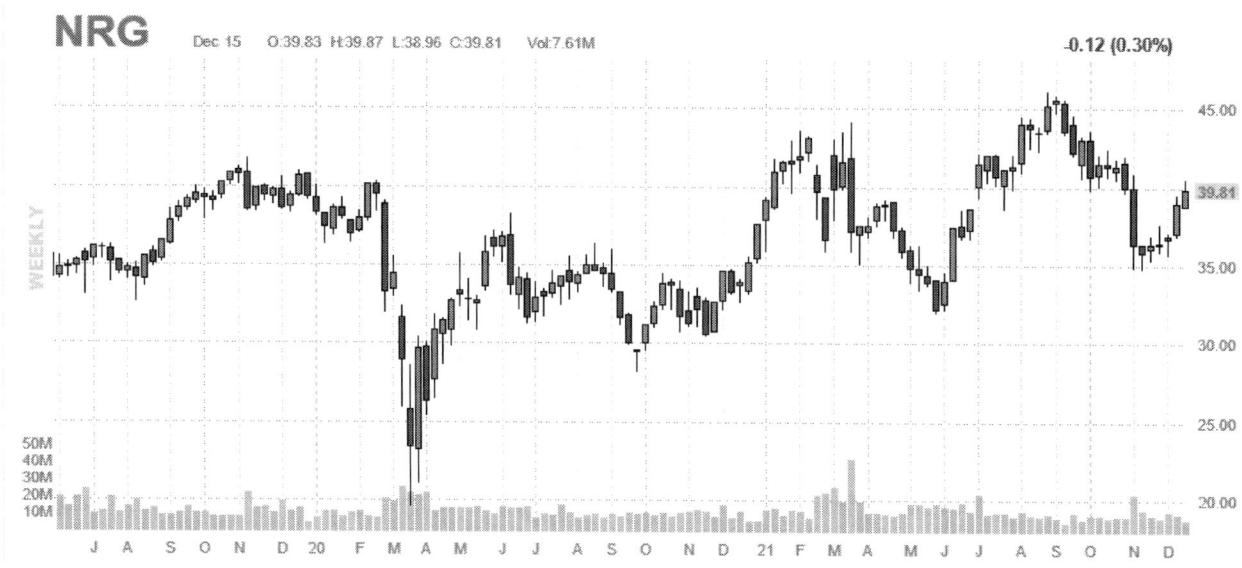

## Company details

| Index | S&P 500 | P/E | 4.01 | EPS (ttm) | 9.96 | Insider Own | 0.70% | Shs Outstand | 245.00M | Perf Week | 2.75% |
|---|---|---|---|---|---|---|---|---|---|---|---|
| Market Cap | 9.68B | Forward P/E | 10.91 | EPS next Y | 3.66 | Insider Trans | -1.07% | Shs Float | 242.54M | Perf Month | 11.85% |
| Income | 2.44B | PEG | 0.09 | EPS next Q | -0.01 | Inst Own | 98.50% | Short Float | 4.25% | Perf Quarter | -9.31% |
| Sales | 21.97B | P/S | 0.44 | EPS this Y | -86.70% | Inst Trans | -0.86% | Short Ratio | 4.54 | Perf Half Y | 8.15% |
| Book/sh | 16.64 | P/B | 2.40 | EPS next Y | -55.81% | ROA | 11.70% | Target Price | 45.30 | Perf Year | 22.37% |
| Cash/sh | 1.07 | P/C | 37.37 | EPS next 5Y | 43.10% | ROE | 99.40% | 52W Range | 31.94 - 46.10 | Perf YTD | 6.34% |
| Dividend | 1.30 | P/FCF | 5.66 | EPS past 5Y | 16.10% | ROI | 8.00% | 52W High | -13.64% | Beta | 0.84 |
| Dividend % | 3.26% | Quick Ratio | 1.20 | Sales past 5Y | -5.90% | Gross Margin | 31.10% | 52W Low | 24.64% | ATR | 1.06 |
| Employees | 4104 | Current Ratio | 1.20 | Sales Q/Q | 135.30% | Oper. Margin | 17.00% | RSI (14) | 62.55 | Volatility | 2.33% 2.55% |
| Optionable | Yes | Debt/Eq | 2.07 | EPS Q/Q | 549.80% | Profit Margin | 11.10% | Rel Volume | 0.65 | Prev Close | 39.93 |
| Shortable | Yes | LT Debt/Eq | 1.95 | Earnings | Nov 04 BMO | Payout | 12.80% | Avg Volume | 2.27M | Price | 39.81 |
| Recom | 2.30 | SMA20 | 6.63% | SMA50 | 3.05% | SMA200 | 1.61% | Volume | 1,138,624 | Change | -0.30% |

The most important are:

- **Market Capitalization:** 9.68B
- **Dividend Yield:** 3.26
- **P/E ratio:** 4.01
- **P/B Ratio:** 2.40
- **EPS past 5 years:** 16.10%
- **ROA:** 11.70%
- **ROE:** 99.40%
- **Debt/Equity:** 2.07
- **Net Profit Margin:** 11.10

What is most striking here is the crazy low P/E ratio. When you see the P/E as low as this then it's most likely not a Holy Grail company, but there is something you are missing. There is probably a reason why the P/E is so low.

What I recommend doing in such a case is going to the stock description page and reading the related news. Ideally, some analyst comments on the company will tell you in simple words what's going on there.

This is what the recent NRG news/articles look like (screenshot from Finviz):

```
Dec-09-21 08:38PM  NVIT Jacobs Levy Large Cap Growth Fund Buys Alphabet Inc, Veeva Systems Inc, Markel Corp, Sells ... GuruFocus.com
Dec-08-21 07:00PM  Fear of Outages Is Boosting Chinese Battery Unicorn on IPO Track Bloomberg
           04:11PM  NRG Energy Inc (NRG): Hedge Funds Are Snapping Up Insider Monkey
           04:00PM  NRG Energy (NRG) Concludes Sale, Announces Repurchase Plans Zacks
Dec-07-21 11:31AM  NRG Energy Recognizes Business Customers During Annual Excellence in Energy Awards News Direct
Dec-06-21 10:12AM  NRG Energy's stock surges after $1 billion stock repurchase program announced MarketWatch
           09:45AM  NRG Closes 4.8 GW Asset Sale and Announces $1 Billion Share Repurchase Program Business Wire
Dec-03-21 03:07PM  WEC Energy (WEC) to Reward Shareholders Via 7.4% Dividend Hike Zacks
Dec-02-21 05:21PM  NRG Energy and Smart Energy Decisions Publish 2021 State of Distributed Energy Resources Study Business Wire
Nov-29-21 01:40PM  Top Utilities Stocks for December 2021 Investopedia
Nov-18-21 09:03AM  NRG Energy Joins the EV100 Initiative News Direct
Nov-17-21 02:44PM  NRG Energy Recognizes Business Customers During Annual Excellence in Energy Awards Business Wire
           10:44AM  Alliant Energy's (LNT) Arm to Refinance, Price Debt Offering Zacks
Nov-15-21 12:28PM  NRG Energy's (NRG) Direct Energy Buyout, Green Goals Bode Well Zacks
Nov-11-21 11:57AM  11 Best Utility Stocks To Buy Now Insider Monkey
           09:58AM  NRG Energy (NRG) Aims for EV Fleet by 2030, To Cut Emission Zacks
Nov-10-21 02:18PM  NRG Energy Joins the EV100 Initiative Business Wire
Nov-09-21 11:15AM  Was The Smart Money Right About NRG Energy Inc (NRG)? Insider Monkey
Nov-08-21 11:10AM  Is It Time To Consider Buying NRG Energy, Inc. (NYSE:NRG)? Simply Wall St.
Nov-04-21 04:31PM  NRG Energy, inc (NRG) Q3 2021 Earnings Call Transcript Motley Fool -11.10%
           04:10PM  Why NRG Energy Stock Slumped Today Motley Fool
           10:03AM  NRG Energy (NRG) Q3 Earnings Beat Estimates, Revenues Rise Y/Y Zacks
           06:59AM  NRG Energy, Inc. Reports Third Quarter 2021 Results Business Wire
Nov-03-21 10:54AM  Utility Stock Q3 Earnings to Watch on Nov 4: DUK, SO & More Zacks
Nov-01-21 01:06PM  NRG Energy (NRG) to Post Q3 Earnings: What's in the Cards? Zacks
Oct-28-21 11:18AM  NRG Energy Recognized for Excellence in Greenhouse Gas Management at the 2021 Climate Leadership Awards News Direct
Oct-27-21 05:50PM  UPDATE 1-New York state denies permits for two proposed natural gas-fired power plants Reuters
           04:01PM  New York state denies permits for two proposed natural gas-fired power plants Reuters
Oct-24-21 06:26AM  11 Best High Dividend Stocks To Buy According To Billionaire Cooperman Insider Monkey
Oct-18-21 02:06PM  Hedge Funds Are Souring On NRG Energy Inc (NRG) Insider Monkey
Oct-15-21 01:28PM  NRG Energy, Inc. Announces Quarterly Dividend Business Wire
Oct-14-21 04:28PM  NRG Energy Recognized for Excellence in Greenhouse Gas Management at the 2021 Climate Leadership Awards Business Wire
           09:00AM  NRG Energy's (NRG) Transformation Plan, Green Goals Bode Well Zacks
Oct-12-21 05:15PM  NRG Energy, Inc. to Report Third Quarter 2021 Financial Results on November 4, 2021 Business Wire
Oct-08-21 04:29AM  7 Oil and Gas Stocks to Buy According to Billionaire Leon Cooperman Insider Monkey
Oct-07-21 05:41PM  NRG Energy Named Champion of Board Diversity by The Forum of Executive Women Business Wire
           01:52PM  NRG Energy (NRG) Partners Google to Meet Clean Energy Goals Zacks
Oct-06-21 07:15AM  NRG Energy Partners with Google to Support Clean Energy Business Wire
```

Apart from this, the other details look pretty much okay. The company pays a nice dividend and even the Debt isn't too terrible - given the industry that it operates in.

# Picking the Right Time to Make Your Investment

When I was showing you how to pick the right stocks, I said that it's important to wait for the price to drop and then buy the stock when it's "discounted". Being able to pick the right price for your investment is crucial and now I am going to show you how to go about it.

We won't focus on stock fundamentals anymore. Instead, we will do this using technical analysis. First, I will show you the basics of reading a price chart, and then I will show you how to implement our secret weapon - the Volume Profile.

Even though Volume Profile is a professional tool, learning to use it is not too hard. Even if you are a beginner. Once you have learned how it works, you will never look at the markets the same way you did before! I can promise you that.

Let's not get ahead of ourselves though, and let's talk first about the simple Price Action chart, and what it tells us. We will need it later when we go into the Volume Profile part.

# Price Action – How to Read a Simple Chart

Price Action is the art of understanding naked charts without using any indicator. It is the first thing I recommend learning before jumping into anything else.

To understand Price Action, you need to understand the reason "why the price moves."

## Why Does the Price Move?

What we hear very often is that the price moves because there are more Buyers or more Sellers. People on television news say it and so-called "experts" say it, but it's not true. It makes no sense. Because every Buyer who wants to buy a stock needs a Seller who wants to sell it. It's never about the number of Buyers vs. Sellers.

The thing that moves the price is the aggressivity of Buyers or Sellers. If Buyers are more aggressive than Sellers, then the price rises. If Sellers are more aggressive than Buyers, then the price declines.

What is this aggressivity though? Let me give you a simplified example of an uptrend:

**EXAMPLE: How an uptrend is formed?**

A biotechnology company called BIO has its current stock price of $100. They have just announced that they have a new cure for cancer. What investors do is they immediately want to buy shares of this company. They want it now – because the news is just groundbreaking. So, they start buying. However, everybody who was willing to sell their stocks for $100 has already sold them. What now? If an investor still wants to buy this stock, he will need to offer more than $100. Let's say that the cheapest price anybody is willing to sell their BIO stocks for is now $105. But it doesn't stop there as there are too many investors who want to buy BIO now. When those guys willing to sell for $105 sold all their stocks, the stock price will rise again. Now buyers will be forced to buy from Sellers who offer their BIO stocks for $110.

This will go on and on and the price will rise and rise. It will be driven up by aggressive buyers.

It could look for example like this price chart:

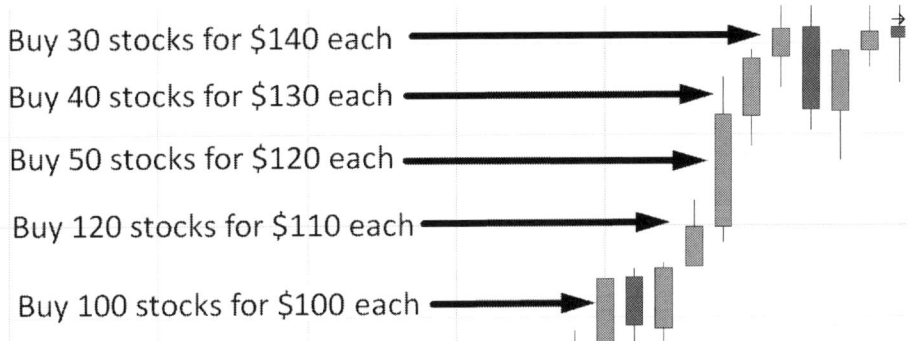

In the example above, people are willing to sell 100 stocks of the BIO company for $100. Then nobody wants to sell their stocks for $100 anymore and Buyers need to offer more. So, they offer $110. Some sellers are okay with selling their BIO stocks for $110, and they sell 120 stocks. Then, if Buyers still want to buy, they need to raise their offer again. This time to $120 per stock. This is the mechanism that moves the price.

**EXAMPLE: How a downtrend is formed?**

If the price is dropping, then it's exactly the opposite case - Sellers are more aggressive. They want to get rid of their stocks now – as fast as possible.

For example – a company GTR selling guitars reported that their huge storehouse with the most expensive wood just burned to the ground. This is a huge blow to their business and many shareholders want to sell their stocks as the future of the company is not so bright anymore. The stocks were $140 before the bad news came out. Unfortunately for the current shareholders, nobody wants to buy the stocks for $140 anymore (there is nobody they could sell their Stocks to).

Consequently, Sellers are forced to offer their stocks for $130 to find a Buyer. But there are not too many investors willing to buy for $130. For this reason, the price needs to drop even more to $120 to attract more Buyers. This goes on and on and the downtrend continues until it reaches a balance. A balance where the Supply = Demand. This is where the trend stops moving.

The example below shows a balanced price followed by bad news. This news was the impulse investors started aggressively selling, desperate to find Buyers.

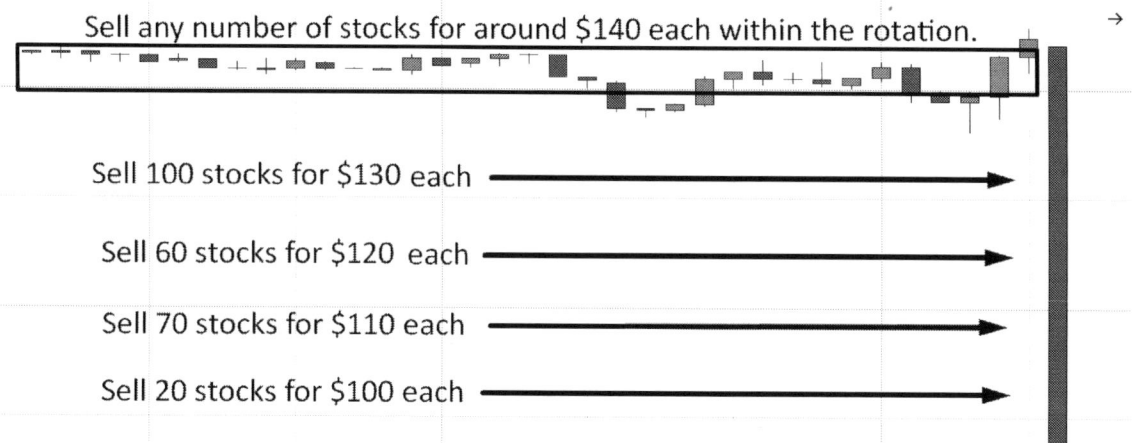

### EXAMPLE: When the price doesn't move

If there are no aggressive Buyers or Sellers, then the price moves only in a tight, side-ways rotation. Or it doesn't move at all. In such a case, Buyers are willing to buy for $100, and for this price, Sellers are okay with selling any number of stocks.

It's like when you go shopping – you go to the store and you start buying apples. The store has a lot of apples to sell and they are okay to sell you an apple for $1 no matter whether you buy 1 or 100. The price remains the same. Both sides are happy. You are happy to buy for $1, they are happy to sell for $1. The price of apples doesn't change.

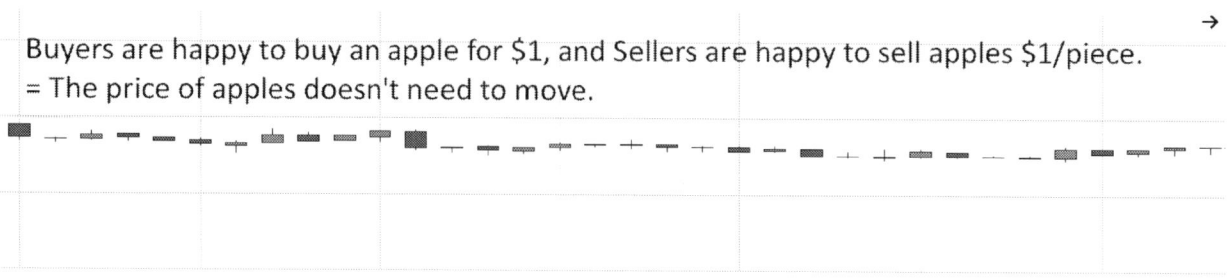

The price of apples would change if the store manager came in, and said "oh, boy those are great apples! And our supply is running low! We best raise the price to $2 per apple."

Trend and rotation are the cornerstones we are going to build upon. Remember this:

**Aggressivity** = Trend (price moves)

**Passive market participants** = Rotation (price doesn't change much)

# The "BIG" Guys

When it comes to the question: who are the market participants who move the prices? then in most cases, it's the BIG guys.

The BIG guys are institutions and institutional traders. Its banks, brokerages, hedge funds, pension funds, insurance companies and mortgage companies. Each of those have a bit different roles and strategies, but it's them who move and manipulate the markets most of the time.

Me, and you, and all those guys from investing forums, we are just small fish. We usually can't move or manipulate the prices (with some exceptions when retail guys like us get organized and pull the rope together).

The BIG guys who move the markets are the ones we need to keep our eyes on. We need to track their actions and predict what they are going to do in the future.

We can spot institutional trading activity using Price Action and Volume Profile. Even though many people don't realize it, those two are connected. For this reason, we will cover both, starting with Price Action.

# How to Spot Institutional Activity with Price Action

In this chapter, I would like to show you how to spot areas where the big financial institutions were active. Those areas are extremely important because they help us understand where institutional interest was and with high probability will be again. A place that is significant for institutions should be significant for us too because our whole method is based on following the BIG guys.

There are three main signs of institutional activity we can spot with Price Action:

1. **Rotation (price goes sideways)**

2. **Trend**

3. **Strong rejection (of higher or lower prices)**

## Rotation

One of the biggest differences between us (small retail investors) and the BIG guys (financial institutions) is the amount of capital we manage.

Remember when I was talking about the thing that for each of your trade/investments you need a counterparty? When you want to buy, you need to find somebody willing to sell. And when you need to sell, you need somebody willing to buy from you.

Because we are only small fish with no big trading accounts (compared to those institutions) it's relatively easy for us to find somebody who will sell/buy the stocks we need - because we don't need many of them. If you, for example, wanted to buy 50 Apple stocks it wouldn't be a problem and you would get a counterparty immediately. However, if you were a hedge fund buying 5.000.000 Apple stocks then good luck finding a counterparty for that! In the end, you would be able to buy the whole amount, but it would take some time. Especially for stocks that are not as popular (not traded so much) as Apple.

Why am I telling you this? Because when the BIG guys want to enter their huge trading positions, it simply takes time. For this reason, the institutions like to do their transactions within a rotation (when the price goes sideways).

In the rotation, they can Buy or Sell whatever amount they need, because they have time to do so. They can also do this secretly and unnoticed without giving anybody a hint of what they are doing.

Why is it so important that they accumulate or get rid of their stocks in secret? Imagine what would happen to stock if a huge bank started to sell insane amounts of it all of a sudden! It would cause panic and others would likely start selling that stock as well. Not only would it cause the stock to plummet, but it would also make it very difficult for the 1st huge company (that huge bank) to sell for a decent price (because prices would be falling).

That's why it's always best for the BIG guys to do their business within a rotation – slowly, unnoticed, and in secret. Only after that, it's okay to manipulate the market to go into a trend. But only when they are finished and ready. Not before.

Here are two examples that should make this a little easier to understand:

**Example A:** The right way to enter a huge trading position (in a rotation, slowly, unnoticed):

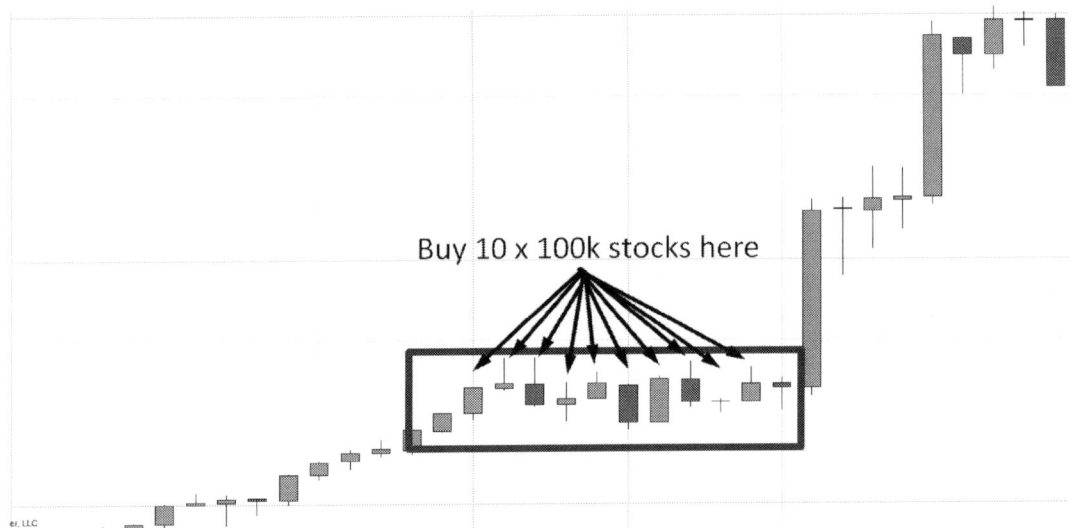

In this example, a bank is slowly buying stocks in a rotation, unnoticed, and without starting a trend.

**Example B:** The bad way to enter a huge trading position. A bank started to buy too aggressively and other market participants noticed it. They started buying too, and this caused the prices to start rising = trend.

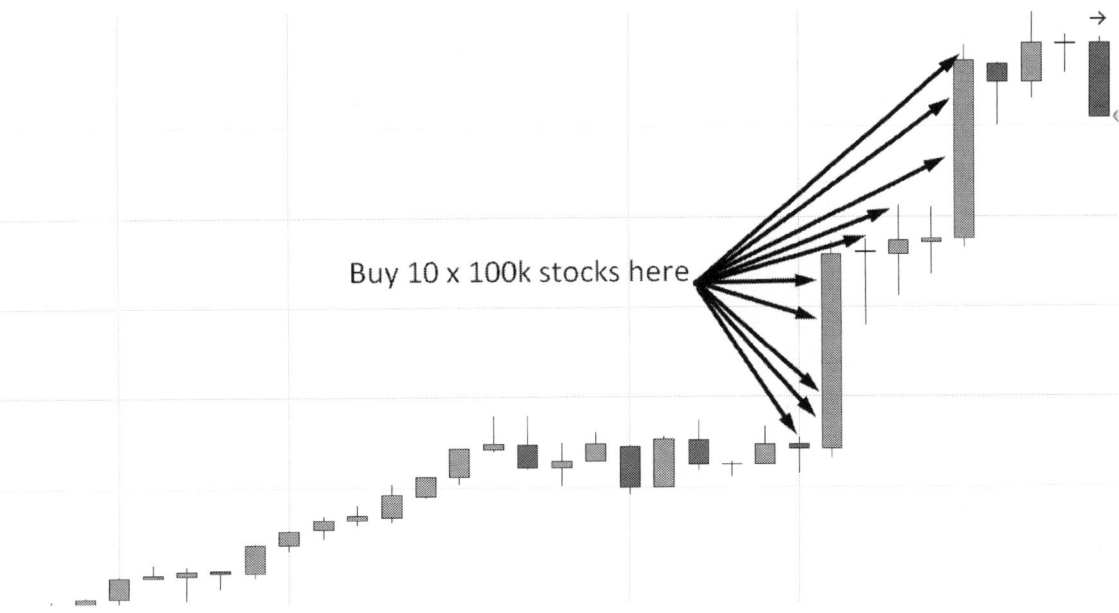

In this case, the price of the stock started to rise rapidly and the bank which wanted to buy 10 x 100k stocks must buy them for a much higher price now.

With all this, I wanted to demonstrate the reason why big trading institutions prefer to Buy/Sell within rotation areas

When there is a rotation it's quite likely that many stocks were traded there and that the BIG guys were active. This is important! That's the reason why I always look for such areas when analyzing any chart.

Remember Rotation = the BIG guys entering/exiting their huge trading positions.

Here is a chart with some rotation areas highlighted:

Let me go ahead and show you the same chart with Volume Profile – a tool that shows volume distribution (how many stocks were traded). Right now, it will suffice to say that the wider the Volume Profile histogram, the heavier volumes (more stocks) were traded in that area.

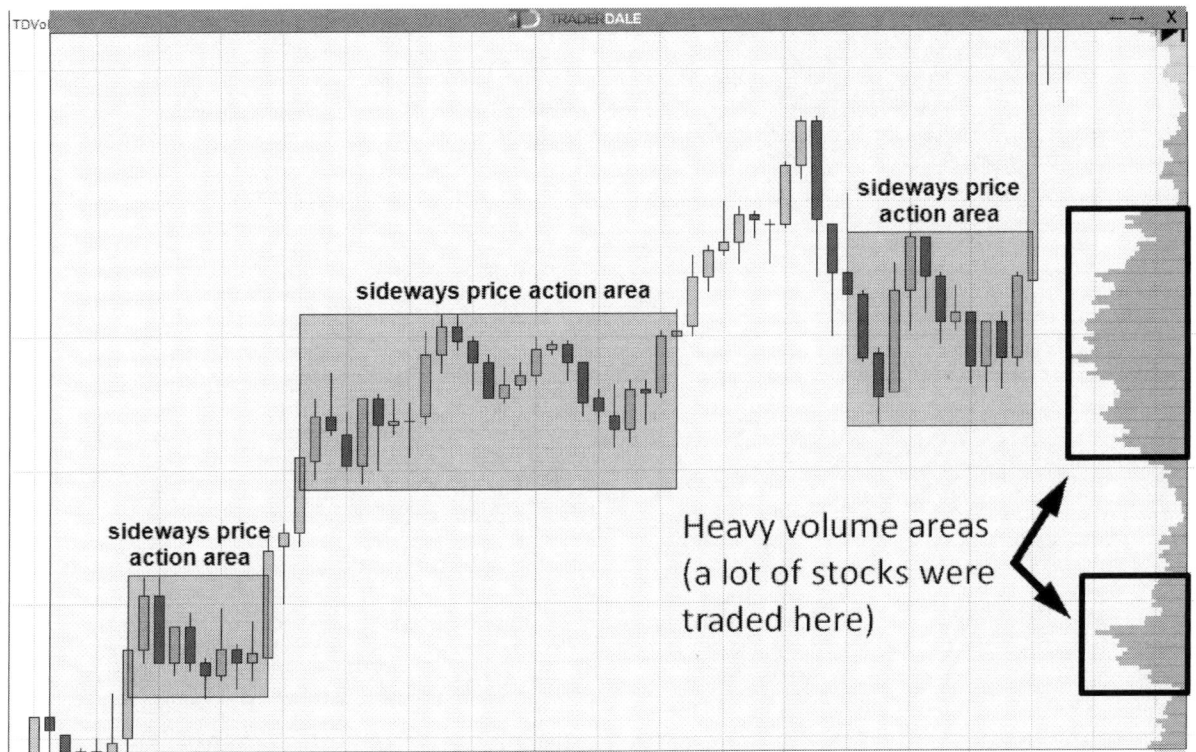

As you can see, most of the trading activity took place at the price levels, where the rotation areas were.

This is why rotation areas are important – they show where the BIG guys were active and where they were buying/selling huge amounts of stocks.

## Trend

A trend is when the price moves fast in one direction. It is caused by aggressive buyers pushing the price higher (uptrend) or by aggressive sellers who are pushing the price lower (downtrend). This sort of aggressive buying or selling often takes place after the rotation.

A typical scenario is that big institutions are building up their positions in rotation areas, and when they are done with that, they start aggressively buying or selling to move the price in the direction they want. This is how they make money. They build up their positions slowly and unnoticed, and then they start a trend to make those positions profitable.

The big institutions need to accumulate their positions before the move because when the price is moving in a fast trend, there isn't time to place their big trading positions anymore.

Below are two typical examples of sideways price action areas followed by a trend:

Strong trends are significant because they show us the intentions of the big institutions. We can't tell those intentions when the price is rotating. We need to see a trend to know if the BIG guys were buying or selling their stocks earlier.

If there is a strong uptrend after a sideways price action area, then we know that the BIG guys were buying stocks. If, on the other hand, there is a sideways price action channel followed by an aggressive sell-off (a downtrend), then we know that the BIG guys were selling their stocks earlier (in that rotation area that occurred before the trend).

Now you know two significant pieces of information that the market gives us and which we should always consider in our market analysis. It is "sideways price action" and a "strong trend." There is one more piece of information that price action gives us and that I find important. It is the "strong rejection."

## Strong Rejection (of Higher or Lower Prices)

Strong rejection of either higher or lower price levels is a sudden reversal. This pattern is made when the price goes aggressively one way, then turns quickly and with the same aggression and speed goes the other way.

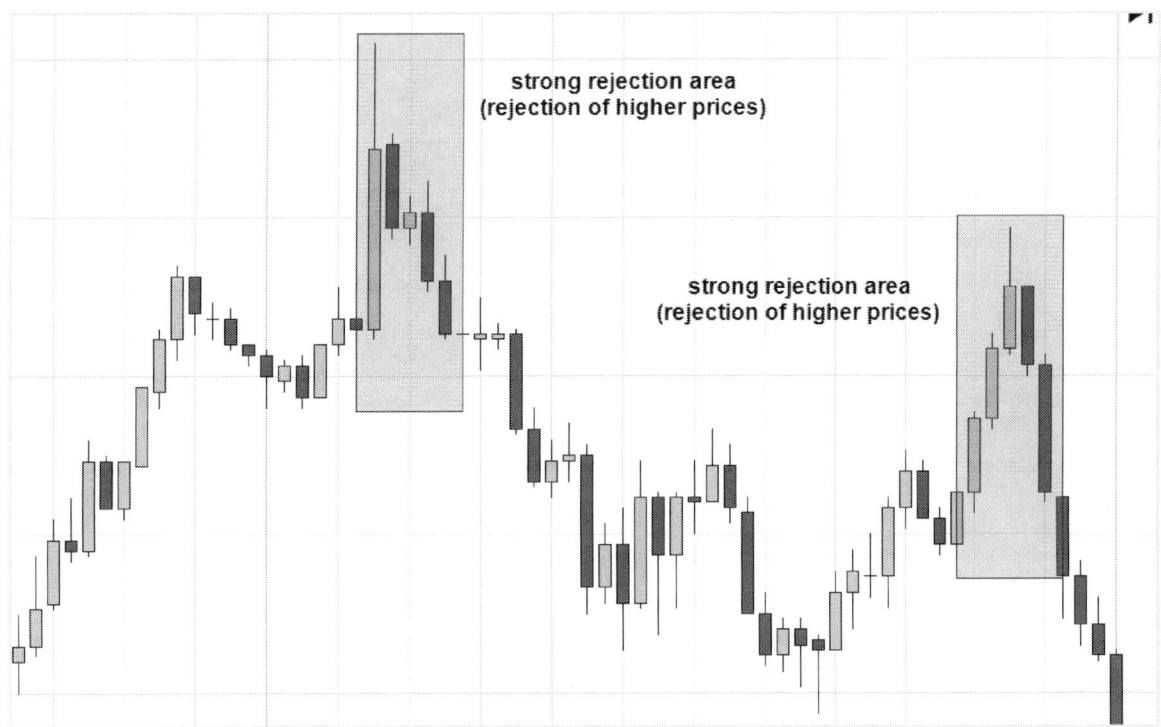

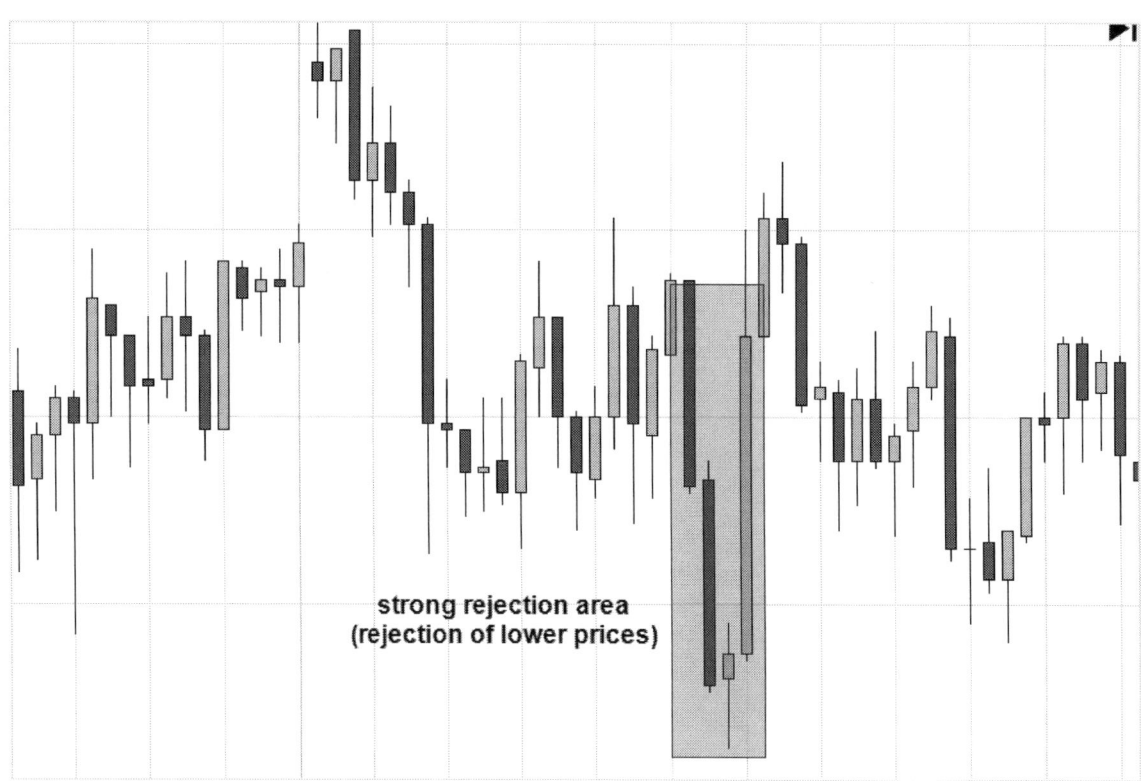

What happens in such strong rejection is this: One side of the market (for example buyers) is aggressive and pushes the price in a trend (up). Then it clashes with the other side (strong sellers) which is even stronger and more aggressive. The price turns quickly, sellers take over and the price starts to drop. The area where the trend changed is significant because it marks the place where strong market participants aggressively rejected the current trend and started a strong countermove.

The rejection point often plays a significant role in the future as well. When the price gets near such a place, a very similar scenario will likely occur again – that the price will react there again. It is because places, where the price made a significant turn in the past, are always watched by the big guys and often become a new battlefield between buyers and sellers in the future.

It takes some time to be able to spot and recognize strong rejections and tell them from rejections that are not so significant. But in time, you will be able to do this, and you will look at the chart, and you will read whole sentences instead of separate letters.

# The Complete Picture

The three Price Action signs of institutional activity I showed you are the core of my strategy. Those three are the most significant patterns I look for in every stock chart. They are also the first thing I notice when I look at any chart. After some practice, you will be able to recognize them quickly, and the whole process of identifying those zones will come to you quite naturally. For now, try actively looking for those areas. You should learn to visualize the charts in your head to look like this:

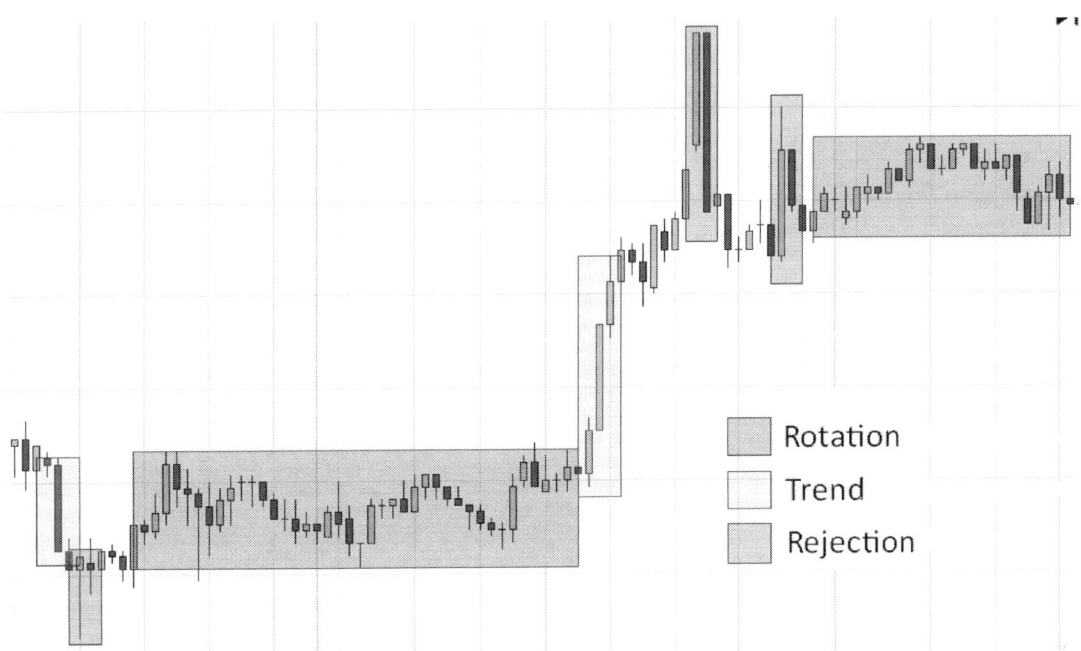

You split the charts into separate areas in your mind. Every area will give you a piece of information about the institutions.

In the next part of this book, I will use those three formations along with the Volume Profile indicator to identify the best places for stock investment entries.

# How to Use Volume Profile in Stock Investing

In the previous parts of this book, I was talking about how to do stock screening, how to filter out the bad stocks and how to create portfolios from the good ones. If you remember, I said that it's not enough to just pick the right stocks, but it is also important to time the trade entry (= that's <u>when</u> you buy that stock). And this is what I am going to teach you now. In this chapter, I am going to teach you how to pick ideal price levels where to buy your stocks. For this, I am going to use the Volume Profile indicator.

## Volume Profile Introduction

Volume Profile is a trading indicator that shows Volume at Price. It helps to identify where the big financial institutions put their money and helps to reveal their intentions. Volume Profile reveals strong Support zones which are places where the stock price is very likely to stop falling and start rising again. Our main intention of using Volume Profile is to find such Supports and buy our stocks there.

## What Does Volume Profile Look Like?

Volume Profile can have many shapes depending on how the volumes get distributed. It is created using horizontal lines (it is a histogram). The thicker the profile is the more volume was traded at the given level. If a profile is thin in some places, it means that there was not much volume traded there.

We are going to focus mostly on areas, where the Volume Profile is the widest as those areas represent places where the BIG guys were active the most. Those places are strong supports where we will want to place our trade entries.

Here is an example of what a Volume Profile can look like:

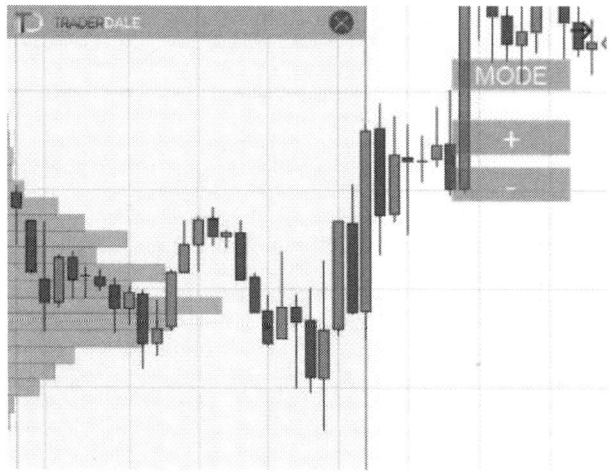

# What Does Volume Profile Tell Us?

Volume Profile tells us how the volume was distributed over a given price range. This is very useful information. Let me demonstrate with an example.

In the picture below, you can see two heavy volume zones and one zone where the Volume Profile is thin.

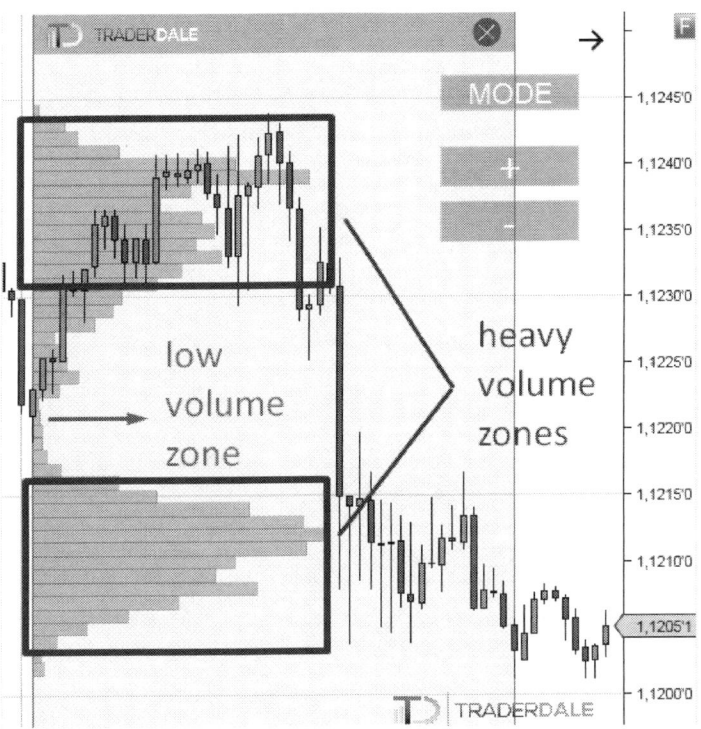

What does this particular picture tell us? It tells us that big financial institutions were interested in trading in those two heavy-volume zones. On the other hand, they did not care for trading too much in the middle zone where the volumes were weak.

This scenario could be a sign that big institutions were:

1. Building up their huge selling positions in the heavy volume zone (1.1230 –1.1240).

2. Manipulating the price to go into a sell-off (that's the thin profile).

3. And, finally, quitting their positions (or adding to them) in the heavy volume zone around 1.1205–1.1215.

Heavy volume areas are the key. They represent areas where the BIG guys were active and areas that will work as significant zones in the future.

# Different Volume Profile Shapes

There are many shapes a Volume Profile histogram can print and many different stories it can tell. However, the shapes and the stories behind them tend to repeat themselves, and in the end, it comes down to just a few basic shapes the Volume Profile can take:

## D-Shaped Profile

It corresponds with the letter "D" and this is the most common shape. It tells us that there is a temporary balance in the market. Big financial institutions are building up their trading positions and they are getting ready for a big move.

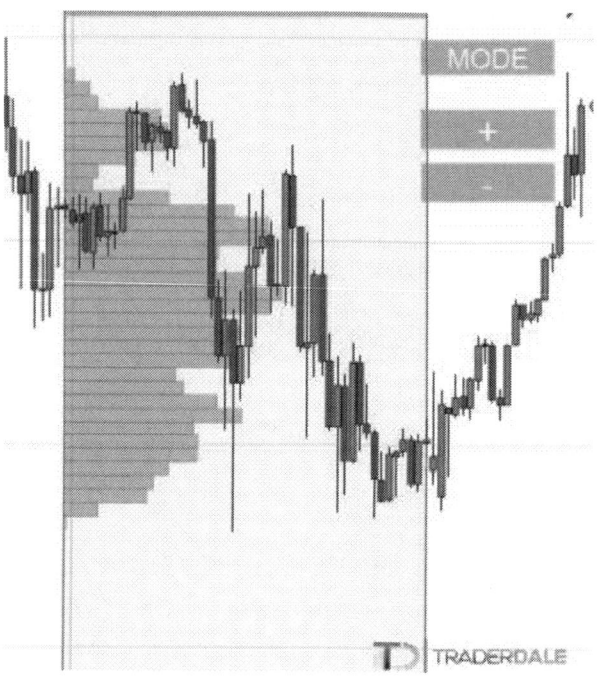

## P-Shaped Profile

It corresponds with the letter "P" and this is a sign of an uptrend. Aggressive institutional buyers were pushing the price upwards; then the price found fair value and a rotation started. In this rotation, heavy volumes were traded, and the market was getting ready for the next big move. P-shaped profiles are usually seen in an uptrend or at the end of a downtrend.

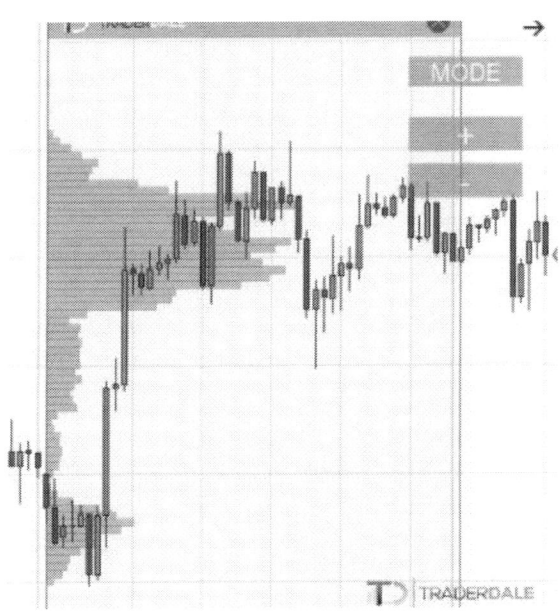

## b-Shaped Profile

It corresponds with the letter "b" and is the exact opposite of a P-shaped profile.

b-shaped profiles are usually seen in a downtrend or at the end of an uptrend.

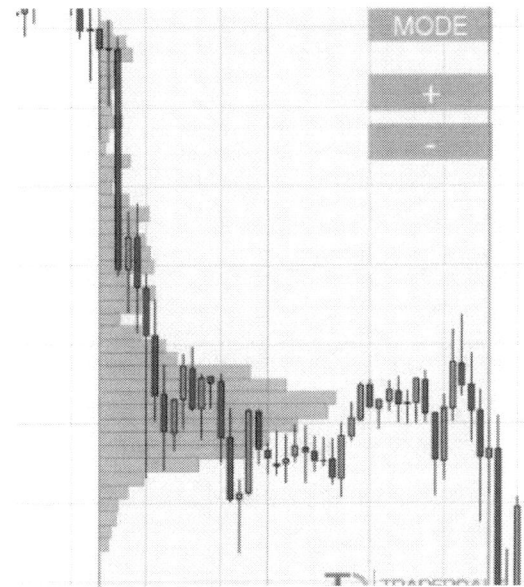

## Thin Profile

It corresponds with the letter "I" (with little bumps in it).

A thin profile means a strong trend. There is not much time for building up trading positions in an aggressive price movement. Only small Volume Clusters (sort of "bumps") are created in this kind of profile.

One of my favorite strategies is based on those Volume Clusters!

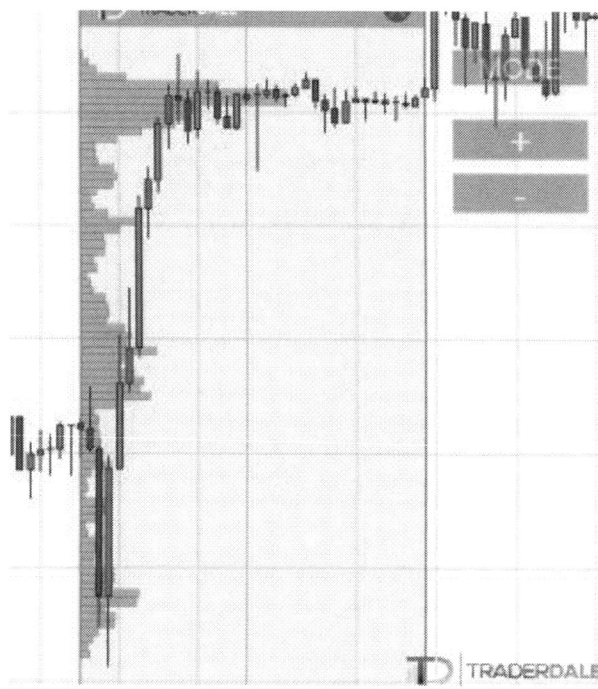

# What Makes Volume Profile Different from Other Trading Indicators?

No other indicator apart from Volume indicators can show you where the big trading institutions were likely buying/selling! Why? Because 99% of all standard indicators are calculated only from two variables: Price and Time. Volume Profile gets calculated using three variables—Price, Time, and Volume.

In other words, 99% of standard trading indicators only show you how the price was moving in the past. The only difference between those hundreds of indicators is how they visualize it. It does not matter whether it is EMA, Bollinger bands, RSI, MACD, or any other indicator... All those only show a different visualization of a price movement in the past (they are delayed—they visualize something that has already happened).

YES – they are pretty useless, which is the reason investors keep jumping from one to the other without having any real success.

On the other hand, Volume Profile points you to zones that were and will be important for big trading institutions. Simply put – Volume Profile can show you what will happen in the future!

## Why Care About Volumes and What the Big Institutions Are Doing?

There is a straightforward reason why we need to know what the big financial institutions are doing. The reason is that they dominate, move, and manipulate the markets. It is they who decide where the price will go, not you or me. We are too small.

Take a look at the following picture. It shows the 10 biggest banks and how much volume they control. Together it is almost 65% of the market. Just 10 banks! This picture shows the currency market, but it is pretty much the same with stocks or with any other instrument.

| Rank | Name | Market share |
|---|---|---|
| 1 | JP Morgan | 9.81 % |
| 2 | Deutsche Bank | 8.41 % |
| 3 | Citi | 7.87 % |
| 4 | XTX Markets | 7.22 % |
| 5 | UBS | 6.63 % |
| 6 | State Street Corporation | 5.50 % |
| 7 | HCTech | 5.28 % |
| 8 | HSBC | 4.93 % |
| 9 | Bank of America Merrill Lynch | 4.63 % |
| 10 | Goldman Sachs | 4.50 % |

With stocks, it's just 10% of all volumes that are traded by retail investors like us. The rest (90%) are big trading institutions.

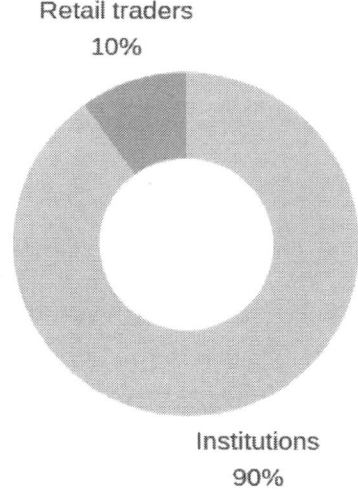

It is those BIG guys who own this game. Those are the guys we need to track and follow. And how do we follow them? We track their transactions (trades they executed) using Volume Profile.

## Where to Get Volume Profile
You can get my Volume Profile indicator on this page:

https://members.trader-dale.com/checkout/?rid=pn8KB0

What I recommend though is not only getting the Volume Profile indicator, but also a complete pack that includes the Volume Profile indicator, stock investing video course (15+ hours), more unique tools and extras, and dedicated tech support, Check it out here:

https://www.trader-dale.com/stock-investing-with-volume-profile/

## Where to Get Data
Since we are doing a long-term analysis and investment planning, we don't need too detailed data feed like we would need for example for day trading. What I recommend is doing your analysis on a chart with Daily or Weekly candles (1 candle = 1 Day, or 1 Week). For those purposes, it's ideal to use the built-in data feed that the NinjaTrader 8 platform offers for free. This data feed is called "Kinetick - End of Day". It provides free Daily data to all major US stocks. This means that the fastest time frame you can use here is the Daily time frame, which is enough for our purposes.

You connect to it through the Control Center → Connections:

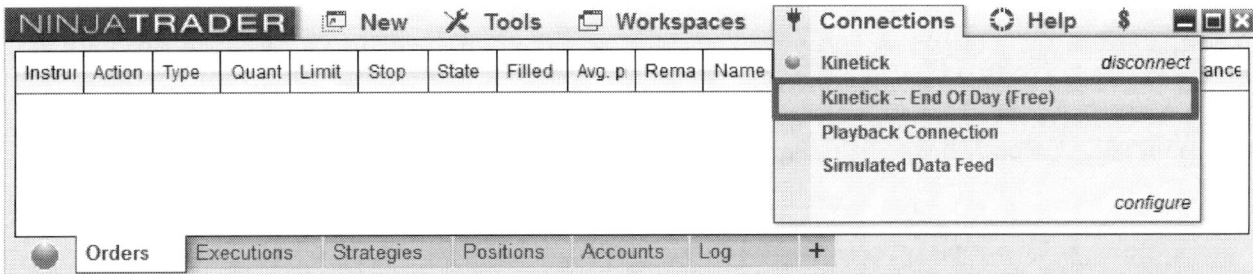

There is a downside to this connection that I need to mention. The thing is that the data feed only gives us the price chart but not the volumes. This would be a problem if we wanted to do day trading and pick exact spots to trade from. However, we will only be looking for the most important zones – those that stand out. For this reason, we can use a special TPO feature my Volume Profile indicator.

This feature can estimate volume distribution over any price action chart even if we don't get the exact information about volumes. I won't go into details about how this is done, but if you would like to find out, then you can check out this video, where I explain it:

https://www.trader-dale.com/volume-profile-vs-market-profile-what-is-the-difference/

## Where to Get Data for Non-US markets

The majority of you who read this book probably won't need this, but in case you are interested in stocks that are not included in the NinjaTrader data feed (stocks not listed in the major US exchanges), you will need to import a stock symbol list into your NinjaTrader platform. It's quite simple and you can learn how to do this in a video I uploaded on the bonus webpage:

https://www.trader-dale.com/investing-book

Password: happy trading

# Volume Profile Trading Setups

In this chapter, I will teach you how to pick the best price levels for investment entries. We will do this using my Volume Profile setups.

The main logic behind those setups is:

1. Never buy a stock when it is at its historical highs (maximum price ever). Smart investors don't do that. What you need to do instead is to wait for the price to drop. Then buy it. But drop where? See point n.2.

2. The best place to make your investment is in heavy volume areas. You simply wait until your desired stock drops to such a heavy volume area, and then you buy it.

Check out this example before we jump into the Volume Profile setups:

Agilent Technologies (A); Daily chart:

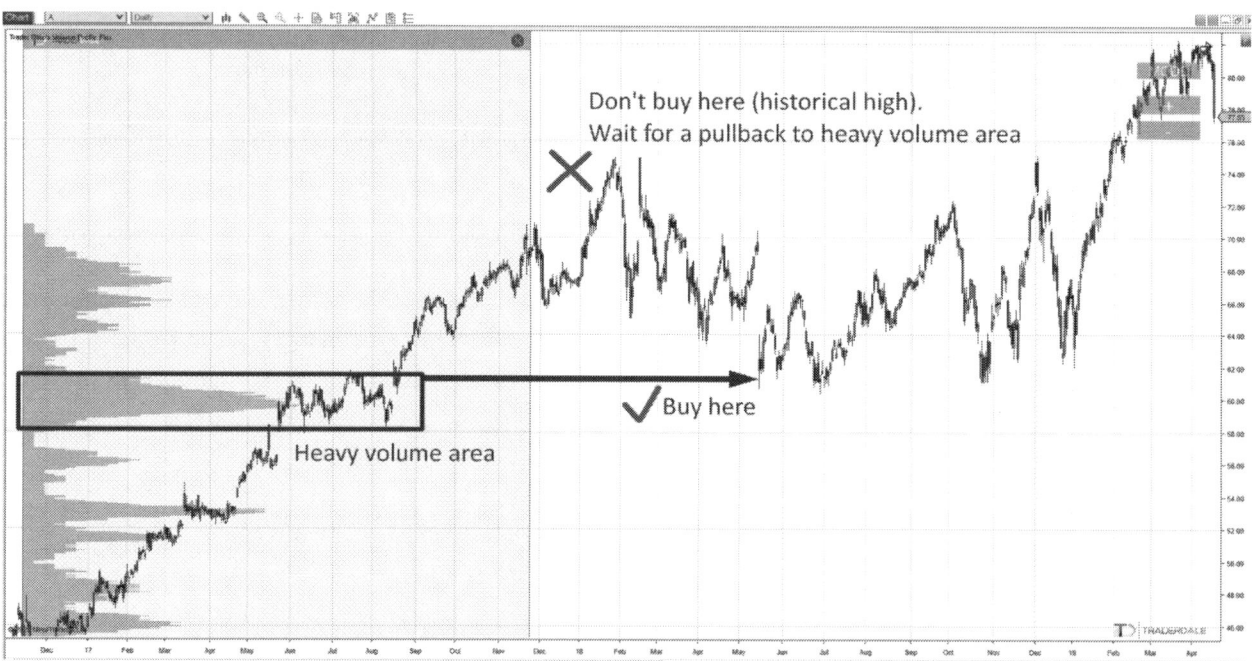

The Daily chart above shows the stock of a company called Agilent Technologies (A). A stock I randomly picked to show you how we will go about all this. As you can see, the price was rising and creating new highs. It wouldn't be clever to try and chase the market by buying the stock as it was going up. It's better to wait for a pullback (a discount).

I used Volume Profile to identify a place where heavy volumes were traded – in other words where trading institutions placed a lot of their orders. This area represents a good place to buy stock. You only need to be patient enough and wait for the price to drop back to this price level. In this case, it took almost a year. But that's fine. It's worth the wait.

Let me give you one more example, and then we jump right into the setups and the concrete steps on how to trade them.

AbbVie (ABBV); Daily chart:

The chart above is another random stock I picked to show you how to use the Volume Profile to pick the right spot to make your investment.

The chart shows a very long rotation in which massive volumes were traded (= big institutions were active there). Then the price started to rise sharply. It would not be a good idea to join in and start buying as the price was reaching new historical highs. Instead, it would be best to wait for the price to make it back into the heavy volume zone (wait for a discount). Then make your investment there.

So, that was a little snippet of what we are going to do. Let's now break down the Volume Profile setups so you can start using them yourself!

# Volume Profile Setup #1: Volume Accumulation Setup

This is my favorite setup. It is based on the fact that big trading institutions first need to enter their huge trading positions before manipulating the market into a new trend. They enter their huge positions in a rotation. This is the only place where they can accumulate large volumes without being seen and without their intentions being recognized.

The setup has three steps:

1. Look for a price rotation/tight channel that is followed by a strong uptrend. What happens in such formation is that big institutions are accumulating their trading positions (in the rotation) and then they start the trend.

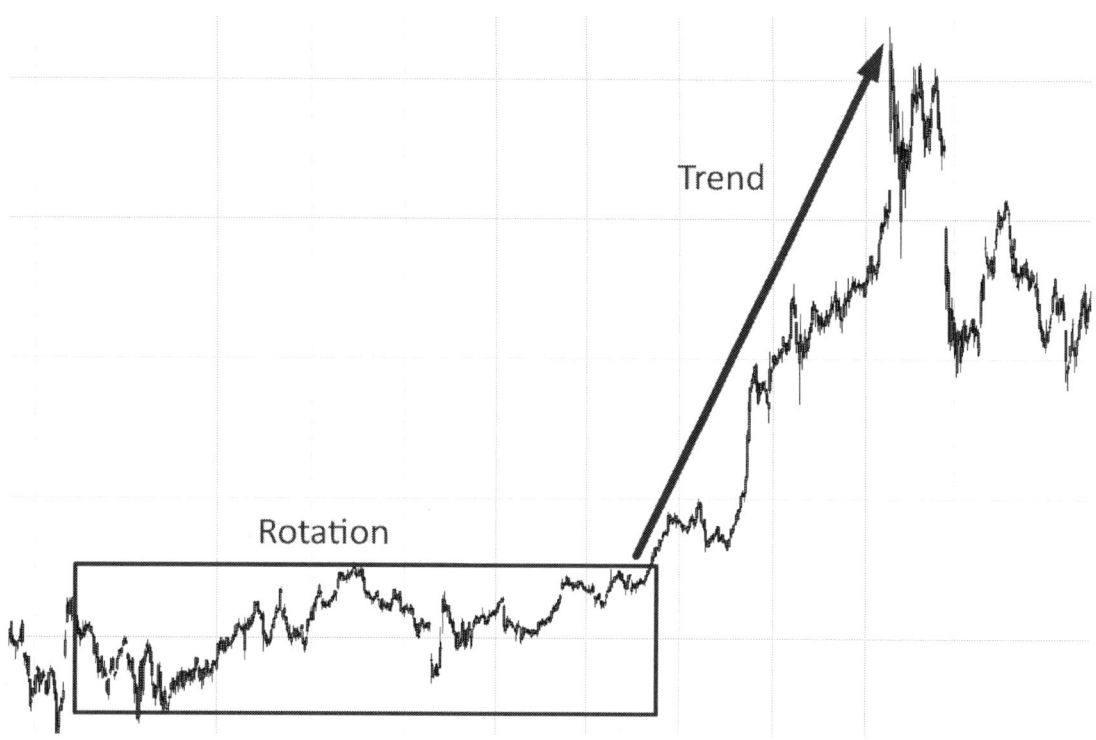

2. Use Volume Profile in the rotation area to identify where the heaviest volumes were. The area where the heaviest volumes got traded is a strong Support.

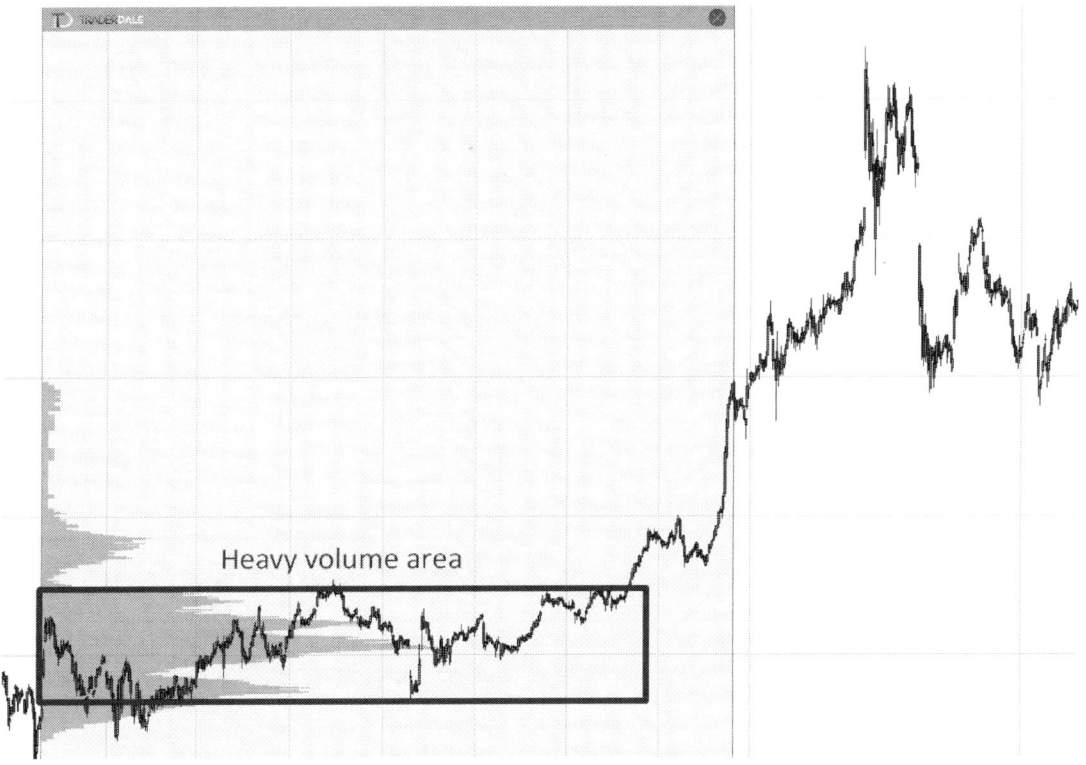

3. Wait for the price to make it back into the heavy volume area again and buy your stock there. BTW do you recognize the chart? It is the chart from the example I showed you on the AbbVie (ABBV) stock earlier.

You need to be patient. Sometimes this will take months, or even years for the price to make it back. It doesn't matter how long it takes though. Markets have a great memory. You only need to set an alert or a limit order there so that you don't miss the opportunity.

Don't worry, you are going to have a watchlist with for example 30-50 stocks with limit orders like this, so it's not going to be like you waiting a year for one single investment opportunity.

*NOTE: An important rule is that the heavy volume zone hasn't been tested yet. This means that the price hasn't made a pullback to that volume zone yet. If it has already been tested, then it's no longer viable to trade. 1$^{st}$ tests have a better chance of a successful reaction.

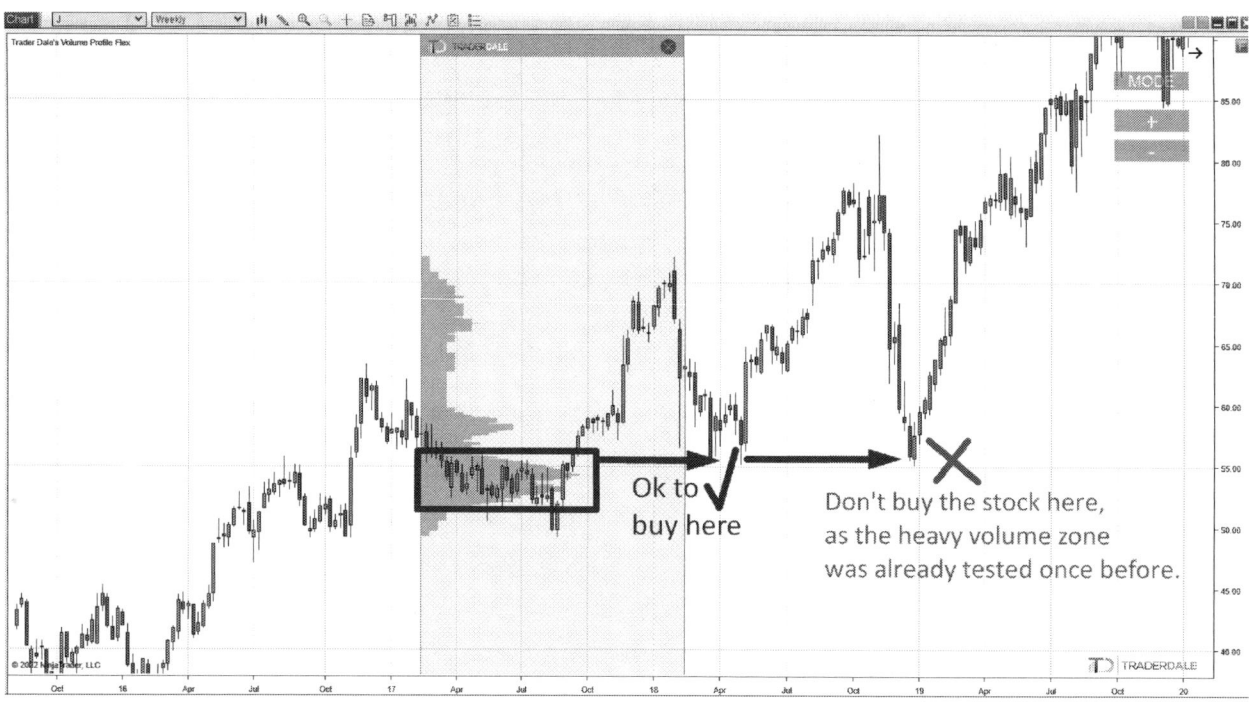

**Where exactly to enter the trade?**

There are two viable options to invest in:

The 1st option is to do it at the beginning of the heavy volume zone. That's the place where the volumes start to rise significantly.

The 2nd option is to do the trade at the place where the volumes were the heaviest (where the Volume Profile is the widest). This place is called the Point of Control (POC).

Either way is fine. I used to trade from POC in the past, but then I started to use the 1st option (trade from the beginning of the heavy volume zone). The reason is that sometimes the price turns a bit earlier and it doesn't make it as far as the POC, resulting in a missed opportunity. Nobody likes a missed opportunity, right? For this reason, I prefer entering the trade a bit earlier so I can be sure my Limit order gets hit.

## The Logic Behind Volume Accumulation Setup

Let me now explain the logic behind this setup. There are two reasons (factors) why the price reacts to these volume zones so nicely. This reasoning also applies to the other volume setups I am going to show you later.

**Reason #1:** Strong institutions who were buying stocks in a heavy volume area are likely to defend this area. The area is important for them as they were massively buying there before.

When the price returns to the volume accumulation area, they start to buy more. They often buy aggressively and by this, they try to move the price upwards again.

**Reason #2:** Nobody wants to risk a fight with strong institutional Buyers

Let me demonstrate this by using an example: First, strong Buyers accumulated their positions in a sideways rotation. Then they pushed the price aggressively upwards. After that, the Buyers stopped pushing the price upward for a while, and Sellers took over. They were pushing the price lower and lower, but when they approached the strong rotation where the aggressive Buyers had accumulated their massive positions before, the Sellers stopped their selling activity and closed their positions. Why? Because they didn't want to risk a fight with strong and aggressive Buyers.

When somebody is in a Short position and wants to close their position, they buy. So, when those Sellers start to buy to get rid of their Short positions, they help to drive the price upwards.

Let me make this clearer with a picture:

It is the combination of these two factors that drive the price upwards from the heavy volume zones. That's why they work as strong supports.

## Why Not Trade This as a Breakout Strategy?

A typical question I often get is why not buy the stock when it starts to move away from the rotation area where heavy volumes were (a breakout strategy). Like this:

The reason I don't recommend this is that there are often many "false breakouts". This means that the price leaves the rotation area but then quickly returns to this area again. Such a strategy simply gives too many bad signals.

For this reason, I prefer to do it the way I showed you earlier and avoid doing those "breakouts."

## EXAMPLES: The Volume Accumulation Setup

The theory is one thing, but in my opinion, it's always better to show real examples and real market situations to demonstrate the trading setup I want you to learn. So, in this place, I am going to give you a couple of examples of the Volume Accumulation Setup.

As you can notice, I am using only the Daily or Weekly chart. I don't recommend using faster time frames because we want to see the big picture to plan our investments. If I had to pick whether to use Daily or Weekly time frames, then I would recommend the Weekly time frame because it gives us the bigger picture.

Another thing I would like to tell you before we go into the examples is that I picked examples that nicely represent what I am trying to teach you. In reality, there will be many occasions when the setups fail and when the price drops even below the best-looking volume-based Supports.

This is a game of probability, and we will never be 100% right. If we are right in about 65 – 70% of cases, then I take it as a success!

Also, picking the right price level is only half of the strategy. The other half is picking the right stock. If you pick the right stock and if you mess up the trade entry, then it's quite likely that in a couple of years you will still be happy with the outcome. Good stocks recover well from failures and tend to grow better than bad stocks. A bad trade entry with good stock is not a disaster. It's better than a bad trade entry with a bad stock.

One final note I would like to say is that stocks are a very volatile trading instrument. They sometimes overshoot heavy volume zones that are supposed to work as Supports only to react later. In other words, the reactions are not as precise as we would like. So, don't despair if the reaction to a heavy volume zone is not immediate.

Also, stocks are very dependent on the whole economy and the economy index. If there is something big happening (COVID-19 pandemic for example) then everything falls – indexes and stocks as well. Everything falls and there is not much to do about it. If you already own stocks that start falling sharply as a result of such an event, then I recommend holding your horses and don't panic. Hold your stocks as they will most likely recover back sooner or later. If you don't own any stocks and the markets start to collapse, then it could be a nice opportunity for making a new portfolio of currently discounted stocks.

**Example #1:** The PNC Financial Services Group (PNC), Weekly chart:

Notice how strongly the price went up from the heavy volume area. This is a sign of strong and aggressive institutional buyers. I always like to see such strong activity commencing from heavy-volume areas. It confirms the strength of the buyers.

**Example #2:** Church & Dwight (CHD), Weekly chart:

The reaction to our Support was a quick one. Sometimes it is like this and that's why I recommend using Limit (pending) orders for your trade entries. If it happens too quickly, then you may miss the opportunity if you didn't set a Limit order.

**Example #3:** Bank of America Corporation (BAC), Weekly chart:

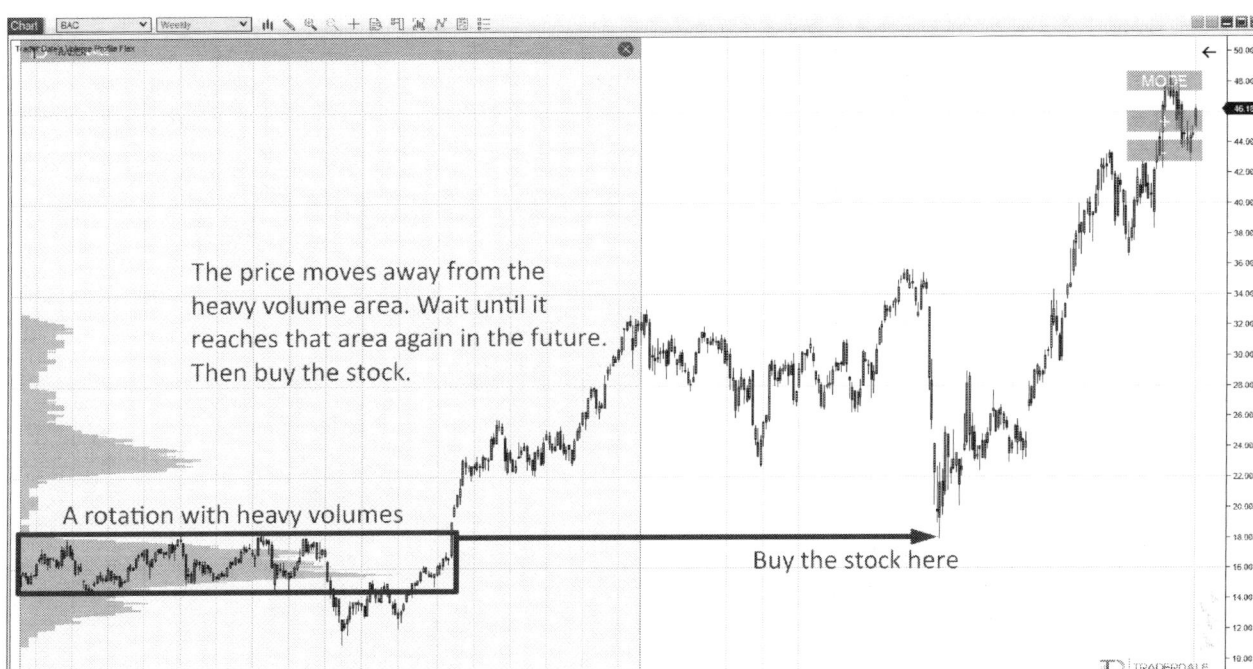

If you wanted to buy your stocks at the Point of Control (POC), then you would miss the opportunity here because the price reacted to the beginning of the heavy volume zone and missed the POC.

Also, this would be quite a risky investment as there was a really strong sell-off on the BAC stock caused by the COVID-19 pandemic. As I said earlier, if there is any significant problem with the economy, banks and financial institutions are the first ones to fall, and they fall the hardest. In this case, the Bank of America recovered because the FED saved them by lending them huge amounts of money almost for free.

**Example #4:** Booking Holdings (BKNG), Weekly chart:

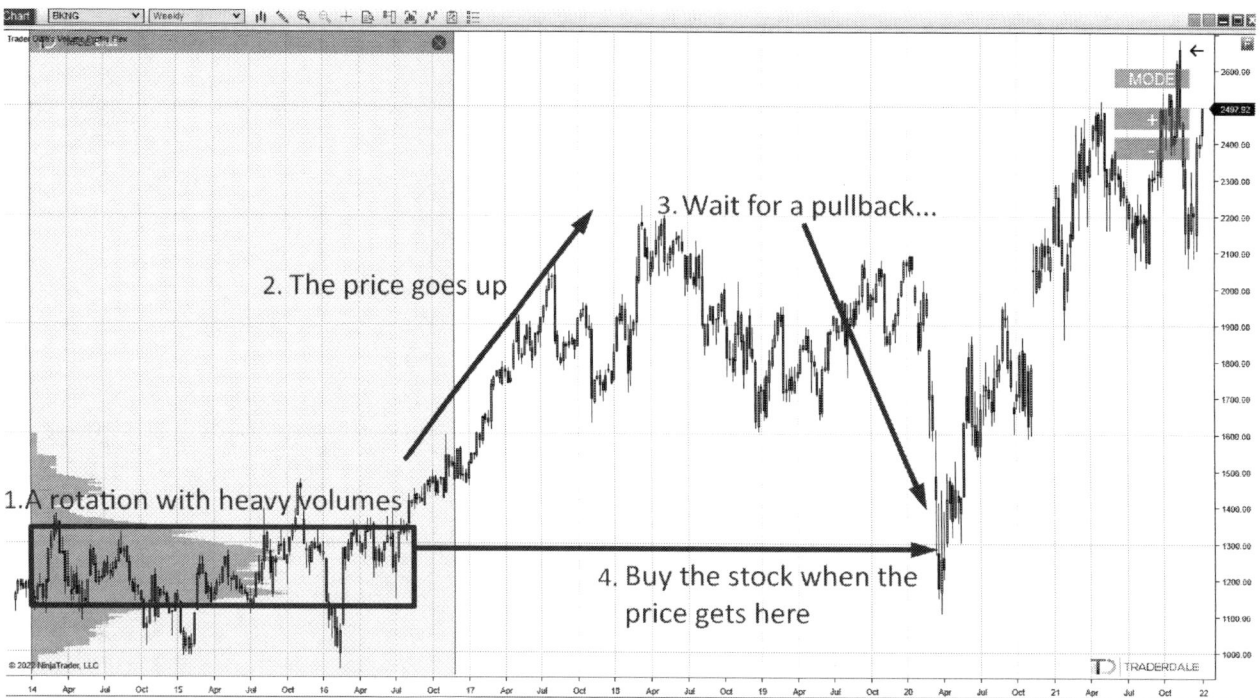

In this case, the price overshot the Support zone but then recovered quickly. When there is a sell-off like this (again, caused by the COVID-19 pandemic-related problems), then you need to be fine with the price not reacting exactly to the level. The price could overshoot your Support or even completely ignore it. However, if it is a solid company then it would be a good investment even if the price went past the Support and fell even lower.

**Example #5:** Hanesbrands (HBI), Weekly chart:

**Example #6:** Vertex Pharmaceuticals (VRTX), Weekly chart:

Quite a tight rotation followed by a steep trend. That's how I like this setup to look. The reason is that a tight rotation often gives a clear place for a trade entry, and the strong trend confirms the strength of buyers.

**Example #7:** Amazon.com (AMZN), Weekly chart:

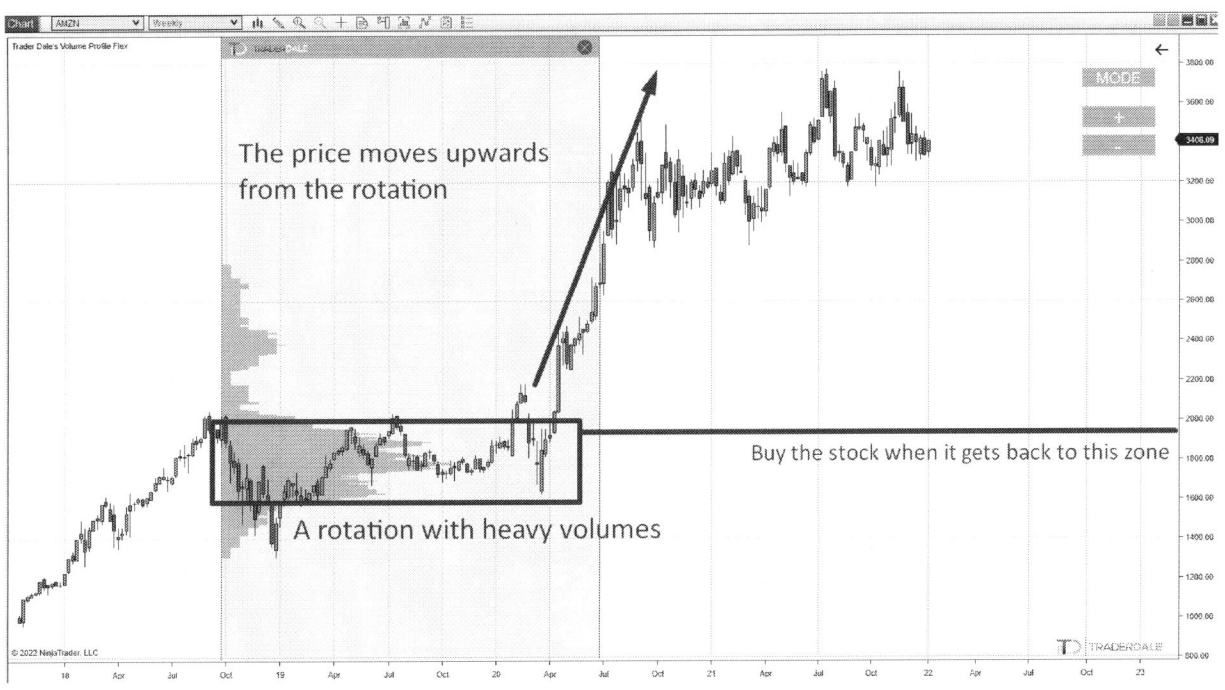

In this case, the trade has not played out yet (at least not when I was writing this). There was a rotation with heavy volumes, then a really strong, easy-to-identify trend. The next step is to wait for a pullback and make your investment when it hits the Support.

**Example #8:** Deere & Company (DE), Weekly chart:

A similar scenario as with Amazon above. There is a rotation followed by a strong trend. The Support has not been tested yet, so we need to wait and be ready to jump in!

# Volume Profile Setup #2: Trend Setup

This setup is based on the fact that there is not much time for buying huge amounts of stocks when there is a trend. As I said earlier, the BIG guys need time to allocate their money. But, sometimes, the trend movement halts for a bit and the BIG guys have some time to buy bigger amounts of stocks.

Such areas show as a little "bump" on the otherwise thin Volume Profile. Those "bumps" are called Volume Clusters. Those Volume Clusters often work as strong support zones. The price tends to react to them and bounce off them. That's why such places are ideal for buying your stocks.

Marriott International (MAR), Weekly chart:

Here are the exact steps on how to go about this:

1. There needs to be a clear and strong uptrend. It needs to be easy to see and easy to identify. Ideally on a Weekly chart.

2. When you have found that uptrend, use the Volume Profile indicator to see the volume distribution within the uptrend.

3. Look for a significant Volume Cluster (or more Volume Clusters) that were created within the trend. The Volume Cluster represents a place where huge volumes were traded, and where institutions bought most of their stocks.

4. Wait for a pullback. Ideally set a Limit order so you don't miss your opportunity. Buy your stocks when the price drops and hits the area where the Volume Cluster was.

5. An important rule is that the Volume Cluster hasn't been tested yet. This means that the price hasn't made a pullback to that Volume Cluster yet. If it has already been tested, then it's no longer viable to trade.

Bank of America Corporation (BAC), Weekly chart:

### **Where exactly to enter the trade?**

Very similar to the previous setup (the Volume Accumulation Setup), there are two options for where to buy your stocks. It's either at the beginning of the heavy volume zone (that's what I prefer), or the 2nd option is at the place where the volumes were the heaviest (the Point of Control).

The reason I prefer the 1st option is that this way I miss fewer opportunities than with the 2nd option. I prefer to invest a bit sooner, than miss the opportunity.

Costco Wholesale Corporation (COST), Weekly chart:

## EXAMPLES: The Trend Setup

**Example #1:** Cerner Corporation (CERN), Weekly chart:

There was a nice and tight rotation in the middle of the trend and heavy volumes were traded in the rotation before the uptrend continued aggressively upwards. I like the aggressive start after the rotation. That's what I always like to see because it nicely shows the aggressivity & strength of Buyers who started to manipulate the price to shoot upwards. I also like the shape of the Volume Profile (in the rotation area) that makes it very easy to spot the price level to make your investment making this situation very clear to read and trade.

**Example #2:** General Mills (GIS), Weekly chart:

There was a rotation on the GIS stock before 2020, but when the COVID-19 pandemic started in the 1st quarter of 2020 the price went wildly up & down. This is a scenario where traders trading breakout strategies would suffer losses. After the situation had settled down, the price went upwards in a strong uptrend showing us that it was Buyers who were in control and that the uptrend would continue. That's information worth the wait. The next step was just to wait for the pullback and buy the stocks for a discounted price at the beginning of the Volume Cluster.

**Example #3:** Illinois Tool Works (ITW), Weekly chart:

I would like you to notice the strength of the uptrend that continues after the Volume Cluster (those 4 steep green candles). I always look for aggressive starts of trends like this because it shows the strength of Buyers – those Buyers who would defend this zone in the future.

**Example #4:** Jacobs Engineering Group (J), Weekly chart:

In this case, the buying activity after the Volume Cluster was super strong and the trend was steep. A perfect scenario! What is also nice to see is how slowly the price went back to the Support level. I like this because it shows strong and aggressive Buyers in contrast with slow and shy Sellers with no real determination behind the pullback. Who will win when those two start fighting at the Support? Yes – the Buyers!

**Example #5:** Jack Henry & Associates (JKHY), Weekly chart:

Once again, notice how aggressively the trend shoots upwards after the Volume Cluster has formed. That's a sign of strong Buyers. That's what I like to see at a Support zone.

**Example #6:** The Coca-Cola Company (KO), Weekly chart:

There are more Volume Clusters in this example, but the one I marked is the strongest. That's the one to trade. In this case, the trade entry is very easy to see. It's not always like this, unfortunately.

**Example #7:** The Home Depot (HD), Weekly chart:

In this case, the Volume Profile shows two significant Volume Clusters formed within the uptrend. Both represent viable Supports. I recommend waiting for the price to make a pullback to the 1st one and invest ½ of your trading position there. Then, if the price continues to drop (which is possible), consider it an even bigger discount and enter the 2nd half of your trading position at the lower Volume Cluster.

This is a method I recommend doing in most cases. Identify two strong Supports (no matter which setup you use), ideally not too close to each other, then split your investment into halves and if the price continues to drop you will still have money to buy for an even better discount.

You can even have some more free money ready for a scenario when the price drops even more and hits 3rd Support, which should be at some ridiculously low price (super discount). Such a scenario won't happen too often, but if you have for example 30-50 stocks on your watchlist, then chances are that a couple of them could offer you such a chance to buy cheap.

# When to Sell Your Stocks?

So far, I have been talking about how to pick your stocks and determine the best place to invest. Now I will show you when to sell your stocks.

Generally speaking, you want to get rid of your stocks when the whole economy index is too high and stocks are generally overpriced. Also, when stock prices no longer correspond with their fundamentals.

## The Stock Index is Too High

The first clue that you should start thinking about selling your stocks, is when the economy index is skyrocketing. So, if we talk about US stocks, then you look at the S&P 500 index. If we talk about European stocks, you best check the Euro Stoxx 50 index, if we talk about UK-based companies, then you check FTSE 100, German companies would be DAX, and Chinese would be Hang Seng index, etc. You can find the corresponding indexes here: https://countryeconomy.com/stock-exchange

A simple glance at the index should give you at least a rough idea of what is going on with stocks generally. If the index is at its historical highs (it has never been higher), then it's time to think about selling your stocks. Not all of them at once, but you should start thinking about slowly reducing your portfolio.

I know that this advice may sound weird because indices have been growing steadily for the last couple of years now, creating new and new highs. However, this growth was driven by the central bank's "free money" policy, and this policy won't last forever.

If the stock index is climbing to new all-time highs, I recommend having only about 50% of your funds invested in stocks and reducing that number the more the stock prices continue to rise. You may even end up with for example 10-20% capital invested.

By this time, you should simply be waiting for a drop to invest your money again. In the meantime, you can invest your free capital elsewhere. For example, corporate bond ETFs. Another option to allocate your money is you can look for different markets (different countries) to invest in. Those countries obviously shouldn't have their indices at all-time highs either. Pick the ones that present an opportunity for a cheap investment.

## Company P/E Became Too High

Another reason to start selling your stocks is when the company's market valuation grew way above its real value. The simplest way to determine this is to check the company's P/E.

The P/E ratio represents the current market price versus earnings. For this reason, it's a good tool to measure whether a stock is overpriced or not. It is not a Holy Grail as I have already shown you before, but it is a good indication.

An average or "normal" P/E is different for each sector so I cannot give you an exact P/E value to start selling. What you can do is use this general rule which should give you at least some guidelines to start with:

First, go to this site and learn what the average P/E in your sector is:

https://www.gurufocus.com/industry_overview.php

If for example, you have stocks from the Basic Materials sector, then the chart shows that the average is somewhere around 15-20.

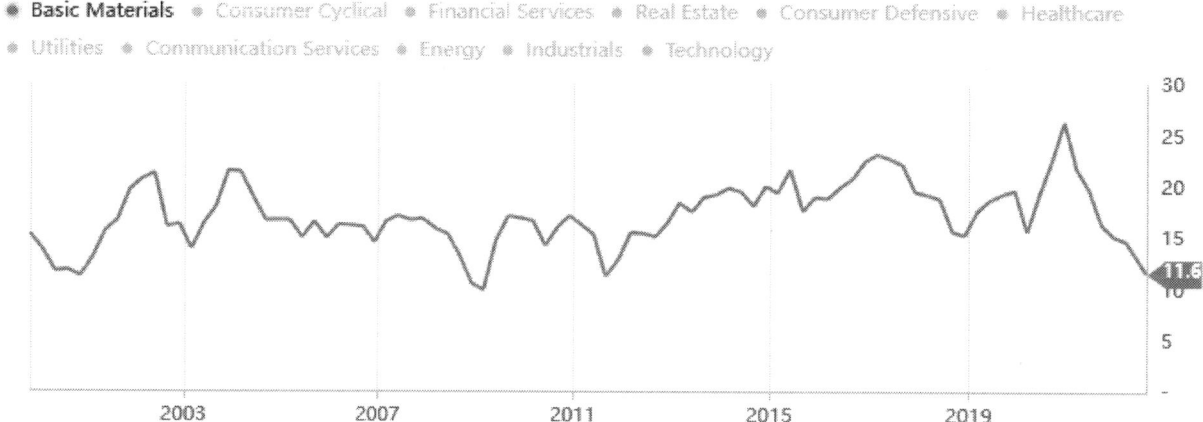

When the P/E of your stock goes way above this, roughly +50% or more over the average, then it may be a good time to start thinking about selling.

## It's the Combination of Warning Signals That Tell You When to Sell

Don't base your decision only on P/E though. It's a combination of these events that should make you sell:

1. A stock index is too high, making new all-time highs.
2. The price of the stock has made a solid performance and you made a lot of money on it
3. The company's P/E is above 50% of the sector average P/E.

At this point, you should get rid of at least a portion of your stocks. Then if the index, stock price, and P/E continue to grow, you should be selling some more until the point where you hold just a tiny fraction of the shares you initially bought, or until you sell them all.

## Sell When a Stock Has No Bright Future

You won't need this too often but there is also another reason when you can sell your stocks. This is the reason I picked it up from Warren Buffet. He says that you should sell your stocks if the company or the industry has fundamentally changed (= you see no bright future for the company or industry anymore). Two examples of when he did such a thing: 1st was when he sold his Washington Post shares (newspapers). The reason is pretty obvious from today's perspective – newspapers are a medium that has no bright future. Internet media replaced it, no doubt about that. The second example was when he sold airplane company stocks because of COVID-19. Remember when covid hit hard the first time and airports just shut down? That's exactly it. Even now, there are restrictions on traveling and airplane companies simply don't have the income they used to.

In permanent changes in the industry like these, it's simply best to get rid of your stocks. It's a waste of money that could be invested elsewhere.

# Recap of the Steps We Have Already Taken

Let me do a little recap of the steps we have made so far.

At this point, you should have a list of stocks that you would like to own – a list that you created using the Finviz screener. You should have that saved as a portfolio in the Finviz platform.

## Fundamental Criteria

Those are the stock lists for each sector. Each list met the fundamental criteria I showed you before:

**Communication Services sector**

| No. | Ticker | Company |
|---|---|---|
| 1. | ATHM | Autohome Inc. |
| 2. | CMCSA | Comcast Corporation |
| 3. | FOXA | Fox Corporation |
| 4. | NXST | Nexstar Media Group, Inc. |
| 5. | TEF | Telefonica, S.A. |
| 6. | TGNA | TEGNA Inc. |
| 7. | TKC | Turkcell Iletisim Hizmetleri A.S. |
| 8. | VIAC | ViacomCBS Inc. |
| | Total | 8 Stocks |

**Consumer Cyclical sector**

| No. | Ticker | Company |
|---|---|---|
| 1. | KBH | KB Home |
| 2. | LKQ | LKQ Corporation |
| 3. | RUSHA | Rush Enterprises, Inc. |
| 4. | THO | Thor Industries, Inc. |
| 5. | WGO | Winnebago Industries, Inc. |
| | Total | 5 Stocks |

## Consumer defensive sector

| No. | Ticker | Company |
|---|---|---|
| 1. | ADM | Archer-Daniels-Midland Company |
| 2. | IBA | Industrias Bachoco, S.A.B. de C.V. |
| 3. | NUS | Nu Skin Enterprises, Inc. |
| 4. | TSN | Tyson Foods, Inc. |
| Total | | 4 Stocks |

## Energy sector

| No. | Ticker | Company |
|---|---|---|
| 1. | CNQ | Canadian Natural Resources Limited |
| Total | | 1 Stock |

## Financial sector

| No. | Ticker | Company |
|---|---|---|
| 1. | BEN | Franklin Resources, Inc. |
| 2. | CINF | Cincinnati Financial Corporation |
| 3. | FAF | First American Financial Corporation |
| 4. | FHI | Federated Hermes, Inc. |
| 5. | FNF | Fidelity National Financial, Inc. |
| 6. | MCY | Mercury General Corporation |
| 7. | ORI | Old Republic International Corporation |
| 8. | RDN | Radian Group Inc. |
| Total | | 8 Stocks |

## Healthcare sector

| No. | Ticker | Company |
|---|---|---|
| 1. | ANTM | Anthem, Inc. |
| 2. | COO | The Cooper Companies, Inc. |
| 3. | EBS | Emergent BioSolutions Inc. |
| 4. | FLGT | Fulgent Genetics, Inc. |
| 5. | LH | Laboratory Corporation of America Holdings |
| 6. | SAGE | Sage Therapeutics, Inc. |
| 7. | UHS | Universal Health Services, Inc. |
| Total | | 7 Stocks |

## Industrials sector

| No. | Ticker | Company |
|---|---|---|
| 1. | MATX | Matson, Inc. |
| 2. | OSK | Oshkosh Corporation |
| 3. | SNA | Snap-on Incorporated |
| 4. | SNDR | Schneider National, Inc. |
| 5. | SWK | Stanley Black & Decker, Inc. |
| 6. | TKR | The Timken Company |
| 7. | WERN | Werner Enterprises, Inc. |
| Total | | 7 Stocks |

## Real Estate sector

| No. | Ticker | Company |
|---|---|---|
| 1. | ABR | Arbor Realty Trust, Inc. |
| 2. | GLPI | Gaming and Leisure Properties, Inc. |
| 3. | HIW | Highwoods Properties, Inc. |
| 4. | IRM | Iron Mountain Incorporated |
| 5. | KIM | Kimco Realty Corporation |
| 6. | SLG | SL Green Realty Corp. |
| Total | | 6 Stocks |

## Technology sector

| No. | Ticker | Company |
|---|---|---|
| 1. | DOX | Amdocs Limited |
| 2. | HPE | Hewlett Packard Enterprise Company |
| 3. | INTC | Intel Corporation |
| 4. | UMC | United Microelectronics Corporation |
| 5. | VSH | Vishay Intertechnology, Inc. |
| Total | | 5 Stocks |

## Utilities sector

| No. | Ticker | Company |
|---|---|---|
| 1. | AQN | Algonquin Power & Utilities Corp. |
| 2. | CIG | Companhia Energetica de Minas Gerais |
| 3. | NRG | NRG Energy, Inc. |
| 4. | UGI | UGI Corporation |
| Total | | 4 Stocks |

**Basic materials sector**

| No. | Ticker | Company |
|---|---|---|
| 1. | AU | AngloGold Ashanti Limited |
| 2. | BBL | BHP Group |
| 3. | BHP | BHP Group |
| 4. | GFI | Gold Fields Limited |
| 5. | GGB | Gerdau S.A. |
| 6. | HMY | Harmony Gold Mining Company Limited |
| 7. | RIO | Rio Tinto Group |
| 8. | SBSW | Sibanye Stillwater Limited |
| 9. | TX | Ternium S.A. |
| 10. | VALE | Vale S.A. |
| **Total** | | **10 Stocks** |

In total, that's 65 stocks that made it through our criteria filter. However, we are not going to need all of them. We should get rid of some sectors first. I recommend getting rid of Financials and Technology stocks – which is 13 stocks. This brings our basket of selected stocks down to 52 stocks.

If you spread your investments too wide across many sectors and stocks, then you may as well buy the whole index and it will be cheaper. For this reason, I recommend considering crossing out more sectors. I would personally cross out the Real Estate, and Consumer Cyclical sectors. If we do that, then we are down to 41 stocks.

Those are the sectors that remain after we crossed out a couple of risky ones:

- **Communication**
- **Consumer Defensive**
- **Energy**
- **Healthcare**
- **Industrials**
- **Utilities**
- **Basic Materials**

These sectors currently include 41 stocks that meet our fundamental criteria. Those are the stocks we will work with further.

# Volume Profile Criteria

The next step is opening a chart of each stock from the 41-stock list and looking for a good place (Support) to buy that stock. You have learned how to do this in the "Volume Profile" part of this book.

When you go through the stock charts then there will be cases where it will be very difficult or impossible to identify viable Supports. Don't force it. If there is a stock without a clear heavy volume Support, then it's best to skip it and just move to the next one.

My very rough estimate is that you will be able to find good volume-based Supports in around 50% of stock charts.

This would bring down the number of stocks you can use for building your final portfolio to around 20 stocks (50% from 41 stocks).

20 stocks are an okay number to work with. Not too few, not too many. If you want more, I recommend lowering the criteria in the Finviz screener. Not too drastically though. If there are not many stocks that make it through our criteria, then it is a sign that now is not a good time for investing.

# Building a Portfolio

We are now at the point where we have around 20 stocks with strong volume-based Supports. When the price drops to those Supports, we buy our stocks.

I recommend having two Supports on each stock. When the price drops to the 1st one, then you buy, but only with half of the position. Then, if the price continues to drop even more, and hits your 2nd Support, you enter the 2nd half of your position.

Example:

The more the price drops, the bigger the discount and the better the opportunity to buy good stock cheap! That's why I recommend splitting your position into two halves.

# Money Management

With 20 viable stocks, I recommend having 4% of your investment capital available for each stock. This means that when the price makes a pullback to the 1st Support, you buy for 2% of your capital. When the stock falls even more and hits the 2nd Support, you buy for the remaining 2%. At this point, you have invested 4% (2% +2%).

If the market starts to drop and you buy at all your Supports, then you will have invested 80% of your capital: 20 stocks, 4% risk/each = 80%.

This should be clear but let me make it crystal clear: Each stock gets the same amount of capital. Don't risk more on stocks you like somewhat better than on others. Your money should be equally diversified among your stocks. In my experience, your favorite picks may not perform as well as some other stocks from your list. So, don't play favorites here. Every stock gets the same share of capital.

If your capital is $100.000, and you have 20 stocks on your watchlist, then each stock gets $4.000. Additionally, there is a $20.000 reserve for stocks that get super discounted. That's $80.000 + $20.000 reserve.

## 20% Reserve

I recommend having 20% as a reserve for extra opportunities. If there happens to be a huge market crash (and I believe there will be), then there will be many opportunities to buy good companies dirt-cheap. It would be a shame having no money to invest at this point, right? That's why I recommend having the 20% reserve.

I recommend going through the stock charts and looking for a 3$^{rd}$ Support additionally to the two Supports you already have. Such 3$^{rd}$ Support should be really low. I mean crazy low! That would be the one where the stock is dirt cheap. For example, if a stock is currently selling for $100, then your 1$^{st}$ support could be at $70, 2$^{nd}$ Support at $40, and 3$^{rd}$ Support (the catastrophic scenario Support) at $10.

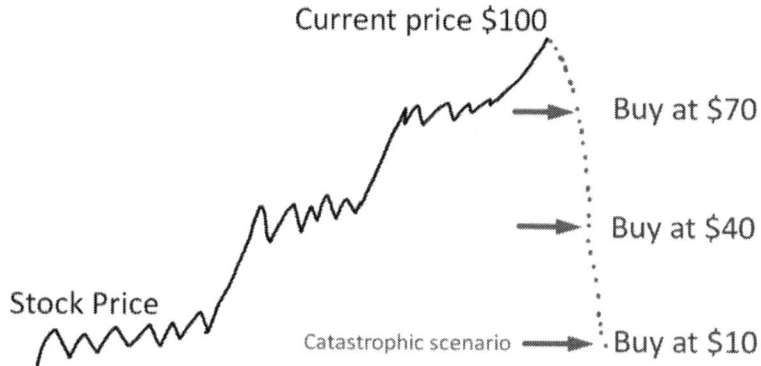

A good thing about this is the more the price drops the more stocks you can buy - with the same amount of money.

If 2% of your capital is $2.000, then when the 1$^{st}$ Support (from the example above) gets hit, you could buy **28** stocks ($2000/$70). When the price drops to the 2$^{nd}$ Support, then you could buy **50** stocks ($2000/$40). If the price drops as low as $10/per share, and the stock fundamentals remain more or less good, then you can use the money from the "20% reserve" and buy **200** stocks ($2000/$10).

The "20% reserve" is here just for extreme cases though. You shouldn't be using it too much.

Some people may say this approach is risky because it is somewhat close to "Martingale" (increasing your risk after each unsuccessful attempt). I say it's exactly the opposite! The cheaper the stock gets, the better opportunity for a buy it is. The stock is just being discounted.

The fundamentals of the stock must not be changing drastically. We only want good stocks that are discounted. We don't want bad cheap stocks.

## The Problem With the "Standard Portfolio Theory"

My approach goes against the "standard portfolio theory" which measures risk using Beta. This theory would say that buying a stock that is dropping fast in a market crash is super risky and portfolio managers following this theory would never do it. What they would do – based on this theory is they would buy an overpriced stock right at its peak just before the drop (because it was growing steadily in the last 5 years) – because at this point Beta would assess the stock as a low-risk stock.

## No Leverage

I strongly recommend using no leverage when investing in stocks. The reason is that when there is a market crash, all stocks fall rapidly. They will most likely return to the original prices after some time, but if you were using leverage, then a market crash could simply wipe your account out.

## No Stop Loss

I don't think it's necessary to use Stop Loss. It's because if you don't use leverage, then the worst-case scenario is that the stock price drops to its book value (more or less). The book value acts like your Stop Loss.

If the company goes under, then what remains (after the company's debts are covered) goes to shareholders (you). That's what you get in the worst-case scenario. The bigger the book value, the more you get.

## Limit Orders

I recommend using limit orders (pending orders) for buying your stocks. The reason is that it is too time-consuming to follow for example 20 stocks every day to see if the price hit an important Support or not.

With a limit order, your trade will get filled automatically and you won't need to sit at the computer all the time, waiting for the trade entry.

Another advantage is that you won't miss any opportunities. What happens sometimes is that the pullback is only a quick one and you only have a couple of minutes or hours to invest. If you miss it, then you might not get a second chance. Such a situation won't happen if you use limit orders as your stocks will be bought automatically, even if your computer is shut down.

Limit order/pending order/waiting order is a standard feature every stockbroker has in its trading platform.

## Alerts

Another way to monitor your selected stocks is through alerts. An alert is a notification that lets you know when the price of a given stock reached a certain price level (this could be for example your volume-based Support).

If you don't want to use limit orders, then you can use alerts instead. When the alert goes off you go to your computer, check the situation out and decide what to do.

Stockbrokers often offer an alert service on their platform. A viable alternative is using a stock alert mobile app. Here are a couple of very simple apps you can use:

**Stock Alarm:** Not free, but with a 7-day trial. Has various paid subscription plans.

https://apps.apple.com/us/app/stock-alarm-alerts-screener/id1465535138

**Stock Alert:** Has 10 free alarms. The full version costs $34.99/year.

https://apps.apple.com/us/app/stock-alert-market-alarm-app/id1245243443

**MarketCue:** Free. It is quite simple, only with mobile push notifications but it does the trick.

https://apps.apple.com/us/app/marketcue-stock-price-alerts/id1477346603

## Free Capital Allocation

The approach I showed you - where you wait for the opportunity (discount) and buy only when the price is good, will sometimes mean that you will have a lot of free, unallocated capital. Some people may see this as a disadvantage, because nothing is more boring than just sitting on a big pile of cash, waiting for your moment, right?

If you don't want to sit and wait on that big pile of cash, then you can make use of it in the meantime. There are a couple of things you can do with your money.

You can have your money in a bank account (which generates only a very little interest), you can buy dividend stocks, or you can invest in corporate bond ETFs. The important thing is that you always have immediate access to your money. This means you can withdraw it anytime and use it to buy stocks when a good opportunity arises.

I advise getting ETFs that invest in corporate bonds over getting dividend stocks. The reason is that most opportunities on stocks will arise when the stock market drops. When the whole market is dropping, it usually drags down all stocks with it - including dividend stocks. This means that you would need to sell your dividend stocks cheap to buy some other stocks that also fell. That doesn't make too much sense, does it? That's why I recommend getting corporate bond ETFs.

## Bond ETFs

I recommend allocating your free capital into corporate bonds ETFs, as they are not correlated to stocks too much. Most often they don't correlate at all or there is a negative correlation (this means that when stock prices are falling, bond prices are rising – which is exactly what you need).

Here is a table that compares stocks (S&P 500 index) and a big corporate bond ETF:

*The rising light blue line is the S&P 500, and the black, more or less steady line is the bond ETF.

Note that the black line (corporate bond ETF) is only showing the price of the ETF, not the income it generates regularly.

Here is a couple of corporate and one government bond ETF you can check out:

### AGG

This one has made around 3.9 %/year on average since it was founded in 2003.

https://www.ishares.com/us/products/239458/ishares-core-total-us-bond-market-etf

### JNK

This one made over 5%/year on average since its inception in 2007. It invests in riskier corporate bonds (rating (Ba1/BB+/BB+ or below) that generate quite high returns.

https://www.ssga.com/us/en/intermediary/etfs/funds/spdr-bloomberg-high-yield-bond-etf-jnk

### HYG

This one has made around 5.44%/year on average since it has been founded in 2007

https://www.ishares.com/us/products/239565/

### VTIP

VTIP is not a corporate bond ETF, but a government bond ETF. This means that it invests in government bonds, which are generally safer than corporate bonds. I mention this one because it is inflation protected. This means it is to outperform inflation. I think this could become quite handy as inflation is now becoming a big threat.

The average annual return is only 1.8% since its inception in 2012, but for example, in the last 3 years, the average return was over 5%.

https://investor.vanguard.com/etf/profile/VTIP

## Other Markets to Diversify

In this book, I have only mentioned stocks that are quoted in the main US exchanges. However, it doesn't have to stop there. You can also build your portfolio from other stocks. To do this you need to use other stock screeners (apart from Finviz which is only for stocks quoted on AMEX, NASDAQ, and NYSE).

I recommend using **Yahoo Finance**, or **MarketInOut** screeners to expand your search to other exchanges (Canada, Australia, China).

The only thing you need to make sure of is that your broker has access to those other exchanges. Not many brokers have access to all the main exchanges. In my experience, each broker offers only a couple of exchanges to pick your stocks. For example, you may end up with a broker that has access to the US, and Australian exchanges, but not to Canadian exchanges, …

Still, there are hundreds and hundreds of stocks to pick from on each exchange so I wouldn't be worried about not having access to all exchanges too much. I just wanted to point it out so that you are not surprised when you pick a Chinese company and then find out that your broker doesn't have access to the Chinese exchange where this company is listed.

## Difference Between Stocks and Stock CFDs

Should you invest in stocks or stock CFDs? Stockbrokers often offer not just stock trading, but also CFD trading. So, what's the difference?

With CFD products you don't invest in the stock itself, but you only "speculate" whether the stock price will go up or down. You don't own stocks and you are not a shareholder. This isn't such a big deal as stock CFDs copy the price development of the underlying stock and most brokers also pay out dividends you would get if you owned the stock.

What is a big deal though, is that you need to pay a fee for holding CFDs overnight (it's called swap). This is the main reason I don't recommend investing in stocks through CFDs. Even though those fees are very small, they pile up. Investing is about holding your stocks for years and paying those fees every day would just ruin your account.

*NOTE: *You always pay a swap, even if you use no leverage.*

There are some positives in trading CFDs – like high leverage, but we don't need that. High leverage is useful if you want to day trade stocks (quick in & out trades, often a couple of trades per day), but that's not the strategy this book is about.

The bottom line is – stock investing through CFDs is too expensive because of the swap fees you are charged every day you hold the stock. For this reason, I recommend investing in actual stocks rather than CFDs.

## How Much Money You Need

A couple of years ago I would tell you that you need at least $5.000 - $10.000 to start with. But times change and you can now do it with far less.

I am not saying you SHOULD do it with less. I would recommend doing it with more. But if you are just getting started and you are not comfortable throwing $10.000 in the game right away, then there is a way.

The thing is that there are stocks that are quite expensive, for example, Tesla (TSLA) which is currently around $1.000 per share. If you were to invest 2% in this stock, how would you do that if your total capital was $5.000? The problem is that a single TSLA stock would cost you $1.000 which is 20% of your capital.

There are three options/compromises you could do:

- Avoid expensive stocks
- Choose far fewer companies to invest in
- Disregard money management that tells you to invest a max of 2-4% in a single company

But that sucks, right? We need a wide variety of stocks to choose from, not just the cheap ones. We need a broad portfolio of stocks and we need to have solid money management.

The solution? A bigger account (and maybe avoid super expensive stocks like Tesla, because $1.000/stock that's too much).

Another solution (and this is a big thing) is "Fractional Shares"

## Fractional Shares

Fractional shares are a solution for small investors with limited capital because they deal with the problem of expensive stocks. If your broker offers fractional shares, then you can simply buy a fraction of a stock instead of the whole stock. That's it.

**Example:** If your account is $5.000 and you want to invest 2% of your capital (that's $100 investment) to Tesla, then you simply go to your trading platform and you type in that you want to buy TSLA stock for $100. What you will get is 0.1 of TSLA stock (provided that the current TSLA stock price is $1.000). Simple as that.

A cool thing is that as a shareholder you will also be getting dividends (you own a part of the company).

## Where is the catch?

The catch is that not all stockbrokers offer fractional shares as this product is relatively new. The good thing is that the brokerage industry is highly competitive, and I expect that most stock brokers will catch up and start offering fractional shares as a standard feature soon.

Another small catch is that brokers that do fractional shares offer this only for some stocks. The variety is very high, don't worry, but there are still some limits. For example, Interactive Brokers (a major US broker) offers fractional shares only on stocks that have an average daily volume over $10 million or a market capitalization greater than $400 million.

I am pretty sure those small problems will get better over time. Give it a year or two and I think fractional shares will become a common thing, and most brokers will offer them on a standard basis.

# The Most Common Mistakes

By now, you should be able to pick fundamentally good stocks, use Volume Profile to identify strong price zones (Supports) to invest in those stocks, and you should also be able to build and manage your stock portfolio.

What I would like to address next are some common mistakes people keep repeating over and over. Let's now go through them one by one.

## Don't Extrapolate the Past

Extrapolating means that you look at a chart and you assume that it will continue developing more or less the same way in the future as it was developing in the past. For example:

The picture above shows the extrapolation of the S&P 500 index. Beginner investors often look back and expect that it will continue the same way in the future. History has taught us many times that it is very rarely like that. We simply cannot count on it. It is a mistake. The world is changing and the conditions that drove the S&P index upwards in the last decade most certainly won't be the same in the next decade. S&P was driven upwards by huge stimuli of the money supply. Now, the central bankers are starting to cut that down by rising interest rates. With this, the S&P 500 might not continue growing like it did in the last 10 years.

This doesn't apply only to S&P 500. It applies to all indexes, stocks, and trading instruments. My advice is – don't try to predict the future based on past development. Don't extrapolate.

Another example of an extrapolation is when a stock or another trading instrument is moving sideways in a price range and investors assume that it will continue like this in the future as well. Like here:

The picture above shows a Gaming and Leisure Properties (GLPI) stock and its development in the last 5 years. The range that moved in was roughly $26 to $38. Beginner investors would assume that it would stay in this range in the future as well - which would be a mistake. This is how GLPI development looked after those 5 years:

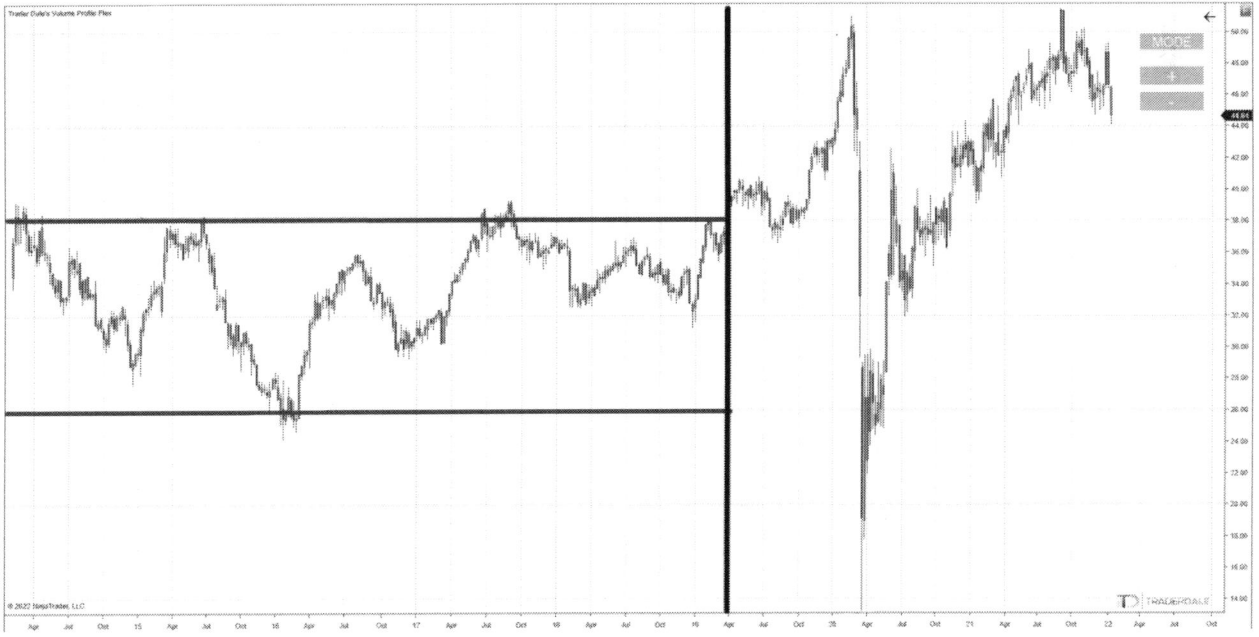

Extrapolating past results simply doesn't work, and my advice is that you should never count on it.

# Don't Buy at All-Time Highs

Buying at high means that you buy a stock that is around its historical highs (all-time highs). Smart money doesn't do that as when something is at its high it is too expensive to buy (because it has never been so expensive before).

It's not only amateur investors who make mistakes but also fund managers. However, each makes mistakes for different reasons.

**Amateur investors**

Amateur investors buy stocks at their highs because they are greedy and don't want to miss an opportunity (which they think is there). Nothing is worse than seeing everybody else making money on that stock that is now skyrocketing, and which you don't own, right? That's why beginner investors fall into this trap and buy at the high. Most of the time, their timing is terrible and their stocks start to fall the very next day after they have bought them.

This is funny but true (Bitcoin, Weekly chart):

With amateur investors, it's all about greed, lack of discipline and a lack of a trading plan.

**Fund managers**

The reason fund managers buy at highs is that they simply need to do this. They need to follow their disclaimers which could for example state that 95% goes into stocks and 5% is cash. What they do is once they get money from their investors, they immediately throw it into the market.

No matter where the market is. They spend it immediately – even if the stocks are at their all-time highs. They rarely sit on cash waiting for their opportunity.

It would sound pretty funny if you gave your money to a fund manager, and then asked him 6 months later about what he was doing with your money, and he would tell you that nothing, because he had been waiting for a good opportunity.

On the contrary, to fund managers, we can afford to sit on a pile of money and wait for our moment. They can't... That's one of our advantages.

I am pretty sure that if you read this book, you won't make this beginner's mistake. If anything, this book should have taught you that you need to wait for your moment and pick a good, discounted stock when the time comes. Not at all-time highs.

## Don't Invest in Pink Sheets or Penny Stocks

Pink sheets or Penny stocks are shares of small companies, whose stocks are very cheap. They often don't meet the requirements to be listed on an exchange and for this reason they are sold at OTC markets (Over-the-Counter) where the requirements are not as strict as on major stock exchanges.

The most common sign of such stocks is that they are small, young companies that are sold for cheap. The way investors hope to make money on those is to buy such a company for cheap, and then watch the company grow massively, and its stock price skyrocket.

The problem is that it's about 1 out of 100 companies that make it.

I know it's very tempting when you read articles about companies that grew from garage companies into giants—those are articles that sell. Unfortunately, there are thousands of small companies that didn't succeed and went bankrupt.

What are the chances you pick the right stock that will skyrocket? Even if you buy stocks of a hundred penny stock companies, chances are very low. Also, keep in mind that the one company that makes it and makes you a lot of money needs to pay for all the expenses you paid for the companies that didn't make it.

My advice is to avoid such trading strategies and rather focus on big companies with history. Don't try to find a hidden gem in a pile of rubbish.

NOTE: I should point out that I am not saying that penny stock trading doesn't work. I know people who do it, who have solid penny stock strategies and who can make money with this. But they all are experienced traders with proven trading strategies who still need to buy hundreds of stocks to get a couple of good ones.

## Don't Bet It All on One Stock

Another thing beginners do is pick one or two stocks they like and they spend all their capital on them without any diversification. If you read this book then you know it's nonsense to do this, but still, I wanted to warn you.

No matter how you like one company, no matter how strong it looks to you, don't bet all your money on it. You never know what can happen in the future. Especially if you are investing in the long-term. Diversification is the key.

## Don't Invest Just in One Sector

Talking about diversification – not only should you diversify between more companies, but you should also diversify across various sectors. No matter how good a company is, if a whole sector gets hit and it gets down, so will all the companies within the sector.

If you bought for example 20 companies, but all just from the Consumer Cyclical sector, then when the economy goes into recession chances are that all those 20 companies you bought would be in trouble. Your portfolio wasn't diversified and your investments turned out sour.

That's why I recommend investing across at least three sectors. Ideally in sectors that are not too dependent on the economic cycle.

## Don't Look at the Charts Too Often

Many beginner investors check their portfolios too often. They check it every day or even a couple of times each day. Is there any benefit to this? Absolutely no. I guess it only gives them a false feeling that they are in control (they aren't). Such behavior only leads to frustration and hasty and bad decisions that are based on emotions rather than on a solid investment strategy.

If you have your alerts or limit orders set, then there isn't any reason to check your portfolio more than once a week. Checking your portfolio only once a week will save you time, you will sleep better, and you will make way better investment decisions.

## Don't Switch to Faster Time Frames

This goes hand in hand with the previous tip. If you are a long-term investor, and you base your analysis on a daily or weekly chart, then I recommend you don't ever switch to faster timeframes (like 4-hour chart, 1-hour chart, …). It will serve you no good. Long-term investors need to see the big picture. Details and the noise from the faster timeframes are just a distraction that could potentially sway you towards some hasty and bad decisions.

If you based your investment decision on a Weekly chart, then you should stick to it. Don't switch to faster charts.

## Don't Change Your Predetermined Time Horizon

One of the mistakes beginners tend to make is cutting their profits too early while trying to sit out the bad-looking investments.

I don't see a problem when you hold an underperforming stock even for years if you picked that stock for a good reason. The market could just be in a bad phase and eventually, the stock could still prove to be a good investment. Especially if you managed to buy that stock cheaply, or if you did a 2$^{nd}$ or even 3$^{rd}$ buy. So, I don't mind holding onto a stock that is in red numbers. Even for months or years.

What I advise against though is selling good-performing stocks too soon. People often fear that they will lose the gain they got. It's hard not to cash out an investment that has already made a nice gain. I get it. However, you should stick to your original plan and not sell your stocks unless there is a very good reason for it.

If you are making an investment portfolio for the next 5-10 years, then don't sell your stocks after a couple of months just because they have already made some gains.

## Don't Change Your Plans at the Last Minute

Once you have done your fundamental and Volume Profile analysis and the time comes to the point where the price is about to hit your Support, then don't change your plans all of a sudden. By this time the planning and analysis phases are over and now you are in an execution phase. Now you only need to execute the plan you have made before – not change or alter it. All the last-minute decisions are usually pretty bad ones as they are often based on emotions.

I am talking about scenarios where you say things like: *"Oh boy, the price is falling so quickly that I best not buy that stock as the price will most likely continue to fall."* Or *"It takes so long for the price to reach my Support. I should buy the stock earlier."*

I am strongly against those last-minute decisions as their outcome is usually pretty bad. Once you have made your plan, you have to stick to it.

Another thing that people do and that I advise against is switching to a faster time frame before the trade entry to catch the best moment to buy their shares. They want to feel in control, outsmart the market and make the best trade entry possible. In most cases, they fail spectacularly. What they should do instead is enjoy the free time this investment method offers. Not seek out an action. If you want more action, then do day trading. Enroll in my volume Profile or Order Flow course and you will see a lot of action every day. But if you are reading this, then you have picked a different approach. You have picked the way of an investor. In the end, it won't matter if you bought a stock for $49.5 or $49.2 anyway.

Your time should be spent on analysis, not on timing the "absolutely best" trade entry possible.

## Don't Buy Before Dividend to Sell After

I wish I didn't have to say it. But there are still people who need to hear this: After the ex-dividend date, the share price will drop more or less by the same amount as the dividend you are about to receive. There is simply no point in buying stocks before the dividend and selling them after. You will only lose the commission you paid for the transaction.

On top of that, a dividend is a taxable income so you would need to tax that dividend (bummer!). If you want to purchase a stock, then you may want to wait for the post-dividend dip and buy there so you don't need to tax that dividend. In my case though, I don't care about that too much. I simply buy when the price is right.

## Don't Invest Money You Will Need Soon

Investing is a long-run discipline. You may have to wait even a couple of years before you build your portfolio and before it turns into positive numbers. For this reason, you can't do this with the money you are likely to need soon. You should build your portfolio with money that you currently don't need and that you won't need soon.

Under any circumstances it shouldn't be like: "*I have some money now and I am going to need it in half a year, so in the meantime, I'll invest it in some stocks.*" That's a very bad idea.

## Don't Be Afraid to Go Against the Crowd

The strategy I showed you is always against the crowd. You invest when stocks are falling when there is a recession, or major economic problems, when people are afraid and panic...

You need to be okay with that as that's the only way you can buy discounted stocks. It's easily said but in reality, it's frustrating and tough to go against the crowd. But that's what it takes.

You need to be prepared for a situation where the news will be filled with info about a crisis, economic problems, or stock prices falling, … Amid all this, you should be buying stocks and building your portfolio.

I think it's best to avoid articles and news about dropping stocks because they only fuel the fear in people. They never tell you – "*Wow, what a sell-off! Now would be a great time to buy some stocks.*" That would sound almost funny if you read that in the newspaper, right?

Journalists and analysts usually extrapolate past sell offs and economic problems into the future. That's why I don't recommend giving too much weight to the information and projections they make.

# Bonus Content

As a little addition to this book, I've put together a special webpage with bonus content.

The bonus content includes an electronic copy of this book (in case you bought this as a physical copy), webinars, videos, links, and some extras I think you will find useful.

Here is the address and the password:

**Address:** https://www.trader-dale.com/investing-book

**Password:** happy trading

# What to Do Next

In this book, I tried my best to explain my investment strategy in a consistent and beginner-friendly way. As far as written form goes, I believe I gave you all the important info this format allowed me to.

If you liked it, and if you want to give it your best, then what I recommend as your next best step is a special **Stock Investing Pack**, I put together for you.

The pack consists of four main parts:

1. **Stock Investing Video Course:** A 15-hour long video course spread over 70 videos where I cover in detail my investing strategy in an easy, step-by-step guide.

2. **Stock Fundamentals Indicator:** A custom-made indicator that shows the most important stock fundamentals right on your chart!

3. **Volume Profile Indicator:** My favorite indicator that shows the activity of the big financial institutions. Can be used for stock investing, swing trading, and day trading and works with all trading instruments (stocks, forex, futures, cryptos, …).

4. **Portfolio Manager:** A custom-made Excel-based tool to keep track of your stocks and portfolio performance. Everything automated!

**BONUS:** As a special bonus to all of this, our specially trained tech support will do the complete setup for you! They will set up the platform, connect it to data, install all the indicators, and show you around!

**Get the Stock Investing Pack here:**

https://www.trader-dale.com/stock-investing-with-volume-profile

# Stock Investing Pack

### Video Course

- 70 in-depth videos with 15+ hours of training
- Learn how to read the big picture
- Learn how to pick the best stocks
- Learn my complete investing strategy step-by-step
- Beginner-friendy A-Z guide

### Stock Fundamentals indicator

- Custom made indicator
- Shows the most important fundamentals right on your stock chart
- Enables a quick one-look analysis

### Volume Profile Pack

- Custom-made Volume Profile indicators
- Best for tracking institutional activity and the "BIG guys"
- Works with all instruments (stocks, forex, futures, cryptos,...)
- Multiple computers & lifetime license

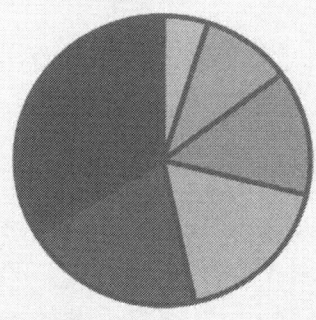

### Portfolio Manager

- Excellent tool to keep track of your stocks and portfolio performance
- Excel-based
- Fully automated and intuitive
- Multiple computers & lifetime license

**The Stock Investing Pack is available at: www.trader-dale.com**

# Thank you!

At this place, I would like to thank you for reading my book. I hope you liked it, and that you found it useful. I hope it helps you in achieving your financial goals and dreams no matter how big they are!

Happy trading!

-Dale

# Publications by Trader Dale

## Available at: www.trader-dale.com

### VOLUME PROFILE:
### The Insider's Guide To Trading

**What will you learn:**

- How to work with Price Action
- Price Action strategies that you can immediately put to use
- How Volume Profile works
- My favorite Volume Profile strategies
- How to find your own trading style and what are the best trading instruments to trade
- How to manage trading around macroeconomic news
- How to do your market analysis from A to Z
- How to manage your positions
- How to do a proper money management
- How to deal with trading psychology
- How to do a proper backtest and how to get started with trading your backtested strategies
- What are the most common trading mistakes and how to avoid them
- The exact ways and rules I apply to my own trading

### ORDER FLOW: Trading Setups

**What will you learn:**

- Choosing the right trading platform for Order Flow trading
- NinjaTrader 8 platform – introduction
- Choosing the right Order Flow software
- Where to get data for Order Flow
- The best instruments to trade with Order Flow
- Order Flow – what it tells us
- Order Flow – special features
- How to set up Order Flow workspace
- Order Flow – trading setups
- Order Flow – confirmation setups
- How to use Order Flow to determine your Take Profit and Stop Loss
- How to use Order Flow for trade management
- How to find strong institutional Supports and Resistances using Volume Profile
- How to combine Order Flow with Volume Profile

Printed in Great Britain
by Amazon